RESTful API Design Patte...
and Best Practices

Master REST API design with real-world patterns, lifecycle
management, and OpenAPI practices

Andrzej Jarzyna

Samir Amzani

‹packt›

RESTful API Design Patterns and Best Practices

Copyright © 2025 Packt Publishing

All rights reserved. No part of this book may be reproduced, stored in a retrieval system, or transmitted in any form or by any means, without the prior written permission of the publisher, except in the case of brief quotations embedded in critical articles or reviews.

Every effort has been made in the preparation of this book to ensure the accuracy of the information presented. However, the information contained in this book is sold without warranty, either express or implied. Neither the authors, nor Packt Publishing or its dealers and distributors, will be held liable for any damages caused or alleged to have been caused directly or indirectly by this book.

Packt Publishing has endeavored to provide trademark information about all of the companies and products mentioned in this book by the appropriate use of capitals. However, Packt Publishing cannot guarantee the accuracy of this information.

Portfolio Director: Ashwin Nair
Relationship Lead: Sneha Shinde
Project Manager: Ruvika Rao
Content Engineer: Nisha Cleetus
Technical Editor: Arjun Varma
Copy Editor: Safis Editing
Indexer: Hemangini Bari
Proofreader: Nisha Cleetus
Production Designer: Ponraj Dhandapani
Growth Lead: Anamika Singh

First published: Sept 2025

Production reference: 1150925

Published by Packt Publishing Ltd.
Grosvenor House
11 St Paul's Square
Birmingham
B3 1RB, UK.

ISBN 978-1-83588-528-4

www.packtpub.com

Foreword

I have had the good fortune of being invited to visit many companies around the world to share what I've learned about how APIs are designed, built, and maintained. I recall standing in front of a whiteboard at a client workshop a few years ago, marker in hand, while a group of engineers tried to sketch how their systems fit together. They started with a few familiar boxes. Customer data here, payments there. All neatly described and carefully laid out. However, within minutes, the board was crowded with arrows connecting boxes, crisscrossing in every direction. Someone in the back piped up and said, "It looks like a roadmap, not an IT diagram." That actually made us all pause for a moment. It wasn't just software we were working on; it was infrastructure. And every line was a road or a bridge carrying something of value from one place to another.

Early on, this book reminds the reader that "APIs are the roads, bridges, sidewalks, traffic lights, signs, and so on of the internet." It's a line that captures the spirit of the book and the state of the world of APIs today. Over the last decade, APIs have solidified their position as the shared infrastructure of the digital world, connecting people, systems, and now, increasingly, AI-driven machines that learn from the patterns we create.

Authors Andrzej Jarzyna and Samir Amzani have put together an excellent guide to this connected world: one that understands both the technical and human sides of the work. They show that API design is, first and foremost, a discipline of communication, an act of translation between business intent and technical implementation. A quick glance at the Table of Contents shows that the book moves naturally from foundations and life cycles to contracts, hypermedia, and change management. And, along the way, Jarzyna and Amzani make a simple but crucial point: APIs thrive when they are able to safely change over time.

I especially appreciate their treatment of hypermedia and affordance-centric design that is found here. For years, these ideas were considered idealistic. Now, with the rise of AI, they're becoming indispensable again. As autonomous agents begin consuming APIs at scale, discoverability and adaptability are no longer optional. As the authors rightly point out, "The APIs you design today need to work for both human developers debugging at 2 a.m. and AI agents that might consume your endpoints in ways you never imagined."

This book belongs to the lineage of work that treats API design as both craft and conversation. It's pragmatic, grounded, and refreshingly aware that good design is not just about stability but about clarity, empathy, and shared understanding. And for me, as I continue to travel the world helping teams find their own way through the ever-growing terrain of the internet, I'm happy to have another fine reference that I can recommend. One more guidebook for those learning to build better roads and stronger bridges.

Mike Amundsen, Author of Design and Build Great APIs and RESTful Web API Patterns and Practices Cookbook

Contributors

About the authors

Andrzej Jarzyna has spent over 14 years navigating the API landscape, from the early days at 3scale helping clients shape their API strategies to his current role as Chief API Architect at PZU, where he's building an API governance program from the ground up. Along the way, he's tackled everything from designing health research platforms in Mozambique to leading API excellence initiatives at Adidas and spearheading policy-as-code approaches at ING Bank. When he's not deep in OpenAPI specifications or mentoring teams on API design, you'll find him organizing API events, because apparently talking about APIs all day isn't enough. He's also co-founded gaming startup Timewarp Inc and somehow finds time to escape the digital world through climbing and mountaineering adventures.

I would like to thank my co-author, Samir Amzani, for making this collaboration both seamless and enjoyable. Special thanks to my partner, Claudia, for her patience and support during the countless hours spent writing this book. I'm grateful to Steve Willmott and the 3scale team for introducing me to the world of APIs, and to the entire API community for being so welcoming and supportive throughout my career.

I would like to dedicate this book to my partner Claudia, my parents, and all my friends around the world. You make my life meaningful.

– Andrzej Jarzyna

Samir Amzani is a Principal API Consultant and strategic advisor who specializes in transforming how organizations design, scale, and govern their API ecosystems. Currently serving on the leadership team at Apideck, he drives the evolution of unified API platforms that seamlessly connect thousands of applications. As a Technical Steering Committee member at AsyncAPI, Samir helps shape the future of open standards for event-driven architectures.

Over 18 years, he has partnered with industry leaders across diverse sectors, from tech giants like Postman to consumer brands such as Adidas and Back Market, guiding their API transformation journeys from fragmented systems to cohesive, developer-first platforms. His expertise spans the full spectrum of API lifecycle management, from initial strategy through implementation and governance at scale.

When Samir steps away from architecting the digital backbone of modern businesses, he finds inspiration in philosophy and travel, pursuits that fuel his ability to see complex technical challenges from fresh perspectives and understand the human stories behind the systems he builds.

*My deepest gratitude to the Packt team for their unwavering support and meticulous guidance throughout this project. Heartfelt thanks to my co-author, **Andrzej Jarzyna**, your expertise and collaborative spirit made this book possible. Working with you has been truly inspiring. Special recognition to **Arnaud Lauret ("API Handyman"), Zdenek Nemec ("Z"),** and **Fran Méndez** for their pioneering work that paved the way for our API community. This book builds on the foundations you established. To all the engineers, product managers, and partners I've worked with over the years. you've shaped my thinking and made this journey possible. This book carries the wisdom of our shared experiences.*

*To my wife, **Asmae,** and my son, **Jad,** your love, patience, and endless support made this journey possible. Asmae, thank you for believing in this project from day one. Jad, this is for the future we're building together. You are my greatest inspiration and my proudest achievement.*

– Samir Amzani

About the reviewer

Akhilesh Tiwari is Director of Product Engineering at InvestCloud and has over two decades of software development experience. He obtained his MTech from BITS Pilani, India. Akhilesh has developed software solutions for leading global organizations such as Merck, Novartis, BNY Mellon, Fujitsu, Cognizant, and Persistent Systems, to name a few. He is a passionate software engineer and, even in his free time, enjoys experimenting with Raspberry Pi alongside his kids. Akhilesh currently resides in New Jersey, USA, where he enjoys a fulfilling family life.

First of all, I would like to thank the Supreme Personality of Godhead, Krishna, for everything. I am grateful to my loving parents for their unconditional love and support. I could not have completed this book review without the support of my loving wife, Sanchita, and my two young children, Osh and Radha. Last but not least, I would like to thank Packt for this opportunity and for their trust.

Table of Contents

Part II: The Wizard's Grimoire — Mastering the Fundamentals of REST   81

Chapter 5: Comparing and Choosing the Right API Style   83

Chapter 6: REST Design Constraints and Maturity Models 105

Chapter 7: Constructing an API Design Domain Model   135

Part III: The Archmage's Circle — Forging and Evolving API Contracts   191

Chapter 9: Understanding the OpenAPI Specification   193

Chapter 10: OpenAPI as a Contract: Best Practices and Implementation   221

Chapter 13: API Change Management: Strategies for Versioning and Evolution 325

Preface

APIs are everywhere, yet many of us have learned to design them through trial and error, often more error than we'd care to admit. RESTful API Design Patterns and Best Practices was born from our collective "aha moments" and, frankly, our mistakes while working with teams across different organizations. We noticed that most API design resources fall into two camps: highly technical guides that assume you're building in a vacuum, or business-focused books that gloss over the nitty-gritty details. The reality? Great API design happens at the intersection of both worlds.

Between the two of us, we've run API initiatives at companies like Adidas, Backmarket, ING, and PZU; watched countless teams struggle with the same challenges; and celebrated when they finally clicked with the right approach. What became clear is that there's a sweet spot between technical excellence and business value, and that's exactly where this book aims. Plus, with AI systems getting chattier and more dependent on well-crafted APIs, the bar for good API design just got higher.

Think of this book as your guided tour through three distinct territories. Part 1: The Apprentice's Study is where we get comfortable with the fundamentals—why APIs exist, how to think about them as products, and how to apply domain thinking that actually makes sense. Part 2: The Wizard's Grimoire is where we roll up our sleeves and dive deep into REST design, comparing different approaches and building solid foundations. Part 3: The Archmage's Circle is where we get practical with OpenAPI, JSON Schema, hypermedia, and keeping your APIs healthy as they evolve.

While you could jump around the book like a choose-your-own-adventure novel, we've structured it with some method to our madness. The Domain-Driven Design chapters in Part 1 build on each other, and the technical chapters in Part 3 are definitely better as a progression. Trust us on this one; we've seen what happens when teams skip the foundation work.

To keep things practical, we follow a "Magic Items store" through Chapters 9–12. This isn't just academic theory; these patterns come from real projects, real deadlines, and real conversations with development teams who needed solutions yesterday.

Here's the thing: we're at a fascinating moment where traditional API design meets AI-driven interactions. The APIs you design today need to work for both human developers debugging at 2 a.m. and AI agents that might consume your endpoints in ways you never imagined. This book gives you the tools to build for both audiences without losing your sanity.

Whether you're designing your first API or you're the person everyone turns to when things get complicated, we hope this book becomes the resource you wish you'd had when you started, practical, comprehensive, and maybe even a little fun.

Andrzej Jarzyna & Samir Amzani

Who this book is for

This book is for professionals involved in the digital product lifecycle who want to deepen their understanding of API design and build future-proof APIs with a product-centric approach. API developers, solution architects and engineers, technical product owners, and software architects looking to extend their skills in creating efficient, scalable, and maintainable APIs will find this book particularly useful. Basic knowledge of APIs and the HTTP protocol is recommended to fully benefit from the design principles and practices covered.

What this book covers

Chapter 1, The "Why" of API Development, Before venturing into the realm of API design and development, it's crucial to address the fundamental question: "Why?" Is it the purpose to unveil functionalities to other applications, broadening your business offerings, or is it the backbone of your enterprise? Crafting APIs also necessitates a clear understanding of the intended target audience.

Chapter 2, API as a Product: Designing APIs with a Product Mindset, This chapter discusses how to approach API design with a product mindset, focusing on the value the API provides to its consumers. It focuses on treating APIs as products rather than mere technical components.

Chapter 3, Understanding Application and API Lifecycles, This chapter explains how a holistic look on the whole API lifecycle influences your API Design. It explains how your API Lifecycle and your Application Lifecycle are interwoven and provides a comprehensive overview of the stages that an application and its APIs go through, from inception to deprecation.

Chapter 4, Applying Domain-Driven Design to APIs, This chapter guides readers on how to incorporate domain-driven design principles into API development. It provides strategies for aligning

API design with business domains, ensuring that APIs accurately reflect and serve business needs.

Chapter 5, Comparing and Choosing the Right API Style, This chapter explores RESTful APIs, their popularity, and unique features. We compare REST with other API styles like GraphQL, SOAP, gRPC, and asynchronous APIs, highlighting their strengths and weaknesses. The choice of API style significantly impacts your application's lifecycle, influencing its design, implementation, testing, and maintenance.

Chapter 6, REST Design Constraints and Maturity Models, This chapter dives into the depths of API Design specifics. It delves into the core principles that guide RESTful API design as originally introduced by Roy Fielding. It explores the main REST design constraints that shape effective APIs.

Chapter 7, Constructing an API Design Domain Model, This chapter provides a comprehensive guide on building a domain model for API design. It emphasizes the importance of a well-structured domain model in creating effective and efficient APIs. It teaches how to understand your API business domain, how to identify key entities in it and define proper relationships between them.

Chapter 8, Designing and Managing Effective API Contracts, This chapter delves into the significance of a well-crafted API design document and its role as a contract in API design. It sheds light on the creation of clear, all-encompassing design documents that act as agreements between API providers and consumers. The objective is to streamline future API usage and cultivate open communication among all stakeholders from the outset.

Chapter 9, Understanding the OpenAPI Specification, This chapter delves into the utilization of OpenAPI Specification (OAS) in the design of REST APIs. It underscores the dual role of the OpenAPI specification as a design blueprint and a binding contract for your API, guaranteeing uniformity and clarity.

Chapter 10, OpenAPI as a Contract: Best Practices and Implementation, This chapter explores practical implementation patterns, from contract validation to tool integration. You'll learn how to design intuitive APIs with consistent resources, error handling, and asynchronous operations while discovering how contract-first approaches transform team collaboration.

Chapter 11, Using JSON Schema to Define Your Object Models, This chapter delves into the utilization of JSON Schema in the design of REST APIs. It builds upon the domain model created in the previous chapters and introduces the reader to how to formally describe those models. It covers the creation, validation, and documentation of complex JSON structures, ensuring consistency and reliability in your API design.

Chapter 12, Don't Hate Your Hypermedia: Creating APIs For Humans and AIs, This chapter explores the concept of hypermedia and its role in API design. It provides insights into how hypermedia can enhance API functionality, improve user experience, and make APIs more adaptable and scalable. It also explains how to design REST APIs beyond CRUD operations.

Chapter 13, API Change Management: Strategies for Versioning and Evolution, This chapter delves into strategies for API change management, focusing on versioning and evolution while balancing stability and innovation. It emphasizes the critical importance of preserving backward compatibility and maintaining a seamless experience for existing consumers.

To get the most out of this book

This book is a valuable resource for professionals involved in the digital product lifecycle who wish to enhance their understanding of API design. It provides insights into designing robust and future-proof APIs with a product-centric approach. Before starting this book, readers should have a basic understanding of APIs and the HTTP protocol. This foundational knowledge will help them grasp the concepts of API design and best practices presented in the book.

Download the example code files

The code bundle for the book is hosted on GitHub at `https://github.com/PacktPublishing/RESTful-Design-Patterns-and-Best-Practices`. We also have other code bundles from our rich catalog of books and videos available at `https://github.com/PacktPublishing`. Check them out!

Conventions used

There are a number of text conventions used throughout this book.

`CodeInText`: Indicates code words in text, database table names, folder names, filenames, file extensions, pathnames, dummy URLs, user input, and Twitter handles. For example: " Let's say we define an endpoint such as `/items/{itemId}` in our OAS document with its operations, parameters, and responses:"

A block of code is set as follows:

```
/items/{itemId}:
  get:
    parameters:
      - name: itemId
        in: path
        required: true
```

```
        schema:
          type: string
          pattern: "^[a-zA-Z0-9-]+$"
    responses:
      '200':
        content:
          application/json:
            schema:
              $ref: '#/components/schemas/MagicItem'
      '404':
        $ref: '#/components/responses/NotFound'
```

Bold: Indicates a new term, an important word, or words that you see on the screen. For instance, words in menus or dialog boxes appear in the text like this. For example: "**OpenAPI Specification (OAS)** is a standardized, language-agnostic way to describe RESTful APIs. Think of OAS documents as clear contracts that spell out exactly what your API can do, just like we talked about in earlier chapters"

Warnings or important notes appear like this.

Tips and tricks appear like this.

Get in touch

Feedback from our readers is always welcome.

General feedback: If you have questions about any aspect of this book or have any general feedback, please email us at customercare@packt.com and mention the book's title in the subject of your message.

Errata: Although we have taken every care to ensure the accuracy of our content, mistakes do happen. If you have found a mistake in this book, we would be grateful if you reported this to us. Please visit http://www.packt.com/submit-errata, click **Submit Errata**, and fill in the form.

Piracy: If you come across any illegal copies of our works in any form on the internet, we would be grateful if you would provide us with the location address or website name. Please contact us at copyright@packt.com with a link to the material.

If you are interested in becoming an author: If there is a topic that you have expertise in and you are interested in either writing or contributing to a book, please visit http://authors.packt.com/.

Share your thoughts

Once you've read *RESTful API Design Patterns and Best Practices*, we'd love to hear your thoughts! Scan the QR code below to go straight to the Amazon review page for this book and share your feedback.

https://packt.link/r/1835885292

Your review is important to us and the tech community and will help us make sure we're delivering excellent quality content.

Free Benefits with Your Book

This book comes with free benefits to support your learning. Activate them now for instant access (see the "*How to Unlock*" section for instructions).

Here's a quick overview of what you can instantly unlock with your purchase:

PDF and ePub Copies | Next-Gen Web-Based Reader

Free PDF and ePub versions

Next-Gen Reader

Access a DRM-free PDF copy of this book to read anywhere, on any device.

Use a DRM-free ePub version with your favorite e-reader.

Multi-device progress sync: Pick up where you left off, on any device.

Highlighting and notetaking: Capture ideas and turn reading into lasting knowledge.

Bookmarking: Save and revisit key sections whenever you need them.

Dark mode: Reduce eye strain by switching to dark or sepia themes.

How to Unlock

UNLOCK NOW

Scan the QR code (or go to packtpub.com/unlock). Search for this book by name, confirm the edition, and then follow the steps on the page.

Note: Keep your invoice handy. Purchases made directly from Packt don't require one.

Part 1

The Apprentice's Study — Preparing for the Craft

In this foundational part of the book, you'll begin your journey as an API apprentice, learning the essential principles and mindset needed to craft exceptional APIs. Just as every wizard must first understand the fundamental forces of magic before wielding powerful spells, every API designer must grasp the core motivations, business drivers, and strategic thinking that underpin successful API development.

You'll discover why APIs have become critical business assets and learn to approach them with a product mindset rather than a purely technical perspective. We'll explore the complete lifecycle of APIs, from conception to retirement, and introduce you to Domain-Driven Design principles that will shape how you think about API boundaries and organization.

By the end of this part, you'll have developed the strategic foundation and conceptual framework necessary to make informed decisions throughout your API design journey. This preparation phase ensures that when you do start designing, you'll be equipped with the right mindset, tools, and understanding to create APIs that truly serve their intended purpose.

This part of the book includes the following chapters:

- Chapter 1, The "Why" of API Development
- Chapter 2, API as a Product: Designing APIs with a Product Mindset
- Chapter 3, Understanding Application and API Lifecycles
- Chapter 4, Applying Domain Driven Design to APIs

1

The "Why" of API Development

APIs are indispensable for any digital business nowadays. They are the roads, bridges, sidewalks, traffic lights, signs, etc. of the internet. This may seem a bold statement, but if you think about it, virtually any digital interaction you have in your everyday life will involve use of APIs. Your map application will fetch data about the route and traffic conditions from dozens of APIs, paying using your phone in a store will involve a few APIs connecting the bank with the credit card company and with the mobile phone application. The examples as endless.

In this book, we will be diving deep into how to design REST APIs – the most common and robust style of APIs. Our approach is to look at APIs not as isolated systems, but instead, from a broader perspective. We will be going through the whole lifecycle process of an API focusing also on how they affect other systems in a bigger ecosystem.

By the end of the book, you will be able to design your API and the processes around it from properly arguing why it should be built, through hands-on design using industry leading tools, to finally putting it into production and eventually planning for sunsetting.

Before venturing into the realm of API design and development, it's crucial to address the fundamental question: "Why?" Is it the purpose to unveil functionalities to other applications and broaden your business offerings, or is it the backbone of your enterprise? Crafting APIs also necessitates a clear understanding of the intended target audience. Pinpointing the precise consumer group is pivotal, as it shapes the API's architecture and informs critical decisions regarding management strategies and security protocols.

In this chapter, we're going to cover the following main topics:

- The "Why" of API development: Exploring the core motivations
- Identifying your API's audience: Tailoring your approach
- APIs as business catalysts: Driving value and innovation

We will start creating our own project, starting from good motivation.

Free Benefits with Your Book

Your purchase includes a free PDF copy of this book along with other exclusive benefits. Check the *Free Benefits with Your Book* section in the Preface to unlock them instantly and maximize your learning experience.

The "Why" of API development: Exploring the core motivations

Before venturing into the realms of API design, we should understand the reasons why. We are at this stage having some sort of business or technical requirements we have to fulfill. Instead of diving straight into API design or development, let's first understand the ecosystem into which we are going to contribute with our new piece of software. It's a system of communicating vessels and seemingly trivial updates can affect multiple of its elements. As the first exercise, let's explore the fundamental reasons that necessitate the creation of APIs.

The essence of APIs

APIs are often built to provide data to our applications without the need to tightly couple the presentation layer with data layer. However, APIs are not just for building applications. They enable data integration across multiple platforms. APIs are commonly used to provide access to various datasets. This way you gain access to the data without any middle agent. APIs can be connected directly to databases, spreadsheets or other business applications. Basically, to any machine-readable data for processing locally.

The reason APIs gained so much traction in the early days of Web 2.0 revolution was that they assure your product, or service is seamless from start to finish. APIs are the connectors that enable most of the communications between the web applications, or apps, that we use today. They work by communicating with, and exchanging data between, other systems. Nowadays you can easily integrate with most of the available SaaS products on the market through their APIs and mash-up data or services from different sources to create a new product.

This is also how APIs enhance businesses. By streamlining operations and offering third-party integration or enabling data analysis APIs drive business growth, create new ways to create genuinely useful products through third-party app integration, expanding offerings, and fostering collaborations. Take the data of your sport activities, your connected scale and an online database of meal recipes and you can build an app helping people to create meal plans in accordance with your energy expenditure and sport goals.

Other advantages of APIs include the ability to move away from monolithic software and toward smaller, easier-to-maintain components. This also allows teams that are responsible for different parts of the application to be split in a more functional manner. Maintaining a huge code base which needs to be updated often is cumbersome and can lead to a lot of potential risks when deploying a new version.

These are only a handful of examples of how APIs enhance both business capabilities not only by opening new possible revenue streams, but also technological ones by making democratizing access to data and functionalities of our applications. They are the catalyst for a more distributed, connected digital economy.

In the next section, we will explore how different types of audiences will define our API design and business approach.

Audience-centric API design

When building an API we have to define its audience. We can roughly classify APIs depending on if their consumers are internal or external to our organization. We can determine whether the consumers are internal to our team/department/company, shared with a curated list of partners or publicly available to anyone who signs up, self-service way, to our API platform.

Creating APIs for internal audience helps to reuse our interfaces and data with more systems, gives visibility to those interfaces and allows us to build a more decentralized and decoupled environment.

Motivations for external APIs mostly focus on the business possibilities they bring. When exposed to third parties, they not only give us a possibility to directly monetize the use of the data we store, but also open our organization to potential integration with other platforms exposing us to more revenue streams.

We can also identify the motivations from a more technical perspective. What kind of device will be consuming our APIs? Is it going to be a computer, a mobile phone or maybe an IoT device? Identifying to which of these groups, maybe several, our audience belongs has a huge impact on our API design constraints. This will hugely impact our security and keys provisioning strategy and also things like API management and documentation.

After identifying our core audience, we have one, immensely powerful, possibility. We can work closely with some of our future consumers during the design process to quickly prototype and verify our designs. This way we will know very early on their exact needs and whether our assumptions were correct. This greatly improves the innovation cycle and allows us to fix any design mistakes early on. We will have a deeper dive into this topic in the next subsection.

Technological drivers for building APIs

If we are about to build an API within a larger organization, it's almost certain that there will already be other elements running within your ecosystem. Your new API may be an extension to one of them or a completely new entity. Either way, if we look at software from the perspective of data, then we realize, applications are data processors applying functions over stored data and fetching and transforming new data. Continuing to look from the same perspective, APIs are interfaces to that data. They allow for interoperability between systems and their elements. It's like a transition from a cubicle-based office to an open space, where information and culture can flow more freely.

Depending on the level of digital transformation at your organization, APIs will allow to greatly improve efficiency by automating previously manual processes. Consider the following real-life scenario at a health research center. The team was generating vast amounts of data from various sources, and researchers frequently had to request specific datasets from their IT department. As you can imagine this was a very arduous, manual process with long lead times affecting their productivity and costs. An API platform for accessing the data in a standardized and self-service fashion allowed them to get an almost instant data availability with improved security (with adequate security policies) and an ability to create real-time data presentations.

The preceding example is also a fantastic showcase of how APIs improve your system's scalability. The case was quite extreme, going from a manual approach to an API-based one. However, because of API's intrinsic qualities like statelessness and loose coupling, they are easily scalable by nature. Statelessness assures that each request from the API consumers will contain all the information needed to process it. Your system won't have to store any session information, and it will allow to easily scale your API horizontally, by adding more machines as no context of previous interactions is needed. Loose coupling, on the other hand, means that you can scale or change any element of your API independently. So, for example, put a more powerful machine on the server side without touching your API gateways or change your authorization method to a more suitable one for external users without affecting your API back-end at all.

APIs also promote the reuse of functionality across multiple applications, reducing redundancy and improving maintainability. You don't need to build your backend for each application type your consumers will operate, but leverage APIs to provide data to all the different client applications assuring the same data on every device.

Last, but not the least, APIs work really well for any modularized and distributed systems. They are a paradigm shift in the way communication between system components occur: from a centralized to decentralized system and eventually distributed and organically evolving one. Technically APIs are agnostic to whether your system is a monolith or a microservice based one. However, if you want to transition from a traditional monolith to microservices or a modularized system, you will probably need to start with building APIs for your core data interactions.

APIs: The Business Game Changers

As we all know very well, technological motivations are rarely the main drivers for building APIs. APIs, however, bring a plethora of great benefits for the business. For one, they enable businesses to innovate by exposing data and functionality that can be used to create new products and services. A great example of this is **Twilio**. By exposing their various communication services via APIs, they spurred a plethora of other companies to be able to leverage their internal systems and create real value to their consumers. For instance, Airbnb used Twilio's API to streamline the communication between guests and rental hosts. By automating SMS messaging, Airbnb made it easier for hosts to connect with guests, providing a better experience for both parties. This also opened new revenue streams to Twilio by monetizing their APIs and is their main revenue driver.

APIs can also facilitate partnerships by providing a means for partners to integrate their services. For example, **Adidas** integrates, using APIs, with online resellers like **Amazon** or **Zalando** to create new revenue streams and gain access to big online selling platforms, thus expanding their market by leveraging the outreach of these big platforms. Adidas was also able to improve customer engagement through integrating via APIs with augmented reality into their mobile app. This way, their customers, without needing to go to a physical store to try shoes, can check at home whether they like the style of adidas product and then order online.

When a business primarily operates through APIs, we refer to this as participating in the API Economy. We will dive deeper into the topic of API Economy in the last section of this chapter: *APIs as business catalysts: Driving value and innovation.*

The balancing act: Creating new vs. extending existing APIs

We have our business and engineers on board with building an API. However, building an API from scratch is not always the best course of action. Maybe we already have a seemingly similar API in our ecosystem? If so, let's ask ourselves a number of questions:

- What style or paradigm does the API use? Is it the same as what we were planning to build?

- What technology stack does it use? Do we still have human resources for supporting and maintaining it long term?

- Is the existing API in the same domain as the one we want to build? Maybe they are operating over similar resources, however in a completely different domain. For example, an order will be a very different thing when talking about e-commerce part of your business and can be different in the domain of manufacturing or logistics.

- Are your new business requirements an extension of what your current API already supplies? Are you able to already deliver some subset of the required functionality with it?

- Would extending your current API break existing clients? This is a tricky question, as with special precautions we can avoid this risk. However, there are situations which will definitely not be backwards compatible, such as a need for a new authorization pattern or implementing previously non existing limits on requests structure.

Remember, these decisions should be made in the context of your specific situation and needs. It's also important to consider the potential impact on your users and to ensure that any changes are clearly communicated and well-documented. Always consider the trade-offs between building new, extending, and reusing. It's not just about the immediate need but also about long-term maintenance and scalability.

Adhering to standards in API development

One of the most important aspects to consider while building or extending an existing API is what kind of standards we are following. We can distinguish two classes of standards for API design: global and singular.

Singular standards

Singular standards describe exactly what an API should be and do not leave much for interpretations. Standards, like **SCIM** for Identity and Access Management, strictly define how an API adhering to it should look like. It specifies all the required endpoints, data models for your resources, response structure, etc.

Read more

Find more information of SCIM here: `https://simplecloud.info/`

While building such APIs you do not have much in terms of design. It is important to adhere to the standard as closely as possible, even if that would mean deviating from your organization's design policies. This way we ensure interoperability between other systems understanding such standard, minimize the learning curve for developers and reduce the design complexity. These standards also tend to have places where you can extend them to adapt to your specific needs. However, all that is defined should stay unchanged. Mind though, that we are talking about the design part. Things like access control, security, etc., should still follow the usual policies.

Global standards

The global standards are the ones which give you a basic structure and guidelines on how to adapt to them but leave you a great deal of flexibility. They work great as policies applied at scale to all your APIs. Some examples of those are **HAL** for the structure of your Hypermedia API JSON documents or **Problem Details** for HTTP APIs which defines the structure of error files while adhering to the hypermedia constraint of REST APIs.

Read more

Find more information, visit the following links:

HAL: `https://stateless.group/hal_specification.html`
Problem Details: `https://www.rfc-editor.org/rfc/rfc9457`

So, when to follow a certain standard or, maybe even, multiple standards? Let's see next.

Selecting the relevant standard

Singular standards are great if you are trying to tackle a well-known problem and want to open your business to partners or other developers who would expect a certain structure for your API. These kinds of standards greatly help to really speed-up the design process and jump straight into prototyping and development. Any additional features can be added later in an iterative process.

Global standards are great if you want to have uniform experience throughout your APIs. Similarly, although to a lesser extent, they also ease the design process by adding a creative constraint to the process and limiting the number of options you have to take. In the case of widely adopted standards, like Problem Details, this will also potentially improve the time to integrate and give you access to some third-party tooling.

However, standards are not always the best way to go. Global standards which tend to be overly constrictive and trying to define too many aspects of your API end up limiting your creative freedom rather than easing the design and development process, so try to avoid them. On the other hand, singular API standards which are very vague do not really speed your API design process that much nor simplify the integration process as the variability of APIs adhering to them may be very wide.

Knowing when to hold back: When not to build an API

This book is about how to design an API, I know. However, a crucial step in this process is to know when not to design one. We have covered some of those motivations in the previous steps. In case we would be duplicating functionality of an existing API it is usually a better idea to extend an already existing API with the new business cases we need, unless the technical requirements are strict enough to restrict this option.

Some of the other important reasons *not* to design an API are:

- **High cost**: If the cost of creating and maintaining an API is not adding sufficiently to user experience or to the revenue, it would be wise to reassess the motivations.
- **High increase of overall system complexity**: This one is tricky as you usually realize about it way too late. A good indicator of this is when your system requires multiple internal calls and references to other APIs creating many dependencies or, worse, recursions. This is a common issue with services running on microservice or serverless architecture where overall system consistency cannot be assured in any given moment.

> Read more
>
> Find more information about Eventual consistency here:
> https://www.wikiwand.com/en/Eventual_consistency

- **Trendiness**: Just because APIs are trendy doesn't mean they're the right solution for every problem. Building an API just to follow a trend can lead to unnecessary complexity. This also applies to specific technologies or styles. Only because some technology, like GraphQL, is currently *hot* doesn't mean that it is a good decision to create an API using it.
- **Overengineering**: If your software is simple and isn't intended to interact with other systems, building an API might be overkill.

- **Regulatory Compliance**: In certain industries, there may be regulations that restrict what data can be exposed through APIs. It's important to ensure that any API complies with all relevant regulations. For example, exposing any health-related data is very sensitive and will require a deep analysis what can and what cannot be shared.

- **Monetization**: While it's not inherently bad to monetize an API, doing so without providing sufficient value to the user can lead to a poor user experience and potential backlash. When you are monetizing data you have via an API, be sure its quality is high enough and remember that this will not only add the required effort on documentation and such, but also will require more complex API management solution.

Creating a new API is usually a good idea. However, as we could learn in this section, there are legitimate reasons not to do so. Going through a short list like the one above and verifying our reasoning and constraints behind this new API may save us some headaches in the future.

Tackling API Sprawl

The last issue we will discuss in this section is so-called **API Sprawl**. It is a phenomenon usually seen in large organizations, where a large number of APIs are being created with little to no governance over them and without following best practices regarding API management and design. If an organization have problems doing any of the following:

- Specifying what APIs do they have in their ecosystem
- Knowing how many APIs they have
- Can't tell where the APIs are deployed and how to access them
- Don't have live monitoring data about all of their APIs
- Can't say why their APIs are failing

Then it is most likely struggling with API Sprawl.

So, API Sprawl is not really the result of too many APIs. It is a deficiency in the API governance program. In case your organization is struggling to some extent with an API Sprawl and really needs that new API, it may also be the harbinger of change which will show how to start a good governance program to tackle the problems you have. If governance and management are done well, having too many APIs is a much better problem to have than having too few.

Read more

More information about API Sprawl here: https://nordicapis.com/api-futures-api-sprawl-to-be-a-pressing-concern-in-2024/

To reiterate - in a rare occasion when your organization may be struggling with the quality of its APIs the questions, the problem does not really come from the number of APIs existing in the ecosystem, it is rather the lack of quality control, observability, and policies management. The first step to fix it is to realize the scale of the issue. With that, our new API may be a beacon of hope and the first API introducing new API Governance standards. Tackling the API Governance challenge is based on communication patterns within an organization. The next section explores in detail how to approach API design centered on your audience and how to leverage good communication patterns to do so.

Identifying your API's audience: Tailoring your approach

In the preceding section, we have briefly talked about the difference between internal and external audience. Now let's dive deeper into the topic of identifying your API's target audience and how it affects API design and our motivations.

As already mentioned, internal and external APIs have many business and technological advantages. We will be able to reuse the data interfaces, give data more visibility, add more revenue streams or monetize our platform. How does the approach to API design differ for internal and external APIs though?

Communication and affordance-centric API design

The requirements with which we usually start to build our new API usually tell us what kind of business requirements we are going to fulfil and how we should do that. However, rarely it is a product of close interaction with the future consumer. One great possibility which internal APIs tend to have out of the box is that we already know who is going to be our consumer. We can work with them from the very beginning to come up with the best design for their needs. This will help creating an affordance-centric API. This means an API whose operations correspond as close as possible with your consumer's needs. This is the most important aspect for REST APIs design and what allows to minimize potential issues like chattiness (what is it), caching, etc. You will be able to create you API data models based on user requirements and thus avoid sending unnecessary or insufficient data or expose database or implementation models. Close communication with future consumers is also crucial to discover limitations on non-design specific aspects, such as performance, security, complexity. Consider also what systems or applications your audience will be integrating your API with. This can influence the design of your API. If possible, you should do a similar exercise with the external or partner consumers. Work as early as possible with those who are interested in using your APIs and design accordingly. You can also create *personas* of different types of consumers and create a design process driven by the requirements for each persona.

Consider also what kind of systems your consumers are going to integrate your API with. For example, in epidemiology researchers commonly do data analysis on information presented in .csv file format, so it could make sense to make your API to provide this type of content. Certain systems expect data to be provided in some specific format. For example, date format is different in US and Europe, similarly decimal number. Units can be provided in metric or in imperial systems. There are many considerations like this, and they are really important for the success of your API. By all means, try to satisfy the needs of your consumers by providing expected data.

> Best practice
>
> Always work with your future consumer. If you already know who that is, reach out and learn their requirements and understand how and what for they want to use your API. If you don't have this possibility, create personas to represent different classes of your consumers and work towards designing your API for their needs. Remember, that your consumers, as well as those personas, may and will evolve with time as both of you better understand the subject matter. *Iterative process and effective communication are crucial to good API design.*

Beyond design

There are also important differences between internal and external APIs which reach outside of pure API design. These include:

- **Security**: Internal APIs may reside within a strictly controlled DMZ zone without any external access. This greatly limits the potential for a breach. Internal APIs can use simpler internal authorization mechanisms in general. However, you still need one in order to be able to manage your access control levels, track the usage of different APIs and their operations and gain observability on any potential issues happening to it.

- **Access control**: External APIs require a fine grain control of who has access to which operations on your API. This is especially important in conjunction with proper rate limiting strategies, where you will limit usage of your API for different type of users

- **Documentation**: External APIs, as a product exposed to external consumers, require great documentation to minimize the confusions on how to integrate and get the necessary value out from it. This works great in conjunction with an easy-to-use keys provisioning mechanism. Together, these allow for the quickest **time to first call** to your API and a painless integration process. The best practice is to create you API documentation the same way for internal as external APIs. Think about your API as a product, and your consumers, no matter whether they are internal or external, deserve great experience using it. The easier and more self-sufficient your consumers will be, the easier maintenance of your API will be, and consumers will be able to take advantage of it to the fullest

    Best practices

    Prepare documentation, feedback channels, design policies, access control, monitoring for internal APIs the same way as you would for external APIs. This way you will assure higher, equal standards for all APIs, better developer experience and onboarding process, and also make the process of externalizing your APIs much easier, as it won't require a complete redesign of the API management strategy.

As we could observe, audience-centric approach to designing and building your API is crucial for its success. It will reinforce both the business value of your API as well as the technical efficiency. Engaging in communication with consumers from the earliest stages of the API lifecycle will also answer doubts about the security mechanisms you can or should implement or how to organize your documentation for the best value added. In the next section, we are going to explore how APIs are driving your business value and enable innovation.

APIs as business catalysts: Driving value and innovation

In this chapter, we delve into the business motivations behind the creation of APIs, arguably the most significant driver of all. The industry truly began to innovate when businesses realized the potential of APIs to enhance revenue and expand market reach. While the technologies enabling APIs to have existed for a long time, it was not until their large-scale implementation that we began to see their true potential. So, what constitutes a compelling business motivation? We touched upon some in the first section of this chapter: *The "Why" of API development: Exploring the core motivations*. Let's explore in greater detail.

If your objective is to externalize your capabilities and foster an economy around your services and data, APIs offer the creative freedom to construct unique solutions tailored to specific user needs, all through straightforward API connections. They facilitate the development of new applications that might otherwise be too complex or time-consuming. APIs streamline the integration between intricate systems, irrespective of the programming language and frameworks employed. This eradicates data silos, ensuring easy access to information. Consequently, the potential consumer market for your API broadens, as the entry barrier is relatively low.

How APIs are creating innovation

In this section, we will go through several examples from different industries about how APIs helped create innovation and improved products.

We are currently experiencing a huge rise in popularity and capabilities of AI systems. AI is being added everywhere to most services we are dealing with. This AI boom was possible because of the advancements of large language models, but also because of APIs. AI systems can efficiently get new data and access external functionality or interfaces exactly because of the APIs they have access to. We can safely say that there would be no modern AI systems in the form we can see them if there were no web APIs. What's more, AI can leverage certain qualities of API design more efficiently than it was possible ever before. Hypermedia APIs, which are self-discoverable and documentable through the use of hyperlinks within their data models, are an amazing feature for systems, which can explore them without the need for tedious implementation of those hypermedia controls.

In the automotive industry, APIs are used to embed efficiency data, driving statistics, maps information, and more. These kind of data is especially crucial to the rise of electric mobility. Charging stations, depending on the country, may not be a very common sight in some places and the ability to plan your route so that you can be sure not to run out of juice is key. To build a solution for route planning car manufacturers had to integrate a number of APIs. You need maps data with charging stations, distances, inclinations, speed limits to plan the path. Weather data to be able to adjust it for temperature, wind, humidity. Your car may also learn your driving style and adjust these predictions based on it. All of that comes from various services, both car manufacturers, as well as third party.

In retail, adidas is a good example of leveraging the API Economy to its benefits. They managed to switch from multiple wholesale and retail channels to a more focused, multiplatform solution by integrating with some of the big online marketplaces and their APIs. They are also using a plethora of internal APIs to track the logistics of apparel manufacture process and shipment. Their apparel design tools use APIs to fetch data about materials and their qualities, colors, pieces, etc., so that designers can easily get information on what is feasible and will create a good product. This is only a snapshot of part of adidas API economy, but already shows how their adoption allowed them to successfully go through digital transformation and be much more agile about how the data is being shared within the organization and with their partners.

In recent years banking, an industry traditionally resistant to changes, has been undergoing a big revolution. With the adoption of the European PSD2 legislative we are experiencing the birth of Open Banking which, in turn, revolutionizes fintech businesses. With banks customers now having the right to access their data in a programmatic way, fintech companies are able to leverage them to provide people with a plethora of new services. By only having access to your banking data with spendings and earnings they can do things like planning your budgets or suggesting investment strategies. Mash these data with some external sources and you can create even more helpful applications to help you save some money or invest in them well.

How good API design impacts API Economy

But how can a good API design impact **API Economy**? After all, this book is about API design and not really about how business can benefit from them. Let's quickly go through some examples of how good API design helps to grow business:

- **Usability**: Good API design makes APIs easy to understand and use. This encourages more developers to use the API, leading to more integrations and a larger user base.
- **Efficiency**: Well-designed APIs can improve efficiency by making it easier for developers to integrate with other systems. This can lead to faster product delivery and innovation.
- **Security**: Good API design also includes robust security measures, which are crucial for protecting sensitive data and maintaining user trust.
- **Scalability**: APIs designed with scalability in mind can handle a large number of requests, allowing businesses to grow without worrying about API performance.
- **Interoperability**: A well-designed API can work seamlessly with other systems, regardless of the programming language or platform. This interoperability can lead to more integrations and collaborations.

As we can see, API design is absolutely crucial for the success of your API. We know very well how important user experience is in consumer applications. In the case of APIs, the consumers are developers, software architects, and other technical people. The user experience in this case is called **Developer Experience** and describes the ease to integrate with your API, maintain this integration for a long time, and the ability to enhance and monitor it. API Design, not unlike classical product design, or game design in case of video games, is what enables positive feedback loop for the consumers of APIs. A well-designed API, providing good value interfaces and which is easy to work with, will assure a long lifetime for your business. Now, let's reiterate what we have learned in this chapter.

Summary

In this chapter, we've delved into the fundamental motivations behind building APIs. One of the key takeaways is that APIs are crafted as products for specific consumer groups. The most effective products emerge from solid communication between API providers - those who build and maintain them - and API consumers. Even when creating an entirely novel API, it's beneficial to engage with potential users to understand their needs and interaction methods.

We've discussed how internal APIs can boost operational efficiency and security, while external APIs can generate revenue and enhance the quality of the API. Both types of APIs play a significant role in the API economy, helping businesses to leverage their unique business logic and data for new uses, deliver value to API consumers, enhance their competitive edge, and speed up time-to-market. Close communication during the API design process is key, whether your API is for external or internal use. While the business motivations may differ depending on whether an API is internal or external, the goals of quality, ease of use, maintainability, and observability are common to all APIs.

We also explored scenarios where it might be more beneficial to update an existing API rather than building a new one. Essentially, if you're considering building a new API when a similar one already exists, it's worth evaluating the difference in cost, both in terms of money and technology, between building and maintaining a new solution versus the current one. Consider the impact on your current clients, whether it will disrupt their integrations, and if your new solution meets their needs. Lastly, consider whether your organization is experiencing API Sprawl. Perhaps your new API could be a step towards addressing the lack of proper governance around your APIs.

We looked at a number of case studies showing that building APIs is key to growing your organization digitally, opening up more revenue streams, and improving internal efficiency. The importance of good API design is now more important than ever with the rise of large language model AI systems which can take advantage of it to an even greater extent.

In the next chapter, we'll discuss the API as a Product approach. We'll show how this represents a paradigm shift in how organizations think about APIs and the value they deliver. We'll break down the building blocks that make this approach work in practice and explore strategies for API monetization, packaging, and the role of the API portal in enabling adoption. We'll also continue developing our small API project and plan its strategy.

Get This Book's PDF Version and Exclusive Extras

UNLOCK NOW

Scan the QR code (or go to packtpub.com/unlock). Search for this book by name, confirm the edition, and then follow the steps on the page.

Note: Keep your invoice handy. Purchases made directly from Packt don't require an invoice.

2

API as a Product: Designing APIs with a Product Mindset

This chapter discusses how to approach APIs with a product mindset, focusing on the value the API provides to its consumers. It focuses on treating APIs as products rather than mere technical components. It emphasizes the importance of designing APIs with business goals and developer experience in mind and creating delightful experiences for API consumers. It covers best practices for designing effective API monetization, API packaging, and an API portal. It provides insights into how these principles can lead to more robust, efficient, and user-friendly APIs.

By the end of the chapter, you'll know the building blocks of an API as a product strategy and understand its mindset and the related benefits. You'll be able to design an effective API monetization and package your API. Finally, you'll learn the role of the API portal and the API product owner.

In this chapter, we are going to cover the following main topics:

- API as a product as a shifting paradigm
- The building blocks of API as a product
- API monetization strategies
- API packaging
- API portal

Shifting paradigm — APIs as products

Historically, many organizations own hundreds or thousands of point-to-point integration interfaces. Adidas, for instance, owns thousands of point-to-point interfaces supporting their internal operations and integration with third parties. Maintaining such a large landscape of legacy APIs has a tremendous cost. For example, Adidas saw an opportunity to shift how they treat these point-to-point interfaces. They decided to change how they treat APIs to achieve operational excellence, speed up how they integrate with their partners, create new revenue streams, and open doors for innovation.

We've also experienced an explosion of software consumption models. Users have swiftly moved beyond browser-based web apps and are now using products across multiple devices and environments.

Etsy, for example, recognized the growing trend of users accessing their services across various platforms. To ensure a seamless experience, they needed to adapt their API accordingly.

> *All of the code that was built for the website then had to be rebuilt in our API to be used by iOS and Android App.*
>
> — *Stephanie Schirmer, Etsy*

Beyond traditional API consumption models, we have also witnessed the rise of autonomous clients, especially with AI agents. This new trend pushes product engineering teams to re-design their APIs and consider APIs as **first-class citizens** instead of just a technical component.

So, **API as a product** is the intention of treating APIs like software products. It's a mindset shift that influences how you see APIs:

- From traditional technical assets to business assets
- From project-based solutions to product-based
- From being managed by project managers to being managed by API product managers
- From afterthought documentation to prototype-based documentation
- From complex integration to simple self-service integration
- From generating zero value to generating unique value for customers
- From slowing your innovation to unlocking new features
- From slowing your team's collaboration to scaling your product organization

The shift towards treating APIs as products emphasizes the need for a consumer-centric approach, which is crucial for their success. This leads us to the next section, where we delve into the building blocks of API as a product, exploring key requirements and practical strategies to ensure APIs meet user needs and deliver value. Let's dive into the main requirements and see how they shape your API as a product.

The building blocks of API as a product

In practice, treating an API as a product involves several key requirements to ensure it meets the needs of its users and delivers the right value. Let's look at the main requirements.

Customer centricity

Consumer centricity refers to a business approach that prioritizes the needs and use cases of your customers. This principle involves talking to your customers, understanding and anticipating their requirements, and designing the APIs together. For example, Stripe has a strong consumer-centric culture as they gather the voices of the customers by using diverse ways and tactics to gain empathy from their users and understand their needs. As a tactic, Stripe performs structured user experience research to answer questions such as *What challenges do developers face when using our APIs?*. They record the developers trying to integrate using Stripe API to find areas of friction and identify unforeseen pains.

In addition to talking to your customers, you have the intention of designing your APIs as packaged products, solving problems not just for one but many customers, and ultimately to an API audience.

Understanding your API audience will enable you to tailor API's design, documentation, support, and marketing efforts to meet the needs and expectations of each user persona, which might be categorized into the following segments:

- **Developers**: They have different levels of expertise, from beginner to advanced; they need clear and easy-to-use documentation, example code, **software development kits (SDKs)**, and frictionless developer experience. To target this segment, you need to focus on developer experience, quick onboarding, and robust API support.
- **Product managers**: They have a good understanding of technical and business aspects, and they need straightforward capabilities, insights, use cases, and what your API has to offer. To target this segment, you need to demonstrate how you can solve their business problems and enhance their products.

- **Business owners**: They are skilled at designing business strategies and making decisions, they need a clear value proposition, **return on investment (ROI)**, case studies, and easy to understand pricing model. To target this segment, you need to show business benefits, potential cost savings, and revenue generation.

- **DevOps and security engineers**: They are skilled at managing infrastructure, and platforms and securing them. They need reliable, scalable, secure, and compliant API features. To target them you need to focus on API performance, uptime, and API security.

- **Support engineers**: They are responsible for community management and API support. They need great documentation, troubleshooting guides, and a supportive community. To target them you need to provide help, explanatory API errors, and detailed troubleshooting guides.

A typical challenge when talking to customers is knowing exactly what they need and deciding whether to solve their problems or not. For instance, you might be known for providing a geo-coding API product, and some customers potentially will ask for map features. The challenge is to balance what you need to solve, what you are good at, and what the customer needs.

To bridge the concepts of customer centricity and design focus in APIs, it's important to emphasize the importance of aligning design principles with user needs. The focus on consumer centricity underscores the necessity of understanding and addressing diverse user requirements, laying the foundation for effective API design. By prioritizing reusability and consistency in API design, we can ensure that APIs are not only easy to consume but also meet the varied expectations of different user personas. Let's explore how reusability and consistency in design enhance the overall API experience.

Focus on design

APIs as products are easy to consume because they are reusable and consistent. Let's take a look at each of these principles in detail.

Reusability

API **reusability** is a design principle where APIs are developed to be used across different applications or services without requiring signification modification. Think of reusability like LEGO bricks. These building blocks are standardized and fit together seamlessly, allowing you to build a variety of structures. For example, Twilio's API is highly modular, allowing developers to add communication features to web applications, mobile devices, and IoT devices using different languages. This reusability makes it the go-to API for diverse communication needs.

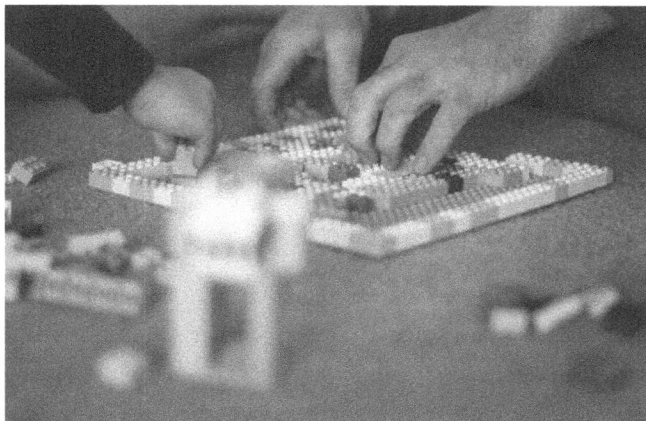

Figure 2.1: Lego (image from Unsplash)

In addition to reusability, API products should be consistent. Like Lego bricks, which follow standard dimensions and connection points, this makes them compatible with other LEGO bricks.

Consistency

Consistency in APIs leads to predictability in how they are consumed, makes them easy to use, and reduces developers' friction. This principle improves your developer's experience in many ways, it reduces your developer's learning curve and reduces time to integrate and failures.

Here are some examples that highlight the impact of missing consistency, leading to challenges for developers:

- **Inconsistent naming conventions**: Inconsistent API endpoint names and parameters. For instance, some endpoints or payload fields use **snake_case** while others use **camelCase**. This practice makes developers unhappy as you increase the likelihood of making errors in their API integrations.

- **Frequent data format change**: For example, an API has different fields or nested structures in different versions without adequate documentation of the versioning strategy. These unannounced changes break existing clients that depend on stable data format, leading to frustration and increased maintenance costs.

- **Unpredictable rate limits and throttling**: API rate limits or throttling rules are inconsistent or not communicated, for example, you might hide a rate limit for security reasons, or instantly change a rate limit without notice. Integrations that rely on your API will suddenly stop working, thus developers will not trust you anymore as they can't build reliable applications.

While effective design ensures APIs are reusable and consistent, having a dedicated API product owner is essential to maintain this focus and drive the API strategy forward. The API product owner ensures that the principles of reusability and consistency are upheld, aligning API development with business goals and customer needs. Let's now delve into the responsibilities and impact of an API product owner.

API product owner

Many organizations adopt API-as-a-product strategies without designating dedicated API product owners, jeopardizing the success and sustainability of their API initiatives. To understand the crucial role and impact of an API product owner, we will explore their key responsibilities and the risks of not having this role in place. Following this, we'll discuss how organizations can build and develop API product owner capabilities.

The role of an API product owner

An **API product owner** is a pivotal figure responsible for steering the API-as-a-product strategy. They ensure that APIs are developed, maintained, and evolved with a product-centric approach rather than a traditional, ad hoc methodology. Their responsibilities include the following:

- **Advocacy and sponsorship**: API product owners champion the value proposition of APIs, securing necessary business sponsorship and funding. They communicate the strategic importance of APIs to stakeholders, ensuring alignment and support across the organization.

- **Customer insight and iteration**: By understanding and decrypting API customer insights, API product owners drive the continuous iteration and improvement of APIs. They support the business in leveraging API potential to maximize revenue and meet evolving customer needs.

- **Defining API roadmap**: From the customer insights API product owners can define and prioritize API features, manage API product backlog, and ensure alignment and engineering teams' commitment to delivering value to customers.

- **Lifecycle management**: API product owners act as the primary customers of the API lifecycle, advocating for its effective implementation. They ensure that the lifecycle processes produce valuable APIs, manage API product bundles, and utilize API management solutions to gain insights on usage, security, and access.

In summary, the API product owner is crucial for bridging the gap between technical development and business strategy. They ensure APIs are not only technically sound but also aligned with market needs and organizational goals. By advocating for API value, driving customer-focused improvements, managing a clear and strategic roadmap, and overseeing lifecycle management, API product owners play an essential role in the success and sustainability of API initiatives. Their involvement helps prevent the risks associated with traditional, ad hoc development approaches and ensures APIs deliver maximum value to both the business and its customers.

Risks of not having an API product owner

Without an API product owner, organizations face several challenges, such as the following:

- **Traditional development approaches**: Without API product owners, your APIs will be built using traditional ways of working, meaning we postpone them or treat them as trivial documentation that potentially will end in an outdated state. Traditional development approaches often involve creating APIs on an ad hoc basis without a long-term strategy, leading to inconsistency and technical debt. These methods treat APIs as one-time projects with minimal documentation and customer engagement, resulting in outdated and difficult-to-use APIs. Additionally, there is little proactive planning or lifecycle management, causing APIs to fall behind in meeting evolving user needs.
- **Siloed APIs**: APIs can remain isolated within organizational silos, making it difficult to secure business sponsorship and funding. The value and potential of APIs are often misunderstood or overlooked.
- **Missed Customer Insights**: Lacking someone to gather and analyze API customer insights results in missed opportunities for iteration and improvement, limiting revenue potential and customer satisfaction.

In summary, the absence of an API product owner can lead to fragmented development, isolated efforts, and missed opportunities to leverage customer insights. This not only hampers the potential value of APIs but also affects their usability, maintenance, and overall effectiveness in driving business success.

Building API product owner capability

Finding and hiring skilled API product owners can be challenging due to the niche nature of the role. However, organizations can also develop this capability internally. This involves identifying current employees who possess a strong understanding of both the business and technical aspects of API development and providing them with the necessary training and resources to transition into the role of API product owner.

For instance, as part of their API-as-a-product initiative, Adidas successfully trained existing product owners to become API product owners. This approach allowed them to scale their e-commerce core APIs and build effective internal API teams. By leveraging the knowledge and experience of their current staff, Adidas was able to foster a deep understanding of their specific API needs and organizational goals, which external hires might take longer to achieve.

To develop API product owner capabilities internally, organizations can take several steps:

- **API training programs**: Implement comprehensive training programs that cover the key responsibilities of an API product owner, including API strategy, customer insights, lifecycle management, and stakeholder communication. This can include workshops, online courses, and mentorship from experienced API professionals.

- **Cross-functional collaboration:** Encourage collaboration between different teams such as development, marketing, and customer support to provide a holistic understanding of how APIs impact various aspects of the business. This can help potential API product owners see the broader picture and understand the importance of their role.

- **Hands-on experience**: Provide opportunities for potential API product owners to gain hands-on experience by involving them in ongoing API projects. This can include participating in the design, development, and iteration processes, as well as interacting with customers and gathering feedback.

- **Mentorship and support**: Pair aspiring API product owners with experienced mentors who can provide guidance, share best practices, and offer support as they transition into their new roles. This can help build confidence and ensure a smooth transition.

- **Continuous learning**: Foster a culture of continuous learning where employees are encouraged to stay updated with the latest trends, tools, and best practices in API development and management. This can be achieved through regular training sessions, attending industry conferences, and participating in relevant professional networks.

By investing in the development of internal API product owner capabilities, organizations can ensure a steady supply of skilled professionals who are deeply familiar with their specific needs and goals. This not only helps in scaling API initiatives effectively but also promotes a culture of innovation and continuous improvement within the organization.

As we have seen, the role of an API product owner is crucial for aligning API strategies with business goals and ensuring the delivery of valuable, user-centric APIs. However, the success of APIs as products also heavily depends on the experience of the developers who use them. A positive **developer experience (DX)** is essential for the adoption and effective utilization of APIs.

DX

To ensure the success of your API strategy, it's crucial to focus on the DX. This section delves into understanding and enhancing how developers interact with and perceive your APIs. We will explore the emotional and psychological aspects of developers, the design of their journey, and practical steps to improve their interactions with your API ecosystem. By optimizing the DX, you can foster positive emotions and productivity, leading to higher adoption and satisfaction.

Understanding your audience

DX revolves around how developers perceive and interact with your APIs. To optimize this, it's essential to understand their emotions and what triggers positive feelings such as fascination and happiness. When developers engage with your APIs, they embark on a journey through your environment, aiming to achieve a specific goal or outcome. This journey has two main facets:

- **Development engagement**: How developers engage with your environment, such as developer programs and API support channels
- **System interaction**: How developers interact with your system to complete their tasks, including API design, documentation, SDKs, and tutorials

Every interaction shapes how developers perceive your API. Your goal is to streamline their journey, ensuring they reach their destination swiftly and enjoyably. Successful API strategies hinge on designing effective developer interactions.

In addition to development engagement and system interaction, the learning curve is a critical dimension. Optimizing for different developer personas—novice, intermediate, and expert—is essential for a holistic DX:

- **Novice developers**: These users benefit from excellent onboarding processes that guide them through their first interactions with the API. Optimizing for first-time-to-hello-world ensures that novices can quickly understand and start using the API with minimal friction.
- **Intermediate developers**: These users require more in-depth documentation, practical examples, and advanced tutorials that help them integrate more complex functionalities.
- **Expert developers**: While many API products excel at catering to novices, they often fall short in providing the flexibility needed for experts. Experts look for comprehensive reference materials, customization options, and the ability to perform sophisticated tasks. Ensuring your API is flexible and robust enough to handle expert use cases is crucial.

By understanding and optimizing the emotional triggers, engagement methods, system interactions, and learning curves for various developer personas, you can create a compelling DX that drives higher adoption and satisfaction. Each touchpoint in this journey must be meticulously designed to reduce friction and enhance the overall experience. In the next section, we will delve into the specifics of designing a developer journey in detail.

Designing your developer journey

Getting your developer journey ready for API as a product is a challenging task—it entails different stages. The nature and number of stages might be different and tightly coupled with what kind of API audience segment you are targeting, for example, your internal developers will experience different stages than external developers.

Let's take a hypothetical API that you're just launching; you notice that you have at least six stages:

Stage	Objective	Steps	Metrics
Awareness	Make developers aware of your API capabilities and its benefits by launching ad hoc marketing campaigns, participating in developer events, and publishing content showing what your API can do.	Marketing materials Blog posts Social media Presentations/webinars	Number of website visits Ad click rate Number of mentions Attendance of events/ webinars
Evaluation	Enable developers to test your APIs and ensure they solve their problems by providing comprehensive and clear documentation, offering example code, showing use cases, and maintaining responsive API support.	API documentation Example code Quick start guides Community forums, FAQ section API support	Documentation page views Sample code number of download/ execution Time spent on documentation page

Stage	Objective	Steps	Metrics
Onboarding	Reduce the time it takes for API developers to get the first value from your API by streamlining API access and developer account creation, providing a step-by-step getting started guide, and offering tips for common issues.	API access Getting started guide Hands-on tutorials Troubleshooting guide	Time to first *"Hello World"* Completion rate for initial setup Number of API key creations Net Promoter Score (NPS)
Adoption	Reduce friction and build trust with your developers by supporting them in their first integration with detailed guides, offering technical support, and making your API support responsive.	Documentation Sandbox Debugging Error management API changelog API support	Active API usage Number of client applications Time it takes users to fix errors NPS
Retention	Keep API developers engaged and maintain trust by continuously improving your API based on feedback, maintaining active communication and superb ongoing support.	API changelog API newsletter Community forums API support	Churn rate API incidents Newsletter click rate NPS
Advocacy	Turn your API developers into advocates, by encouraging them to share their success stories and engaging with them through recognition programs and events.	Case study submission Advocacy program Event organization materials/ merchandising	Number of case studies Advocacy program participation rate Social media mentions

Table 2.1: Example of developer journey

Now that we have covered the building blocks of APIs as a product, let's dive into how to monetize your API products.

API monetization strategies

As we delve into API monetization strategies, it's crucial to understand how turning your API into a revenue-generating asset can significantly impact your business. This section explores the concept of API monetization, various monetization models, and the steps to design an effective monetization strategy. By aligning your API's value with the right pricing model, you can create a sustainable revenue stream and meet your business objectives.

What's API monetization

API monetization is when you turn your API into a profitable stream of direct or indirect revenue. It consists of the entire process of generating this revenue from defining your monetization model to maintaining it over time. This revenue is mainly generated by API access to third-party developers, partners, and end-users. They pay you because you are solving a problem they have and don't have the time or expertise to solve it.

Defining your API monetization model depends on various factors, including the target audience, the API value you provide, and your overall business model. Here are several models you can choose from:

- **Free**: This model helps you drive adoption to your APIs, build your brand, and enable you to foster innovation.
- **Developer pays**: You can charge developers using several pricing models:
    - **Freemium**: In this model, you offer a limited version of your API. For example, Open API offers a limited free tier to allow users to experiment with their APIs and convert them to paid users. This includes a limited number of tokens or a limited amount of time to use the API.
    - **Pay-as-you-go**: API consumers pay per usage (e.g., number of API calls or data volume). This pricing model offers higher usage limits and additional services for paying customers. This model can be attractive to users who want to avoid upfront costs and pay only for what they use. For example, Twilio's WhatsApp Business API offers a pay-as-you-go pricing model and charges $0.0042 for sending a WhatsApp message.
    - **Tiered**: You define different usage tiers (e.g., basic, standard, premium, enterprise, etc.) with different pricing structures based on API call limits or feature sets. API consumers can upgrade to higher tiers as their usage grows. For example, Mailgun API offers Basic, Foundation, and Scale plans, each plan is capped by the number

of emails you are allowed to send per day and a set of features. This model can be combined with pay-as-you-go to create a hybrid pricing structure that offers both flexibility and predictability for your API consumers, who can choose a subscription tier that fits their typical usage and then pay additional fees for extra usage.

- **Transaction fee**: This involves charging API consumers based on the number of value of transactions processed through your API. Each time a transaction occurs (e.g. a payment or a loan request), a fee is applied. This model is particularly common in banking, e-commerce, or some data processing APIs, where the value of your API is not linked to the transaction itself and not the number of API calls. The Stripe API is a good example. As we write, they are charging 1.5% + E0.25 for standard European Economic Area cards.

- **Points-based**: Also called token-based or unit-based, it involves charging users based on the consumption of points or tokens, which are used to consume your API or perform certain API operations. Each type of API call consumes a predetermined number of points, which users can purchase in advance. This model is quite popular in APIs that perform heavy computation behind the scenes. For example, OpenAI uses a token-based pricing model for their services, particularly for its language models; each language model has different capabilities and token points.

- **Developers get paid**: Developers get paid to leverage your web APIs using several pricing models:

  - **Revenue share**: You partner with your API consumer who uses your API to generate revenue and share a percentage of the revenue they generate using your API, this can incentivize both parties to maximize revenue. This model is common in marketplaces or platforms. For example, Shopify API provides APIs that allow developers to build apps for their e-commerce platform. Developers earn revenue from their apps and Shopify takes a fixed commission.

  - **Affiliate**: Your partners include your API content or advertisement to sell your offering, and you compensate them for that with a commission. Amazon Associate API is an example of an affiliate program that allows users to earn commissions on sales.

  - **Referral**: Similar to affiliate, but your partners earn money only if the end user makes a purchase.

API monetization is not just about earning revenue, but also about achieving business goals. This is where indirect API monetization models can enable grow your business:

- **Content syndication and acquisition,** where publishers or users use your content and distribute it to other platforms, publishers, or users. This model is commonly used in the media domain (e.g., the YouTube API).

- **B2B customers and partners**, where you focus on developing your business using partnerships.

- **Internal users**, that use your API to develop other business capabilities, enhance the performance of your software delivery, and foster a lean team collaboration.

API monetization is not just about earning revenue but also about achieving business goals through indirect models such as content syndication, B2B partnerships, and enhancing internal business capabilities.

Now that we have covered different API monetization models, let's see in detail how to choose the right one.

Designing your monetization model

Designing an effective monetization model requires a deep understanding of your customer's needs, the value your API provides, and careful consideration of the pricing models we mentioned in the preceding section. These steps are a walk-through of how to design a successful monetization model:

1. **Understand your customers and define value** by engaging directly with them, understanding their needs, their pains, and their intention to pay you for the value you provide.

2. **Define value proposition** by clearly defining what capabilities your API provides that solve your customers' problems, identifying cost-saving benefits and efficiency improvements.

3. **Choose a monetization model** that aligns with your API business value and matches the insights you gathered from your customers. Many successful API companies use a combination of different models. For instance, you might offer a freemium model to attract users, tiered pricing for predictable revenue, and pay-as-you-go for scalability.

4. **Iterate and improve** on your API monetization model, based on insights, customer feedback, and API consumption patterns.

While it might be tempting to create a complex API monetization model, simplicity is key. Your customers should quickly understand the cost and the value they are transparently getting from your API. Consider also that your API consumers are mainly developers, who don't necessarily own a company credit card, expect to adapt your API monetization model to this reality, and ultimately face some API usage abuse, as some developers might be tempted to create multiple API keys to use your API. Finally, foster trust by offering transparent pricing and calculators to help them estimate costs based on their anticipated usage.

In summary, API monetization is a strategic process that involves turning your API into a revenue-generating asset. By choosing the right monetization model and continuously iterating based on customer feedback, you can create a sustainable revenue stream while achieving broader business goals. Simplicity, transparency, and understanding your customers' needs are key to designing an effective monetization strategy.

API bundling

While monetization models determine how an API generates revenue, **API bundles and plans** organize the API's structure and accessibility by grouping related APIs and defining usage limits, features, and terms for different customer segments. Like any product, APIs need to be thoughtfully packaged for developers through an API portal, where bundles and plans help streamline access, clarify value, and meet a range of customer needs.

For instance, a company might create distinct bundles for **analytics**, **machine learning**, and **data storage** APIs, each with tailored pricing models. The analytics bundle could use a tiered model for steady, predictable revenue, while the machine learning bundle might adopt a pay-as-you-go model to accommodate high-intensity computational usage. This bundling approach enables more flexible and targeted pricing strategies, maximizing value for both the provider and the consumer.

What's an API bundle?

An **API bundle** refers to a collection of APIs bundled together, providing similar capabilities; they help users access related APIs, reduce complexity, and enhance developer experience. For API providers, they streamline management, access, and security. For example, Google Cloud Platform provides various API bundles that cater to different functionalities, such as machine learning, cloud storage, and data analytics, Google Maps Package includes Maps, Routes, and Places APIs, each with its own set of features and pricing.

The majority of API management and API portal solutions help with implementing and structuring your APIs into packages and plans, ensuring an efficient monetization of your APIs.

What's an API plan?

An **API plan** is an offering that defines the terms and conditions of how your APIs will be consumed; in detail, it defines the usage limits, pricing, features, support levels, and **Service Level Agreements (SLAs):**

- **Usage limits**: This includes rate limits and quotas. A rate limit is typically the maximum number of API requests allowed per time unit (e.g. seconds or minutes). A quota is the total number of API requests within a billing period (e.g. daily or monthly).

- **Pricing**: This can be one of the pricing models we discussed earlier in the *What's API monetization?* section.

- **Feature access**: Different plans may have access to different API features; you might restrict access to advanced features for higher pricing tiers.

- **Support level**: Depending on the pricing tier, support may be different; a higher pricing tier may offer 24x7 support, faster response time, and ultimately a dedicated account manager.

- **SLAs**: This encompasses what guarantee you can provide to your customers regarding the performance and reliability of your APIs.

Designing a comprehensive API plan ensures that your customers understand what they are getting and what they can expect from your API offering. By clearly defining these elements, you can cater to different customer needs and create a structured approach to API consumption.

In summary, an API plan is essential for managing how your APIs are consumed, providing clarity on usage limits, pricing, features, support levels, and SLAs. This structured approach not only helps you meet diverse customer needs but also aids in maintaining the quality and reliability of your API services.

Next, we will explore how to effectively implement effective API bundles and plans through an example.

Example – Magic Cloud API packaging

To help you grasp the concepts of an API bundles and API plans, let's take a hypothetical example: **Magic Cloud** is a cloud provider that offers a variety of API products:

- Compute API
- AI and machine learning API

- Storage API
- Networking API
- IoT API

They might structure API bundles and plans like the following:

- **Basic cloud package**: Compute (VMs), storage (object storage), and networking (VPC) APIs
- **Advanced cloud package**: Compute (VMs and container orchestration), storage (object and block storage), database (SQL), and networking (VPC and load-balancing) APIs
- **AI and data analytics package**: AI and machine learning (image recognition and NLP), databases (NoSQL, in-memory, and vector), and storage (file storage)
- **IoT package**: IoT (device management, data ingestion, and edge computing), networking (CDN), storage (object Storage), and database (SQL)

Each package may include one or many plans. For example, the *Basic Cloud API bundle* includes three plans:

- **Free tier**:
  - *Usage limits*: 1 VM, 10 GB Object Storage, Basic VPC with limited bandwidth
  - *Features*: Basic features for testing and development
  - *Support*: Community
  - *Pricing*: Free

- **Standard plan**:
  - *Usage limits*: 10 VM, 100 GB Object Storage, Standard VPC with moderate bandwidth
  - *Features*: Access to the majority of services with standard SLA
  - *Support*: Community + email support
  - *Pricing*: $49 per month

- **Premium plan**
  - *Usage limits*: 50 VM, 1 TB Object Storage, Basic VPC with high bandwidth
  - *Features*: All standard features in addition to premium features
  - *Support*: Community + email support
  - *Pricing*: $149 per month

Next, let's see how the concepts of an API bundle and API plan have been applied in the real world based on a use case.

Real-world use case — Twilio's SendGrid Email API

Twilio's **SendGrid Email API** provides a clear example of how API bundles and plans work alongside a monetization model to maximize value for both the provider and the consumer. SendGrid offers a set of tiered plans—**Free**, **Essentials**, **Pro**, and **Premier**—each designed with specific usage limits, feature sets, and pricing tailored to different user segments and business sizes.

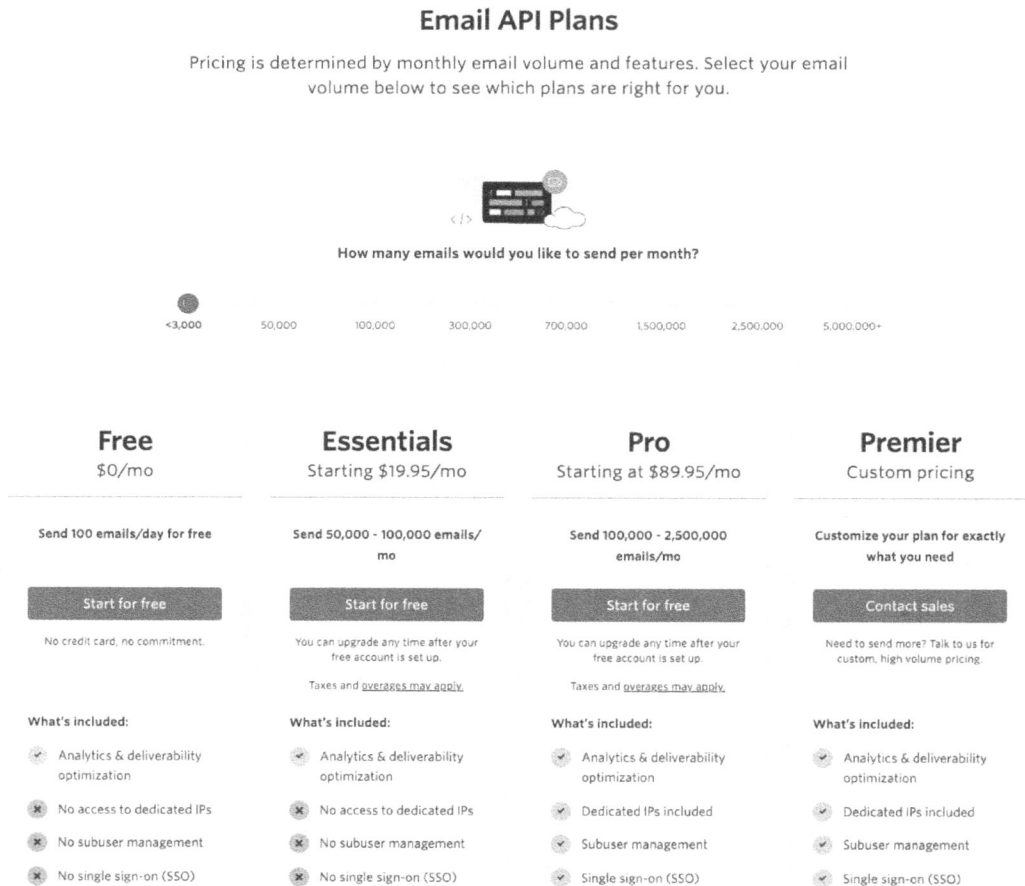

Email API Plans

Pricing is determined by monthly email volume and features. Select your email volume below to see which plans are right for you.

How many emails would you like to send per month?

<3,000   50,000   100,000   300,000   700,000   1,500,000   2,500,000   5,000,000+

Free	Essentials	Pro	Premier
$0/mo	Starting $19.95/mo	Starting at $89.95/mo	Custom pricing
Send 100 emails/day for free	Send 50,000 - 100,000 emails/mo	Send 100,000 - 2,500,000 emails/mo	Customize your plan for exactly what you need
Start for free	Start for free	Start for free	Contact sales
No credit card, no commitment.	You can upgrade any time after your free account is set up.	You can upgrade any time after your free account is set up.	Need to send more? Talk to us for custom, high volume pricing.
	Taxes and <u>overages may apply</u>.	Taxes and <u>overages may apply</u>.	
What's included:	What's included:	What's included:	What's included:
✓ Analytics & deliverability optimization	✓ Analytics & deliverability optimization	✓ Analytics & deliverability optimization	✓ Analytics & deliverability optimization
✗ No access to dedicated IPs	✗ No access to dedicated IPs	✓ Dedicated IPs included	✓ Dedicated IPs included
✗ No subuser management	✗ No subuser management	✓ Subuser management	✓ Subuser management
✗ No single sign-on (SSO)	✗ No single sign-on (SSO)	✓ Single sign-on (SSO)	✓ Single sign-on (SSO)

Figure 2.2: Twillio Email API pricing page

⚲ **Quick tip**: Need to see a high-resolution version of this image? Open this book in the next-gen Packt Reader or view it in the PDF/ePub copy.

▣ **The next-gen Packt Reader** is included for free with the purchase of this book. Scan the QR code OR go to `https://packtpub.com/unlock`, then use the search bar to find this book by name. Double-check the edition shown to make sure you get the right one.

Here's a breakdown of Twilio's SendGrid Email API example, specifying the **Monetization Model**, **Bundles**, and **Plans**:

- **Monetization model**:

  - *Freemium and Tiered pricing model*: Twilio uses a freemium model to attract users with a free plan, allowing them to send up to 100 emails per day at no cost. This approach encourages initial adoption and offers a pathway for users to explore basic features.

  - *Tiered pricing*: Beyond the free plan, Twilio applies a tiered pricing model for paid plans, each offering additional features, larger email volumes, and varying levels of support to cater to different user needs and scales.

- **Bundle**:

  - *Email API bundle*: The SendGrid Email API bundle encompasses all the core email-related services (such as sending emails, analytics, and email validation) that developers and businesses need for email communication. This bundle is structured to provide a variety of email services within one cohesive package, suitable for businesses of all sizes.

- **Plans:**

  - *Free plan*: Provides basic access, allowing up to 100 emails per day with limited features.

  - *Essentials plan* (starting at $19.95/month): Includes access for sending 50,000 to 100,000 emails per month, offering added features such as additional webhooks and analytics, but without dedicated IPs.

  - *Pro plan* (starting at $89.95/month): Supports up to 2.5 million emails per month and adds premium features such as dedicated IPs, subuser management, and advanced analytics.

  - *Premier plan* (custom pricing): For high-volume enterprises, this customizable plan offers extensive analytics, dedicated IPs, high-level security, and up to 1,000 teammates, with pricing adjusted for volume and specific enterprise needs.

This structure leverages a **freemium and tiered pricing model** to gradually upsell users based on their email needs, with the *Email API bundle* providing the essential email functionalities in a range of plans that address different customer segments and usage levels.

In summary, API bundles and plans are crucial steps in structuring your API offerings to meet diverse customer needs while ensuring efficient management and monetization. Clearly defined bundles and plans help streamline access, enhance the developer experience, and align API consumption with business objectives.

Now that you know how to structure your API offering, let's see where to expose it using an API portal.

API portal

API portal is a central hub that serves as a bridge between you and your API consumers. It's typically a web-based interface hosting necessary API documentation, tools, sandbox to interact with your API, API access provisioning, and support.

An API portal is fundamental to your API as a product strategy. It makes your APIs easily discoverable by providing a categorized and searchable catalog of available APIs, where users browse through different API products and understand their functionalities. Once users find what API they need to use, next, you provide a detailed user-friendly documentation section, so they can quickly grasp how your APIs work, test your API using a sandbox or playground, and find necessary documentation that helps them to troubleshoot their issues.

Effective API portals offer the following tenets:

- **Transparency**: Transparency is crucial, particularly regarding pricing. The portal should provide clear and detailed information about pricing plans, along with an API changelog to communicate any potential breaking changes. Additionally, a status page showing the operational status of the API is essential to keep users informed about any incident or upcoming maintenance.

- **Inclusivity**: An API portal must cater to a diverse range of user personas, not just developers. This means understanding and addressing the needs of product managers, business stakeholders, and other non-technical users to ensure everyone can understand and utilize your API offering.

- **Enabling collaboration**: Serving as a hub, an effective API portal should facilitate collaboration between the API provider and its users. It should provide forums, chat tools, and support channels to enable seamless communication and minimize users' frustrations.

Deciding whether to build or buy your API portal involves weighing several trade-offs. Building offers the benefits of full customization and control, allowing you to tailor features to your specific needs, but it comes with higher upfront costs, longer development times, and ongoing maintenance requirements. For example, companies such as Stripe and Twilio built their portals to provide a highly customized experience for their users. On the other hand, buying an API portal provides the advantage of faster deployment, lower initial costs, and ongoing support. Many API management providers and API platforms, include built-in API portals, making it easier for organizations to get started quickly. However, these options may offer less customization, potential vendor dependency, and recurring costs.

In summary, an API portal is a vital component for effectively managing and presenting your APIs to consumers. By ensuring transparency, inclusivity, and enabling collaboration, a well-designed API portal can significantly enhance the developer experience and drive API adoption. Whether you choose to build or buy, the decision should align with your specific needs and strategic goals.

Summary

In this chapter, you have explored the concept of API as a product mindset, emphasizing the importance of viewing APIs as valuable business assets rather than mere technical components. You have learned how shifting from traditional project-based solutions to a product-based approach can enhance business goals and improve the developer experience. By treating APIs as products, you can create more user-friendly and efficient interfaces, ultimately delivering unique value to customers and fostering innovation.

You have gained insights into the importance of understanding the needs of different API consumers, including developers, product managers, business owners, and support engineers. This chapter highlighted the value of consumer-centric design, which involves engaging with customers to gather insights and co-design APIs that address their requirements. You also learned about the significance of API reusability and consistency, which can reduce developer friction and improve the overall user experience, akin to how standardized LEGO bricks fit together seamlessly.

You have understood the risks of not having a dedicated API product owner, such as siloed APIs and missed opportunities for improvement. Additionally, you have been provided with insights into building an effective API product owner capability, either through hiring or training existing team members.

Finally, you learned about API monetization strategies and packaging. Various monetization models, including freemium, pay-as-you-go, and tiered pricing, have been explored, emphasizing the need for simplicity and transparency in pricing to build trust with users. You have learned about the concept of API packaging, where related APIs are bundled together to enhance user experience and streamline management. The chapter concludes with the role of the API portal, which serves as a central hub for documentation, tools, and support, ensuring APIs are easily discoverable and accessible to a diverse range of users.

In the next chapter, we will gain a comprehensive understanding of how a holistic view of the entire API lifecycle influences your API design. You will learn about the interconnectedness of the API lifecycle and the application lifecycle, and how they impact each other throughout their various stages.

Get This Book's PDF Version and Exclusive Extras

UNLOCK NOW

Scan the QR code (or go to packtpub.com/unlock). Search for this book by name, confirm the edition, and then follow the steps on the page.

Note: Keep your invoice handy. Purchases made directly from Packt don't require an invoice.

3

Understanding Application and API Lifecycles

This chapter explains how taking a holistic look at the whole API Lifecycle can influence your API design. We'll cover how your API and application lifecycles are interwoven and provide a comprehensive overview of the stages that an application and its APIs go through, from inception to deprecation.

In this chapter, we're going to cover the following main topics:

- What is the API Lifecycle and how does it relate to your application lifecycle?
- What are the main stages of the API Lifecycle?
- Why thinking about your API design from the perspective of its whole life will make it better
- How to plan your API Lifecycle based on target audience, purpose, and business model

What is the API Lifecycle?

The **API Lifecycle** is simply the process an API undergoes from the moment a decision is made to create it until the moment it must be decommissioned. The API Lifecycle goes through the same process as the application life cycle. APIs expose an application's functionality and data capabilities, and their life cycle shouldn't be treated as a separate entity. The API follows the same life cycle as the application it's part of. A well-managed API lifecycle contributes to the success of the application. Understanding this leads to more efficient development processes, better quality products, and, ultimately, successful digital transformation initiatives.

The API lifecycle is defined as a series of steps that teams follow to successfully design, develop, deploy, and consume APIs. It's one of the fundamental parts of any API governance strategy. If you don't define what your API's life cycle will be like, it will be difficult to establish proper design, process, and publishing policies.

Why knowing about your API lifecycle is important for a good API design

A well-defined API lifecycle establishes a shared understanding and vocabulary for API-related work. In the model we'll be following in this book, a team will create a design for an API, which can then be shared with other stakeholders to start effective communication. This will help team members stay on the same page throughout the API lifecycle. This design will act as a starting point for implementing the API and a source of truth for testing whether the code works as intended. A well-tested application can then be deployed and published to end users. With feedback coming from them and from our monitoring effort, we can add and update the design and its implementation.

This promotes the API-first approach, which is about designing and building applications as a collection of internal and external services that are delivered through APIs. We talked about this in detail in *Chapter 2*.

What are the benefits of API lifecycle management?

Some of the benefits of API lifecycle management include increased productivity, greater visibility into an API's trajectory, and organizational alignment. This allows you to prepare for each stage. The main advantage of establishing a controlled API lifecycle is that you can create and evolve all the processes the API lifecycle will go through in its life. This reduces uncertainties and establishes creative constraints. It also describes how to set proper **continuous integration/ continuous deployment** (**CI/CD**) processes so that we can automate quality control and verify all the steps that are involved.

Understanding the API lifecycle and implementing some best practices for managing it are crucial for good API design for several reasons:

- **Consistency**: Following a well-defined API lifecycle ensures that all APIs follow a consistent design and development process. This makes it easier for developers to understand and use the APIs, leading to more efficient development processes. By starting with the design, we can set expectations publicly within our team and are open to any discussion early on. Referring to the design as a single source of truth, we can validate the implementation and whether it's consistent with it.

- **Quality assurance**: Each stage of the API lifecycle has quality checks. In a well-established API lifecycle, we utilize validations and tests within our CI/CD pipelines – for example, we can contract test our implementation during the deployment phases. We can also publish up-to-date documentation whenever a new design document version is being implemented.

- **Versioning and maintenance**: Understanding the API lifecycle helps in managing different versions of the API and planning for future updates. It helps prevent changes that could break its clients from being introduced to your API. It does so by introducing proper quality assurance in between changes and implementing backward compatibility checks in the life cycle's flow. It also aids in deciding when to deprecate or retire an API.

- **Collaboration and communication**: A well-defined API lifecycle facilitates better collaboration between different teams involved in the API development process. By standardizing a life cycle process, we can establish a common vocabulary, tools, resources, and steps for each API. By utilizing the concept of our design being the single source of truth, we can maximize the number of stakeholders being able to reason about the API. This way, we can create a common language for discussing API design, development, and management.

- **Business alignment**: The API lifecycle starts with planning and designing the API based on business requirements. This ensures that the API aligns with the business goals and adds value to the organization. It adds to the transparency of the process for the business stakeholders.

In summary, understanding the API lifecycle is key to designing APIs that are consistent, high-quality, easy to maintain, and aligned with business goals. It helps organizations maximize the value of their API portfolio and advance their digital strategies.

Next, we'll learn about the various stages of the API lifecycle.

Defining the stages of the API lifecycle

Now that we've learned about the benefits of a well-structured API lifecycle process, let's dive a little deeper into its structure. As mentioned previously, the API lifecycle consists of several stages. You may have seen this division in various places and noticed that it may differ between places and people. The number, naming, and other aspects of the stages are arbitrary and depend on the focus of the program. For example, we're focusing on the design phase and the governance processes, while some organizations or teams may focus on observability and testability. In this book, we'll be using a six-step process, starting with design and finishing with updating. This is an iterative loop and ends with a one-time additional step – retirement. This book will focus almost exclusively on two phases – **design** and **update** – while providing some important comments on other stages, which either are results of your API design or are connected to the quality and reliability of your design-driven API governance program.

Figure 3.1 depicts the stages in the API lifecycle:

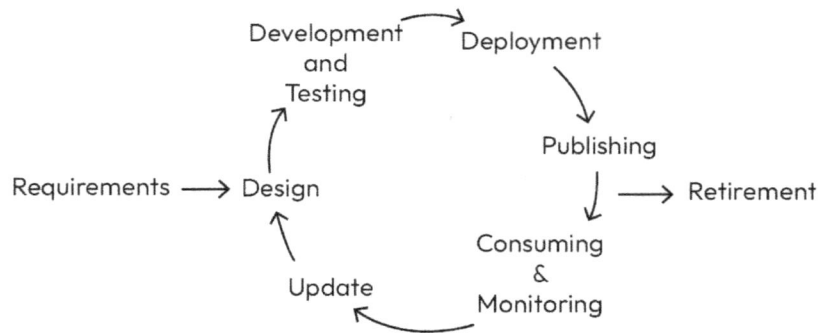

Figure 3.1: API lifecycle stages

Before you can start building an API, we must gather requirements and constraints. It's in this step that we discover and analyze the motivations that we discussed in detail in *Chapter 1*. This is mostly a one-time step, but whenever new business requirements arise, we may need to re-evaluate our motivations and set the path for future development.

Now, let's learn in detail about each step in our seven-step process, starting with **design**.

Design

API design is the first step we go through during our life cycle journey and is the step that this book focuses on. Throughout this book, we'll be arguing that this is hands-down the most crucial step and will also define the steps that follow.

In the design phase, we define our data model, as well as the resources, interfaces, and actions it supports. We also take care of the security model design. The result of this step will be a document that formally describes our API design. In this book, we'll be using the **OpenAPI Specification (OAS)** to achieve this goal.

The OAS

The OAS is a specification for describing API design in a machine-readable manner. By using it, we enable true API lifecycle definition and a design-first approach to API development. In *Chapter 10*, we're going to explore OAS in detail and work on concrete examples of how to leverage it both in API design as well as in other API lifecycle stages.

This way, during the design process, we'll have a tangible outcome that can not only be used to generate code or documentation but can also be used as the single source of truth for interested stakeholders. Such an approach is called **design-first** or **contract-driven development**. This is something we took a much deeper dive into in *Chapter 2*. We'll explore the importance of contract-driven development in *Chapter 8*.

Best practice

If possible, collaborate with your consumers during the API design process. Share your design documents early so that they can prototype creating early proof of concept applications. This way, you'll be able to catch possible technical issues early on, even before your API has been fully designed or implemented. You can work using only API design documents and mock servers to expose your API design.

Development and testing

This phase is about the process of implementing our design. Since we already have a document that formally describes our API, we'll be able to validate and test whether our implementation conforms to what we've designed. This is one of the great advantages of contract-driven development. Of course, we'll be doing other types of testing as well, such as unit testing and, in the case of interdependent APIs, integration testing. The outcome of this step is a workable piece of code that runs in a development environment that we can later deploy on production servers and publish to consumers.

Deployment

During this stage, our API implementation is deployed to the production environment. Because we have our contract document, we can create gatekeepers to ensure that only properly implemented APIs are going to be deployed. This can be done by leveraging the API design document and proper CI/CD processes with tooling that will run our contract tests and any other checks that are important for quality assurance.

Publishing

In this stage, we expose our API to the consumers. This means that we'll be setting up things that are associated with API management, such as the following:

- **Setting the API gateway**: Here, you'll be setting the API gateway or any other network-level infrastructure element that will be processing requests incoming to your API.

- **Authentication and authorization**: These are partly described in your API design document, and the implementation of this functionality is usually covered by your API management platform and/or API gateway.

- **Access control, reporting, and rate limiting**: This is the process of setting what types of users have access to which resources and whether they have any limits on their access.

- **Monetization**: This involves setting the business model for external APIs. You'll be configuring how consumers will be charged for their use: flat fees, pay-per-call, or some sort of tiered hybrid model.

Since we'll be able to consume our API from outside once we've published it, this is also the step where we will be performing integration tests with our API. This ensures that all the configuration effort we've put in here is working as expected.

Consuming and monitoring

This is the stage in which our published API is consumed by client applications. Because we're leveraging API design documents, our consumers can start creating client applications before our implementation is fully ready in production. When referring to only one source of truth, there's no ambiguity between the design and the implementation, so we can speed some processes up without fearing discrepancies.

Once we have our API running in production and client applications are making calls to our system, we need to be able to observe the traffic. Setting up proper monitoring systems is crucial to your API's success. Thanks to good monitoring systems, we can see data related to the consumption of our APIs, their performance, and whether there are any issues with the traffic. By knowing what traffic errors occur, we can easily say what the cause is. This way, we can quickly spot any potential attacks or security threats, any uncaught errors, potential issues with the payloads, and many more. This step, even if setting it up may not be the most resource or time-consuming aspect of the API's life cycle, lasts the longest and, besides the design, is crucial for your success.

The level of detail that's provided regarding traffic monitoring also depends on the quality of your API design. Proper error object body design, usage of the HTTP protocol, and security definitions will determine the quality of the information that's given to your monitoring systems. The clearer and more exact they are, the less ambiguity you'll have in your traffic.

Update

The last stage of our iterative life cycle loop is the update phase. We go through the update phase during both the building phase and the production phase of our API. While building and designing the API, if you're prototyping with future consumers, they will most likely come with feedback regarding your current design. In the production phase, this step occurs due to both user feedback and changes or updates that have been made to the business requirements.

The most important rule while updating your API design is to not break your existing clients. This is much less of an issue if your API isn't in production yet, but once we have live traffic, other systems depend on our API and the fact it can adhere to previous rules.

We must follow a handful of simple rules to ensure our design updates aren't backward incompatible:

- You *must not* take anything away (related to the minimal surface principle and robustness principle)
- You m*ust not* change the processing rules
- You *must not* make optional things required
- Anything you add *must* be optional (related to the robustness principle)

Following these rules will minimize the possibility of introducing breaking changes to your client. We'll discuss the process of updating your API in detail in *Chapter 13*.

> Read more
>
> Minimal surface principle: `martinfowler.com`.
>
> Robustness principle: `https://datatracker.ietf.org/doc/html/rfc761#section-2.10`.

Retirement

Eventually, the moment will come when you'll need to deactivate your API. This may happen due to many reasons, such as there being a new, more efficient API with the same functionality, technical debt leading to a need to create your API from scratch, a change in business goals or requirements, and more. Similarly, as with the update phase, we try to ensure this step will affect our consumers as little as possible. Note that this can't be eliminated completely since we are, at the end of the day, closing our service. This phase is mostly about clear communication, and it should be gradual, and not instant. The process of gradually retiring a service is usually called **sunsetting**. We'll discuss this stage in detail in *Chapter 13*.

Why is the design stage the one that impacts everything?

As mentioned previously, the **API design document** is a formal, machine-readable document that acts as a resource to which every stakeholder can refer. We use it as the single source of truth during our API lifecycle process. The use of structured, unambiguous, and machine-readable documents also helps us test the implementation, create documentation, deploy and publish our APIs, monitor, and more.

There are multiple benefits of using the API design document as the single source of truth:

- **Defines expectations**: The API design stage sets the expectations for what the API will do, how it will behave, and what it will deliver. It outlines the resources, operations, and data models that the API will expose.

- **Facilitates communication**: A well-designed API serves as a contract between the API provider and the consumers. It communicates the functionality of the API to developers, product managers, and other stakeholders, ensuring everyone has a clear understanding of its capabilities.

- **Drives consistency**: A good API design promotes consistency across all APIs in an organization. This makes it easier for developers to understand and use the APIs, leading to more efficient development processes.

- **Impacts user experience**: The design of the API directly impacts the user experience of the applications that consume it. A poorly designed API can lead to a poor user experience, while a well-designed API can enable a seamless and intuitive user experience. The ability to refer to the API design early on and a way to give feedback to the API provider is also crucial to good quality affordance-centric API design.

- **Future-proofs your API**: A well-thought-out API design can accommodate future changes and additions without breaking existing functionality. This makes your API more resilient to changes and ensures its longevity.

In summary, the API design stage is crucial because it lays the foundation for all subsequent stages of the API lifecycle. It serves as the **single source of truth** that guides the development, deployment, and maintenance of the API. Therefore, investing time and effort in the API design stage can pay off in the form of a robust, easy-to-use, and future-proof API.

> Why design and not code?
>
> If you're principally a developer or an engineer, you may be tempted to use code as the single source of truth. It does have some benefits at the beginning, such as cutting the time spent on your design, because you don't have to create a special design document. Additionally, the fact that the code is, in essence, your application, there can be no discrepancy between the code and the design. However, these benefits quickly wane in the long run – for example, it's much more difficult for other stakeholders to reason about your API just from code. Code also tends to lack specific tooling to generate clear and efficient documentation; it may not be clear from the code base alone how the API is intended to be used. By nature, it will also change much more frequently, making it harder for you to version your API properly and keep the documentation and client implementations up to date.

Next, we'll investigate how to successfully manage your application's and API's life cycles.

Successfully managing application and API Lifecycles

Creating a good process within the API lifecycle involves several key steps. Let's look at them in detail:

1. Clear definition of goals: We're building an API for our Magic Items Store, which is core to our business model. The e-store will be accessible via the web and native devices and will integrate with external marketplaces..

2. The next step should be to **adopt a "design-first" approach**. This means designing the API before writing any code. Use an API description language such as the OpenAPI Specification, which we'll cover in detail in *Chapter 10*, to define the API's resources, operations, data models, and security scheme. This will serve as a contract between the API developers and consumers.

It also makes it much easier to **involve key stakeholders.** By engaging them in the API lifecycle, you get valuable insights that improve the API's usability and effectiveness while also matching your organization's business goals. This includes not only developers, but also product managers, business analysts, and even end users.

When using design documents such as the OAS, you can generate your documentation during the design stage. Providing comprehensive documentation for your API enhances your ability to reason about your API to a wider group of stakeholders. This should include detailed descriptions of the API's resources, operations, and data models, as well as examples of how to use the API and the context in which they operate.

> Read more
>
> You can read more about the OAS here: https://www.openapis.org/.

3. Next, consider **implementing API standards.** These are standards for API design, development, and documentation that ensure consistency across all APIs and make them easier to use. Developers tend to have better experience working with familiar systems.

4. **Implementing robust security measures** to protect your API is crucial. This includes authentication, authorization, and encryption. On top of that, leveraging tested and proven security schemes and design patterns will enhance your overall system stability.

5. While designing, **plan for any changes and additions to the API.** What will be your approach to that process? Use proper design document versioning to manage these changes and prevent disruptions to the API's consumers and plan whether you'll need to have API versioning in production. Those are two different things, and we'll talk about them in depth in *Chapters 10* and *13*.

6. While in the design phase, start using **automated testing.** Automate as much of the testing process as possible. This includes functional testing, performance testing, and security testing. This should also include design validations during the process of design document creation. This way, you can ensure the design standards (both external and the ones from your organization) are met. Automated testing saves time and helps you catch issues early.

7. Once the API has been deployed, **monitor its usage and performance.** Use this data to iterate on the API and make improvements. This is a continuous process that is done throughout the API's life cycle and is crucial to its success. You can't reason about data you can't measure.

8. Eventually, you'll have to plan to **retire your API gracefully**. When it's time to retire an API, do so in a way that minimizes disruption to its consumers. Provide advance notice and offer alternatives if possible.

Remember, the API lifecycle is a continuous process. Even after an API is deployed, you should continue to monitor its performance, gather feedback, and make improvements. This will ensure that your API continues to meet its goals and deliver value to its consumers. The API lifecycle is iterative, meaning it's not a one-time process but rather a continuous cycle of stages that repeat over time. Once the API has been retired, the life cycle can start again, with planning and designing a new API. This iterative nature allows the API to continuously improve and adapt to new requirements and technologies. It ensures that the API remains relevant, useful, and effective over time. It's important to note that feedback from API consumers is a crucial part of this iterative process as it informs improvements and changes in each iteration of the life cycle. So, the API lifecycle isn't just a linear process but a feedback loop that promotes continuous learning and improvement. Let's understand this while considering our e-store.

Example of a life cycle model for an e-store

To show a more concrete application of the approach described in the preceding subsection, let's apply it to an e-commerce platform selling magical items:

1. **Clear definition of goals**: We're building an API for our *Magic e-Store*, which is core to our business model. The e-store will be accessible via the web and native devices and will integrate with external marketplaces.

2. **Design-first**: We've chosen a design-first approach, meaning our development will begin with API design. This will be covered in *Chapters 9* and *10*.

3. **Choosing standards**: We've decided to use JSON as the default data format. Additionally, we'll adopt the **Problem Details** standard (RFC 9457) to convey machine-readable error details. Since we aim to build a hypermedia-driven API (discussed in *Chapter 6*), we'll use the **Hypertext Application Language** (**HAL**), which offers a lightweight solution that meets our needs.

> Read more
>
> Problem details: `https://www.rfc-editor.org/rfc/rfc9457.html`.
>
> HAL: `https://datatracker.ietf.org/doc/html/draft-kelly-json-hal-11`.

4. **Implementing security**: For authorization, we'll use OAuth 2.0, while for authentication, we'll use OpenID Connect. All traffic will be encrypted via HTTPS. We also plan to publish our API through an API management platform, which will handle access control, rate limiting, and throttling. *Chapter 7* covers API security in detail.

5. **Planning for changes**: We've decided not to version the API or its endpoints so that we don't break existing consumers. If new versions are needed, they'll be introduced as new endpoints. We'll follow the **You Aren't Gonna Need It (YAGNI)** principle to maintain a minimal API surface while still meeting product requirements. API versioning strategies will be explored further in *Chapter 13*.

Read more

YAGNI principle: `https://martinfowler.com/bliki/Yagni.html`.

6. **Automated testing**: Our first step will be to ensure that our API design adheres to the chosen standards through design validation. We'll also conduct contract testing to verify that the implementation matches the design. This will complement other types of automated testing unrelated to the design itself. *Chapter 12* provides further insight into API testing techniques.

7. **Monitoring**: We want our API management platform to log all API calls, providing visibility into the incoming traffic. Additional monitoring strategies will be discussed in *Chapter 13*.

8. **Planning for retirement**: When deprecating endpoints or sunsetting the API, it's crucial to communicate with API consumers effectively. These topics will be covered in detail in *Chapter 13*.

This way, we can plan the approach we want to have for our API throughout its life cycle. However, one more element is missing that glues the whole process together – the communication between different stakeholders and teams. Let's learn more about it.

The importance of communication

Communication plays a pivotal role in the API lifecycle for several reasons. Firstly, it enables effective collaboration. APIs are developed by teams, not individuals. Clear and effective communication helps to ensure that everyone on the team understands the API's design, functionality, and goals. This promotes collaboration and helps prevent misunderstandings that can lead to errors, delays, or even mismatches of functionality.

Effective communication is also essential for creating clear and comprehensive API documentation. This documentation serves as a guide for developers who will use the API, helping them understand how to effectively integrate it into their applications. It also gives context to external decision-makers about what kind of functionality and in which context your API supplies will be used. Good documentation should also enhance the ability for a feedback loop between the API developers and the API consumers. This way, developers can gain valuable insights from the consumers' experiences, which can be used to improve the API in future iterations.

Communication is also crucial once you've taken your API into production. APIs often undergo changes and updates. Communicating these changes effectively to all stakeholders, including developers, end users, and business leaders, is crucial for managing these changes and ensuring the API continues to meet its intended goals. You should also use your communication channels to communicate any downtimes on your servers and information regarding any deprecation or retirement. When an API is to be deprecated or retired, it's important to communicate this to all affected parties well in advance. This gives them ample time to make the necessary adjustments and prevent disruptions to their operations.

As we've seen communication is a key aspect of the API lifecycle. It facilitates collaboration, helps manage changes, and ensures that the API meets the needs of its consumers. Without effective communication, the API lifecycle can become disjointed and inefficient, leading to inadequate quality APIs and dissatisfied consumers.

Prototyping and quick feedback loop

The ability to quickly validate your design with your future consumers can't be overestimated:

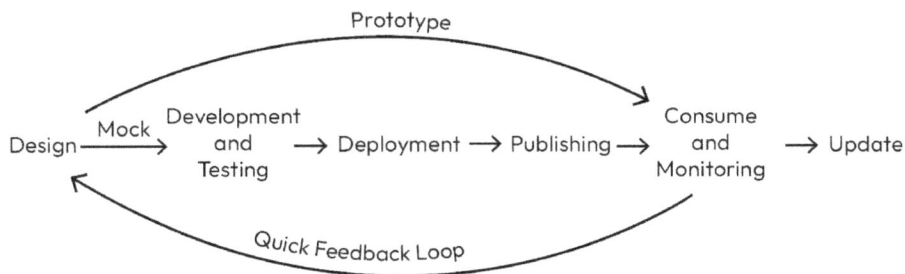

Figure 3.2: A quick feedback loop in the API lifecycle

This is the practical application of the affordance-centric API design process, where the API design team cooperates closely with future consumers. By going design-first and having a design document early on, we can gather feedback during the design process:

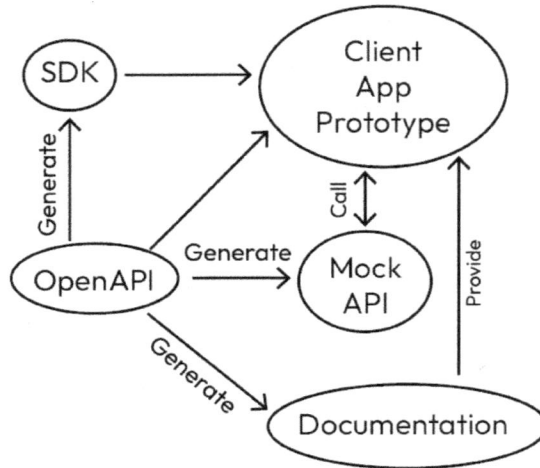

Figure 3.3: OAS is a foundational part of the whole API lifecycle and development

For instance, the OAS is a JSON or YAML document and thus is machine-readable and deterministic. This allows us to leverage it to generate a mock server with some dummy data and calls. We can also generate our API's documentation for all stakeholders. On top of that, we can generate our API's SDKs and collaborate with API consumers who can already start developing their client applications. We'll get a different type of feedback from reasoning about the API based on its documentation than we can get by implementing a client application. Both are equally valuable.

When we can involve our future customers in the design process, we can change our work quickly to meet their needs. Using an OAS document makes our work more visible to others involved and speeds up the creation of prototypes. This is done by making mock APIs for testing or SDKs to make integration faster. There are no negatives to this way of working.

Summary

In this chapter, we delved into the concept of the API lifecycle, underscoring its significance. We emphasized the importance of viewing the API lifecycle and the application life cycle as intertwined entities, recognizing APIs as the fundamental capability of any application.

We also learned about the various stages of the API lifecycle, from creation to decommissioning. A well-defined API lifecycle establishes a shared understanding and vocabulary for API-related work. It serves as the starting point for implementing the API and a source of truth for testing. This promotes the API-first approach, which leads to increased productivity, greater visibility, and organizational alignment.

We also stressed the importance of communication in your API lifecycle processes. The API lifecycle isn't a one-time process but a continuous cycle of stages that repeat over time. So, understanding the API lifecycle is key to designing APIs that are consistent, high quality, easy to maintain, and aligned with business goals.

In the next chapter, we'll introduce the concepts of **domain-driven design (DDD)** in the context of REST API design. We'll recap the core concepts of DDD and help you understand how to align your API functionality with the business domain it sits in. We'll also learn how to apply domain-driven API design in practice and how to avoid anti-patterns.

Get This Book's PDF Version and Exclusive Extras

UNLOCK NOW

Scan the QR code (or go to `packtpub.com/unlock`). Search for this book by name, confirm the edition, and then follow the steps on the page.

Note: Keep your invoice handy. Purchases made directly from Packt don't require an invoice.

4

Applying Domain-Driven Design to APIs

This chapter deep-dives into how to incorporate **Domain-Driven Design** (**DDD**) principles into API development. It demonstrates the benefits of DDD to API design, with a brief overview of DDD. It provides strategies for aligning API design with business domains, ensuring that APIs accurately reflect and serve business needs and ubiquitous language. This chapter is essential for anyone aiming to create APIs that are not only technically sound but also business relevant.

By the end of the chapter, you will understand the importance of aligning business vocabulary and how to materialize your business domains in your APIs. You'll have also learned how to avoid the pitfalls of CRUD-based REST APIs and API design anti-patterns.

In this chapter, we are going to cover the following main topics:

- Domain-driven design overview
- Benefits of design-driven design
- Applying domain-driven design in REST APIs

Domain-driven design overview

In this section, we will introduce the fundamental concepts and benefits of DDD. DDD is an approach to software development that focuses on creating a shared understanding of complex business domains through collaboration between technical and business teams. By aligning software models with business needs and language, DDD ensures that the software accurately reflects the domain and supports business goals effectively. Let's explore what DDD is, why it's important, and how it can be applied in modern software development.

What is domain-driven design?

DDD is an approach to software development that emphasizes collaboration between technical and business teams to create a shared understanding of the problem domain. It focuses on modeling the domain according to the needs and language of the business, ensuring that the software aligns closely with business goals and processes. DDD was invented by Eric Evans and introduced in his seminal book *Domain-Driven Design: Tackling Complexity in the Heart of Software*, published in 2003.

DDD has gained popularity due to its effectiveness in managing and addressing the complexities of software development. By focusing on the core business domain and its intricacies, DDD ensures that software solutions are closely aligned with business needs. This approach is particularly beneficial for complex domains where business logic is intricate and requires deep understanding and precise modeling. The collaborative nature of DDD, which involves both domain experts and developers, also ensures that the software is built with a thorough understanding of the business processes and requirements, reducing misunderstandings and improving the quality of the final product.

Moreover, DDD supports agile development practices, making it suitable for modern software development methodologies. Its emphasis on iterative development, continuous refinement of the domain model, and breaking down complex problems into manageable subdomains and bounded contexts aligns well with agile principles. This compatibility with agile methodologies helps organizations adapt quickly to changes, improve their development processes, and deliver high-quality software in a timely manner. Companies such as Amazon, Netflix, and LinkedIn have successfully implemented DDD to handle their complex systems, demonstrating its practical value and effectiveness in real-world applications.

Why is domain-driven design important?

DDD plays a crucial role in bridging the gap between technical and business teams. It ensures that software development efforts are closely aligned with business objectives and user needs. This section will delve into the reasons why DDD is essential in modern software development, highlighting its impact on communication, scalability, and long-term maintainability.

Bridging the communication gap

DDD addresses the communication gap between technical and business teams by defining a ubiquitous language. This shared language facilitates clear and effective communication, ensuring that both sides understand each other and can collaborate more effectively. This alignment helps in building software that truly meets business requirements.

Enabling microservices and organizational scalability

Many companies use DDD as a driver and enabler for migrating from monolithic architectures to microservices. By breaking down the monolith into smaller, more manageable services, organizations can solve scalability issues and improve their agility. DDD provides the tools and methodologies to identify and define these smaller services within the context of the overall business domain.

Reducing technical debt

While design activities in DDD certainly require time and effort, they pay off by making the software easier to evolve in the future. Neglecting design can save time in the short term but often leads to the accumulation of technical debt, which slows down productivity later. Investing in the design of your software improves the project's stamina, allowing for sustained, long-term development speed.

This design trade-off is well known as the **design stamina hypothesis**, visible in the following pseudo-graph:

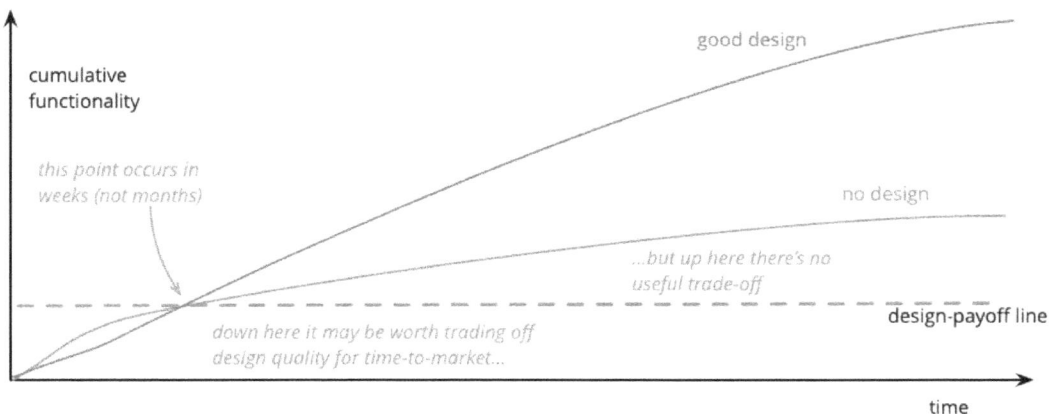

Figure 4.1: Design stamina hypothesis by Martin Fowler

🔍 **Quick tip:** Need to see a high-resolution version of this image? Open this book in the next-gen Packt Reader or view it in the PDF/ePub copy.

📖 **The next-gen Packt Reader** is included for free with the purchase of this book. Scan the QR code OR go to `https://packtpub.com/unlock`, then use the search bar to find this book by name. Double-check the edition shown to make sure you get the right one.

Enhancing maintainability

DDD enhances the maintainability of software by providing a clear structure and separation of concerns. By modeling the domain accurately and dividing it into well-defined components, the software becomes easier to understand, modify, and extend. This maintainability is crucial for long-term project success and adaptability.

Now that we've discussed the importance of maintainability, let's dive into the fundamental building blocks of DDD.

Building blocks of domain-driven design

DDD consists of several fundamental building blocks that help in structuring and organizing the domain model. These building blocks ensure that the system is modular, maintainable, and aligned with business requirements. Let's explore each of these building blocks in detail.

Domain

A **domain** is a broad and high-level area of knowledge or activity within which a software system operates. It encompasses the overall business or problem space that the system is intended to address. It is where the core business functionalities are implemented and is usually divided into smaller subdomains to manage complexity. A domain is also called a **problem space** or **sphere of knowledge**.

In a banking application, the domain would be the entire banking industry, covering aspects such as account management, transactions, loans, customer relationships, and compliance.

Subdomain

A **subdomain** is a more focused and specific area within the larger domain. It represents a particular segment or aspect of the broader domain, often corresponding to a distinct set of business processes or functions. Additionally, it represents the building blocks of a domain, each addressing a particular aspect of the business. Subdomains allow for the decomposition of the overall domain into more manageable and understandable parts.

We can differentiate three kinds of subdomains:

- **Core subdomains**: These are the most critical parts of the domain, providing a competitive advantage or differentiating the business. They often require the most attention and customization. Often, these subdomains are not subject to outsourcing to third parties. For a banking application, transaction processing, loan management, and account management could be core subdomains.

- **Supporting subdomains**: These support the core subdomains but are not central to the business's competitive advantage. They might include generic or less critical functionalities. For example, compliance and reporting, **customer relationship management** (**CRM**), and document management may be the supporting subdomains for the banking application.

- **Generic subdomains**: These are common to many businesses and do not provide any competitive advantage. They can often be handled with off-the-shelf solutions. For our banking application, these might be authentication and authorization, notification system, and content management.

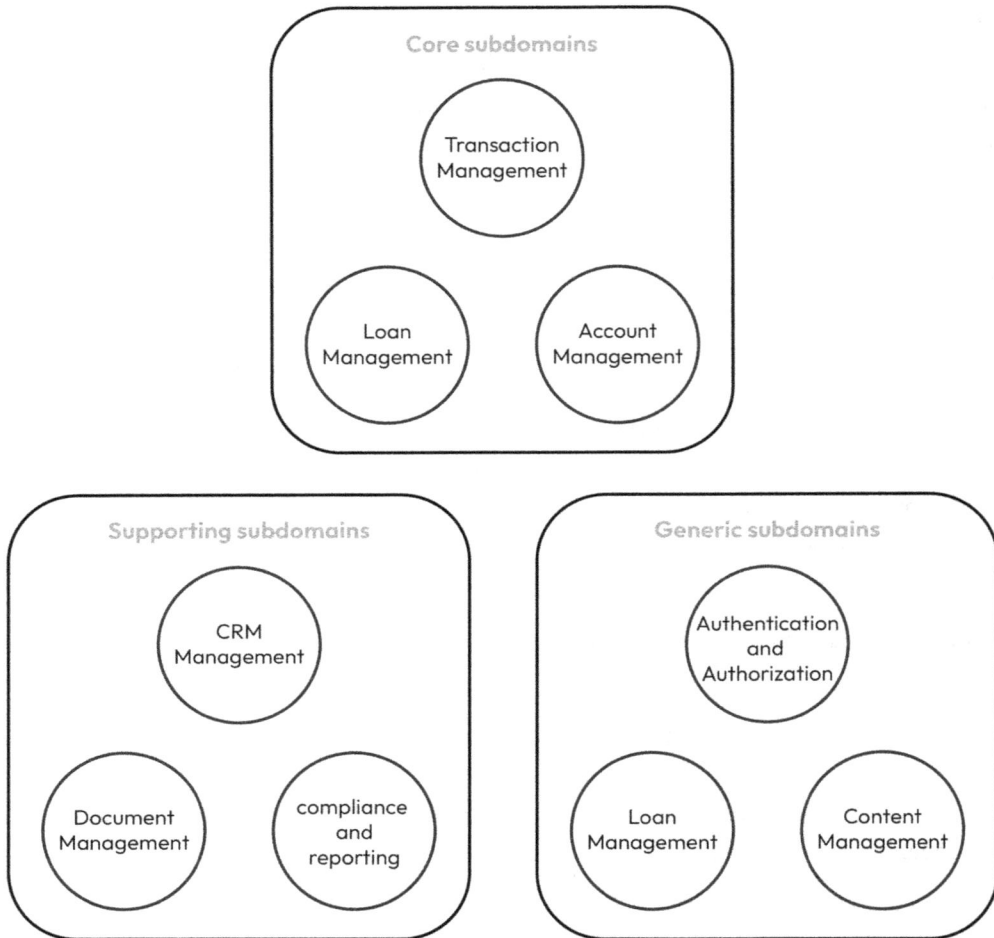

Figure 4.2: Banking domains and subdomains

Defining all your subdomains at once is a challenging task. By using an iterative process, you can achieve a real-world representation of your problem space. Additionally, this approach may reveal that some subdomains are still too large and require further breakdown to reach a manageable size.

Bounded contexts

A **bounded context** is a central pattern in DDD that helps to manage complexity in large software systems by clearly defining the boundaries within which a particular domain model is defined and applicable. Each bounded context has its own distinct models and is responsible for a specific part of the business logic.

Let's break down the key concepts of bounded contexts:

- **Context**: This is the setting in which a word or statement appears that determines its meaning. In DDD, context refers to the scope in which a specific model is defined and used.
- **Bounded**: These are the defined boundaries that limit the scope of the context. These boundaries are explicitly defined to ensure clarity and separation.

Each bounded context must provide the following:

- **Clear boundaries**: Each bounded context has well-defined boundaries that do not overlap with other contexts. This ensures that the language and rules within one context are not confused with those of another.
- **Unified language**: Within a bounded context, a ubiquitous language is used consistently. This language is shared among developers and domain experts to ensure clear communication.
- **Independent models**: Each bounded context contains its own model that is isolated from models in other contexts. Changes in one context do not directly affect another context.

In our banking application example, we can recognize two bounded contexts:

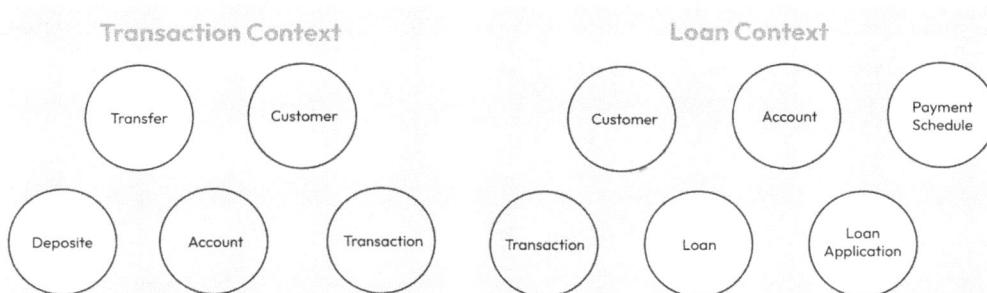

Figure 4.3: Transaction and loan bounded contexts

Different bounded contexts can have similar models, but these models serve different purposes depending on the context they belong to. For example, a customer model in a transaction context might be focused on attributes and methods related to account management and transaction history. Meanwhile, in the loan context, the customer model might be focused on attributes and methods related to loan applications and repayment history.

A **bounded context** can sometimes span multiple subdomains when the team working within that context shares a cohesive understanding of the concepts across those subdomains. This shared understanding ensures consistency in how models and language are applied, even when the context covers a broader area of the business. Such an approach works well when teams are aligned and collaborate effectively within a defined boundary.

In large organizations, it's more common for each bounded context to align with a single subdomain. This is because teams in these companies are often specialized and focused, owning their models, data, and language without significant overlap with other teams. Integration between bounded contexts is managed through deliberate strategies, ensuring that teams can work independently while maintaining overall system coherence.

Smaller companies, on the other hand, often have teams that handle multiple responsibilities, leading to a single bounded context spanning several subdomains. These teams typically have a broader understanding of the business, which allows them to manage overlapping areas effectively. However, this approach requires careful boundary management to prevent confusion and maintain a clear focus on each subdomain's objectives.

In the following diagram, the domain encompasses multiple subdomains, each housing its own set of bounded contexts. This layered structure shows how DDD decomposes complexity into manageable parts, promoting scalability, maintainability, and clear communication between business and technical teams.

Domain

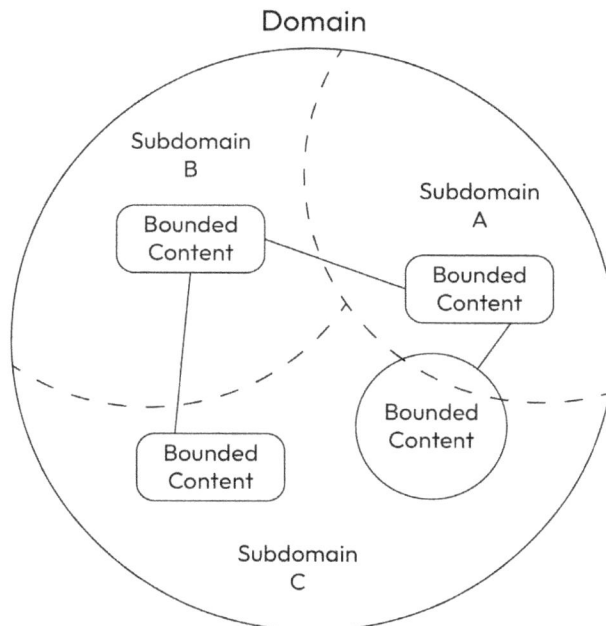

Figure 4.4: Domains, subdomains, and bounded contexts

Ubiquitous language

Ubiquitous language is a critical concept in DDD that aims to create a common, shared language between software developers and domain experts. This language is used consistently across the entire project to ensure clear communication and mutual understanding of the domain.

A successful ubiquitous language should provide three key characteristics:

- **Common terminology**: The language is developed collaboratively by domain experts and developers, ensuring that terms are understood by both parties

- **Consistency**: The same terms are used throughout the entire project, including in code, documentation, and discussions, to avoid ambiguity

- **Domain-specific**: The language is tailored to the specific domain or bounded context, capturing its unique concepts, processes, and rules

Ubiquitous language can be implemented using the following steps:

1. **Definition**: Domain experts work together with developers to define and refine the language. This may involve regular meetings, discussions, and asynchronous feedback.

2. **Documentation**: The language is documented in a way that is accessible to all team members, often including glossaries, concept diagrams, and usage examples. Additionally, using versioned documentation will make your ubiquitous language more flexible for future changes.

3. **Technical implementation**: The terms from the ubiquitous language are used directly in the code and API. This makes your implementation more readable and aligned with the business domain.

Let's illustrate the definition and documentation phase of ubiquitous language, with a banking application focusing on the bounded context of account management.

Business terminology

- **Account**: A customer's account with the bank
- **Customer**: An individual or business holding an account
- **Deposit**: Adding money to an account
- **Withdrawal**: Taking money out of an account
- **Balance**: The amount of money currently in an account

Ubiquitous language in use

- **Definition**:

    - **Domain expert**: "When a customer makes a deposit, we update the account balance."

    - **Developer**: "So, we need a Deposit API endpoint that modifies the balance of an account object."

- **Documentation**:

    - **Glossary**:

        - **Account**: Represents a customer's bank account

        - **Customer**: An entity representing an individual or business holding an account

        - **Deposit**: A transaction adding funds to an account

- **Withdrawal**: A transaction removing funds from an account
- **Balance**: The current amount of money in an account

Documentation may include any relevant diagram that helps users to deeply understand the different terms used.

Entities

An **entity** is an object that is defined not only by its attributes but also by a distinct identity that runs through time and different states. Entities have a unique identifier and life cycle, and their identity remains consistent even if other attributes change.

Each entity has a distinct identifier that differentiates it from other entities. This identifier is often immutable; entities have a life cycle that includes creation, modification, and deletion. Additionally, they encapsulate both data and behavior.

As an example, let's consider the **customer** entity in the bounded context of a transaction context:

- **Attributes**: `transactionId`, `accountId`, `transactionType`, `amount`, `transactionDate`, `status`, `description`, and `currency`
- **Unique identity**: `transactionId`
- **Life cycle**: A transaction is created when an account operation occurs, and it may change state during processing (e.g., pending, completed, or rolled back)
- **Behavior**: `process()`, `validate()`, `rollback()`, and `generateReceipt()`

Value objects

Value objects are another essential building block. Unlike entities, value objects do not have a unique identity. Instead, they are defined by their attributes and are immutable. Value objects are used to represent a descriptive aspect of the domain with no conceptual identity, meaning two value objects with the same attributes are considered equal.

Value objects are identified solely by their attributes. Once created, a value object cannot be changed; if a change is needed, a new instance must be created. Two value objects with the same values for their attributes are considered equal. Finally, value objects can ensure their own validity and consistency.

To illustrate value objects, let's consider the **money** value object in the loan context:

- **Attributes**: `amount` and `currency`
- **Behavior**: `add(Money)`, `subtract(Money)`, `multiply(factor)`, and `equals(Money)`

Aggregates

Aggregates are a cluster of domain objects that can be treated as a single unit. An aggregate consists of one or more entities and value objects that are tightly related. It ensures consistency within its boundaries by enforcing invariants and business rules. Aggregates help in managing and encapsulating complexity within a bounded context.

Aggregates have the following characteristics:

- **Root entity (aggregate root)**: Each aggregate has a root entity, called the **aggregate root**, which is the only entry point for interacting with the aggregate.

- **Consistency boundary**: Aggregates define a consistency boundary. Changes within an aggregate are consistent and transactional.

- **Encapsulation**: Aggregates encapsulate internal entities and value objects, providing a clear interface through the aggregate root.

- **Transaction management**: Aggregates manage their own transactional consistency, ensuring that changes are consistent and valid.

For example, in the loan context, the `LoanApplication` aggregate consists of a loan application and related entities. The `LoanApplication` entity is the aggregate root:

- `LoanApplication` (**aggregate root**):

    - **Attributes**: `applicationId`, `customerId`, `loanType`, `requestedAmount`, `applicationDate`, and `status`

    - **Methods**: `submitApplication()`, `approveApplication()`, and `rejectApplication()`

- `LoanTerms` (**value object**)

    - **Attributes**: `principalAmount`, `interestRate`, `termLength`, and `startDate`

    - **Methods**: `calculateTotalRepayment()` and `equals(LoanTerms)`

Repositories

Repositories are like a bridge between the business logic and the data storage. They help keep our code organized and make it easier to manage how we save and retrieve data. Repositories provide a clean and simple way to interact with the database, so the rest of our code doesn't need to worry about the details of how data is stored.

Here are some key points to note about repositories:

- **Simplified access**: Repositories make it easy to get and save data without needing to know the details of the database
- **Collection-like**: They act like a collection of domain objects, allowing us to add, remove, and find these objects
- **Focus on business logic**: By using repositories, our business logic can stay clean and focused, without getting bogged down by data access code
- **Ensure consistency**: Repositories ensure that the data we work with is consistent and valid

For instance, in the transaction context, AccountRepository helps us manage bank accounts. It allows us to find accounts by their ID, save new accounts, delete accounts, and find all accounts belonging to a customer, like so:

```python
class AccountRepository:
    def __init__(self):
        self.accounts = {}

    def find_by_id(self, account_id):
        return self.accounts.get(account_id)

    def save(self, account):
        self.accounts[account.account_id] = account

    def delete(self, account_id):
        if account_id in self.accounts:
            del self.accounts[account_id]

    def findBycustomerId(self, customer_id):
        return [account for account in self.accounts.values() if account.
customer_id == customer_id]
```

💡 **Quick tip:** Enhance your coding experience with the **AI Code Explainer** and **Quick Copy** features. Open this book in the next-gen Packt Reader. Click the **Copy** button (1) to quickly copy code into your coding environment, or click the **Explain** button (2) to get the AI assistant to explain a block of code to you.

```
                                                              Copy     Explain
function calculate(a, b) {
  return {sum: a + b};                                          1         2
};
```

📖 **The next-gen Packt Reader** is included for free with the purchase of this book. Scan the QR code OR go to https://packtpub.com/unlock, then use the search bar to find this book by name. Double-check the edition shown to make sure you get the right one.

With a solid understanding of DDD and its core concepts—such as domains, subdomains, bounded contexts, and ubiquitous language—we can begin to see how these principles apply to real-world development challenges. But why should API designers care about DDD? What unique advantages does it bring to API design?

How can domain-driven design benefit APIs?

In today's rapidly evolving technological landscape, designing APIs that are both effective and user-friendly is paramount. DDD offers a strategic approach to API development that aligns closely with business goals and user needs. By focusing on the core business domain and the relationships within it, DDD ensures that APIs are intuitive, maintainable, and capable of supporting complex business workflows.

In this section, we will explore the numerous benefits of applying DDD principles to API design. We will delve into how DDD enables the creation of experience-based APIs, helps avoid accidental complexity, and enhances API security. Through practical examples and detailed explanations, we aim to illustrate how DDD can transform your API development process and ultimately deliver better value to your users.

Enabling experience-based APIs

DDD enhances both domain APIs and experience-based APIs, each serving distinct but complementary purposes. Domain APIs, such as an Inventory API used by third-party vendors, directly reflect core business entities and operations, benefiting from DDD's bounded contexts and ubiquitous language to create clear, well-structured interfaces. Meanwhile, experience-based APIs, such as a Checkout API in an e-commerce platform, leverage DDD's focus on business processes to orchestrate complex user workflows rather than exposing pure data operations. The strength of DDD lies in its ability to support and connect both approaches; it helps maintain the integrity of your domain model while enabling intuitive user experiences. For instance, an e-commerce platform might expose both domain APIs for inventory management and experience-based APIs that guide users through the purchase process, with DDD ensuring clear boundaries and relationships between them.

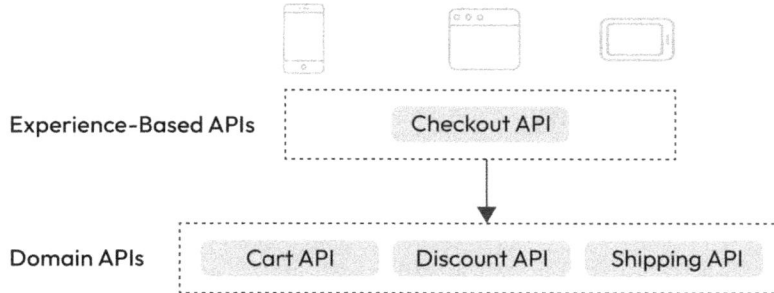

Figure 4.5: Experience-based APIs and domain APIs

Despite REST APIs' constraints, such as URLs, endpoints, and HTTP verbs, thinking in terms of DDD offers strategies to effectively define workflows and processes. REST resources don't need to be confined to domain entities; they can represent business workflows, enabling a rich and seamless experience for your customers. Additionally, you enable a uniform multi-channel experience by design, meaning your customers will enjoy a consistent API interaction across various platforms and devices.

DDD encourages thoughtful API boundary definition, resulting in APIs with clear purposes. Well-designed boundaries enhance API discovery and documentation, making it easier for developers to understand and use them effectively. By embedding business language into APIs, DDD ensures that the API's functionality aligns with business goals, improving usability and flexibility. This abstraction layer prevents breaking changes when internal domain models evolve.

In addition to enabling experience-based APIs, DDD protects you from accidental complexity.

Avoiding accidental complexity

Accidental complexity stems from design and implementation decisions that add unnecessary complications, rather than from the inherent difficulty of the problem itself. This often occurs due to poor design choices, over-engineering, or the misuse of technology.

APIs designed as simple **Create, Read, Update, Delete** (**CRUD**) operations often mirror internal models and schemas, requiring users to read extensive documentation and make multiple API calls to complete a task. This increases the learning curve and makes the API harder to use and maintain. Additionally, different parts of the API might use inconsistent business vocabulary, leading to confusion and errors.

DDD mitigates accidental complexity by focusing on the business domain and reducing low-level details. Developers interact with high-level concepts and workflows, without needing deep knowledge of internal domains. This simplification makes the API more intuitive and easier to maintain.

Improving API security

Applying DDD principles can enhance API security by promoting a clear, cohesive, and well-structured API. This approach mitigates some vulnerabilities as outlined in the **OWASP API Security Top 10**:

- **Broken Object-Level Authorization (BOLA)**: By defining clear domain boundaries and responsibilities, DDD ensures object access is controlled through well-defined services and repositories. Each domain entity enforces its own access control, reducing the risk of unauthorized access.

- **Broken authentication**: DDD advocates for a distinct identity and access management domain. Implementing robust authentication mechanisms such as OAuth and JWT within this domain ensures consistent and secure handling of user credentials across the application.

- **Broken object property-level authorization**: DDD promotes encapsulation and context boundaries, which limit data exposure. APIs designed with DDD principles return only necessary information, minimizing sensitive data exposure. Aggregates and value objects encapsulate internal states, preventing direct manipulation.

- **Unrestricted access to sensitive business flows**: DDD helps manage risks by emphasizing a deep understanding of the business domain and implementing robust, context-specific controls.

> More information
>
> **OWASP** stands for **Open Web Application Security Project**. It is a nonprofit foundation that works to improve the security of software. OWASP provides a wealth of free, open resources, tools, and guidelines for organizations, developers, and security professionals to help them secure web applications and software development. To learn more, visit `https://owasp.org/www-project-api-security/`.

As an example, imagine a tech company releasing a high-demand product such as a gaming console—this company can prevent abuse by defining a bounded context for the purchasing flow. Aggregates enforce limits on purchase quantities, and domain policies restrict the number of items a user can buy within a timeframe. Monitoring and adjusting policies based on domain events helps detect and respond to unusual activity. By leveraging DDD, this company can benefit from the following:

- **Collaborative API design**: Engage domain experts to model business processes accurately, balancing functionality with security

- **Bounded contexts and aggregates**: Define bounded contexts for sensitive flows, enforcing business rules and constraints

- **Domain policies and invariants**: Implement rules that limit high-demand item purchases, encapsulated within the domain layer

- **Monitor and adjust**: Continuously monitor sensitive endpoints, using domain events to detect anomalies and adjust policies

Now that we have covered the benefits of DDD, it's time to explore how these principles can be applied to REST APIs. The next section will guide you through the process of integrating DDD with RESTful services, focusing on how to design APIs that are both user-centric and aligned with business objectives. We'll discuss strategies for defining API boundaries, creating meaningful endpoints, and ensuring that your APIs are maintainable and scalable. Let's dive into the practical application of DDD in the realm of REST APIs.

Applying domain-driven design to REST APIs

Applying DDD to REST APIs ensures that the APIs are closely aligned with business goals and processes. This alignment helps create APIs that are intuitive, maintainable, and scalable.

While DDD is a comprehensive approach that applies to various layers of software development, this section focuses solely on how its principles can shape API design. The goal is to show how concepts such as ubiquitous language, bounded contexts, and experience-based workflows can guide API design, without delving into the details of full DDD implementation in the underlying application or code base. By narrowing the focus, we aim to provide actionable insights for API designers and developers who want to align their interfaces with business objectives.

In this section, we will explore several key aspects of integrating DDD with RESTful services, including aligning APIs with ubiquitous language, defining bounded contexts for APIs, designing experience-based APIs, and making your API discoverable.

Aligning APIs with ubiquitous language

Aligning your APIs with the ubiquitous language of your domain ensures consistency, clarity, and a shared understanding across both technical and business teams.

Let's consider a concrete example in the context of a banking domain. Suppose that the business domain includes concepts such as **Account**, **Transaction**, and **Loan**, with specific actions such as OpenAccount, DepositMoney, and ApplyForLoan.

The following are the concepts included in the business domain:

- **Account**: Represents a customer's bank account
- **Transaction**: Represents a financial transaction
- **Loan:** Represents a loan application and management process

Table 4.1 describes the related API endpoints, actions, and operations for the three concepts:

Business term	API endpoints	Actions	API operation
Account	`/accounts`	`OpenAccount`	`POST /accounts`

Transaction	`/transations`
	
	`/accounts/`
	`{accountID}/`
	`transactions`
		`DepositMoney`	`POST /accounts/`
			`{accountId}/`
			`transactions/`
			`deposit`

Loan	`/loan`
	
	`/loan/{loadId}`
		`ApplyForLoan`
		
		`ApproveLoan`
		
		`RejectLoan`
			`POST /loan`
			
			`POST /loan/`
			`{loanId}/approve`
			
			`POST /loan/`
			`{loanId}/reject`

Table 4.1: Example of business terminology in an API

Defining bounded contexts for APIs

Defining bounded contexts in your APIs is crucial for maintaining a clean and organized API structure, which significantly impacts the developer experience. Bounded contexts ensure that each part of the API has a clear responsibility and aligns with a specific part of the domain. This separation reduces complexity, avoids naming collisions, and makes the API easier to navigate. For example, having separate contexts for transaction and loan operations in a banking API ensures that each set of endpoints is focused and relevant.

By implementing bounded contexts in your APIs, you benefit from the following:

- **Clear separation of concerns**: Bounded contexts help separate different areas of the business domain, ensuring that each context has its own clear responsibilities.

- **Improved scalability and maintainability**: By isolating each context, changes in one context do not affect others, making the system easier to maintain and scale.

- **Enhanced developer experience**: Developers can work on specific contexts without needing to understand the entire system, leading to faster development and fewer errors.

- **Flexibility**: Bounded contexts provide a structured way to manage complexity by dividing a large system into smaller, more manageable parts. This separation helps design APIs that are both flexible and maintainable, accommodating a wide range of use cases and integration scenarios.

Bounded contexts can be reflected in your API in two places:

- **Your API endpoints**: For example, in the banking domain, you might define /accounts, / transactions, and /loans as separate bounded contexts. Each context would handle its specific operations, such as /accounts/{accountId}, /transactions/{transactionId}, and /loans/{loanId}, ensuring clear separation and focus.

- **Your API documentation**: Maintain separate API-as-a-product bundles for each bounded context to avoid confusion and make it easier to navigate. Stripe documentation is a great example.

Now that we have defined bounded contexts for your APIs, let's explore how to design experience-based APIs.

Designing experience-based APIs

As mentioned in the first section, thinking in terms of DDD helps you think about user experiences and workflows rather than purely around data entities.

As an example, consider an e-commerce checkout process. Instead of multiple API calls for adding items to a cart, calculating shipping, applying discounts, and processing payments, a single **checkout API** streamlines the user experience, integrating all necessary steps into a coherent workflow.

Without an experience-based API, you will have the following OpenAPI specification:

```
openapi: 3.0.0
info:
  title: Checkout API
  version: 1.0.0
paths:
  /cart/add
    post:
      summary: Add item to cart
      ...
  /shipping/cost
    post:
      summary: Get shipping cost
      ...
  /discount/apply
    post:
      summary: Apply discount code
      ...
```

```
/payment/process
  post:
    summary: Process payment
    ...
```

Your API customers will make at least four API calls to make a checkout:

- First API call:

```
POST /cart/add
Content-Type: application/json
{
 "items": [{
   "itemId": "123",
   "quantity": 2
  }]
}
```

- Second API call:

```
POST /shipping/cost
Content-Type: application/json
{
 "cartId": "452",
 "address": {
   "street": "39 Rue de la paix",
   "city": "Paris",
   "zip" : "75006"
  }
}
```

- Third API call:

```
POST /discount/apply
Content-Type: application/json
{
   "cartId": "452",
   "discountCode": "SAVE20"
}
```

- Fourth API call:

```
POST /payment/process
Content-Type: application/json
{
 "cartId": "452",
 "paymentType": "Card",
 "paymentDetails": {
   "cardNumber": "232132132423423432423",
   "expirationDate": "02/29"
   "cvv": "123"
  }
}
```

If you leverage DDD and experience-based APIs, you can combine all steps into one call, simplifying client implementation and encapsulating the entire checkout process into a single transaction, making it more robust and easier to maintain, like so:

```
openapi: 3.0.0
info:
  title: Checkout API
  version: 2.0.0
  paths:
    /checkout:
      post:
        summary: Complete checkout process
        requestBody:
          ...
```

The required API call will be as follows:

```
POST /checkout
Content-Type: application/json
{
   "items": [{
     "itemId": "123",
     "quantity": 2
   }],
   "address": {
     "street": "39 Rue de la paix",
     "city": "Paris",
```

```
      "zip": "75006"
    },
  "discountCode": "SAVE30",
  "paymentDetails": {
    "cardNumber": "232132132423423432423",
    "expirationDate": "02/29",
    "cvv": "123"
  }
}
```

Making your API discoverable

Hypermedia and experience-based APIs are two powerful approaches to designing flexible, intuitive, and user-friendly APIs. While experience-based APIs focus on tailoring the API to specific user experiences, hypermedia (often referred to as **HATEOAS,** which stands for **Hypermedia as the Engine of Application State**) emphasizes the dynamic discovery of domain actions through embedded links and controls within the API responses. Both approaches can significantly enhance API design when combined.

Roy Fielding emphasizes that HATEOS allows clients to dynamically navigate and interact with the application, enhancing flexibility and evolvability:

> *The central feature that distinguishes the REST architectural style from other network-based styles is its emphasis on a uniform interface between components, which simplifies and decouples the architecture, enabling each part to evolve independently.*
>
> *— Roy Fielding (2000)*

In *Chapter 6*, we will discuss in detail how to make your API discoverable by using Amundsen and Richardon API maturity models.

Summary

In this chapter, you've learned the foundations and deep insights into how to apply DDD to API design. This chapter began with an overview of DDD, highlighting its importance in aligning software development with business goals through collaboration between technical and business teams. We explored the benefits of incorporating DDD principles into APIs, emphasizing how this approach can create experience-based APIs that improve user workflows and maintain a consistent business language across platforms.

We then delved into the key concepts of DDD, such as domains, subdomains, bounded contexts, and ubiquitous language. These building blocks are crucial for structuring and organizing your domain model to ensure that the system is modular, maintainable, and aligned with business requirements. By using a shared language and clearly defined boundaries, DDD facilitates better communication and understanding between developers and domain experts, ultimately leading to more effective software solutions.

The chapter also covered the practical application of DDD to REST APIs, illustrating how to align APIs with the ubiquitous language of the domain. By doing so, we ensure consistency and clarity, making APIs easier to understand and use. We discussed how bounded contexts can be reflected in API endpoints and documentation, improving scalability, maintainability, and developer experience. This separation of concerns helps in managing the complexity of large systems by dividing them into smaller, more manageable parts.

Additionally, we explored the concept of designing experience-based APIs, focusing on user experiences and workflows rather than just data entities. This approach simplifies client implementation and encapsulates entire processes into single transactions, making APIs more robust and easier to maintain. We provided a concrete example of how an e-commerce checkout process can be streamlined into a single API call, enhancing the overall user experience.

Finally, this chapter highlighted the importance of making APIs discoverable using hypermedia principles. By embedding links and controls within API responses, we enable dynamic discovery of domain actions, enhancing flexibility and evolvability. Combining experience-based APIs with hypermedia principles creates a powerful and intuitive API design that aligns closely with business objectives while providing a seamless and consistent user experience across various platforms.

In the next chapter, we will explore RESTful APIs and compare the different API styles. We'll delve into the popularity and unique features of RESTful APIs, comparing them with other API styles, such as GraphQL, SOAP, gRPC, and asynchronous APIs.

Get This Book's PDF Version and Exclusive Extras

UNLOCK NOW

Scan the QR code (or go to packtpub.com/unlock). Search for this book by name, confirm the edition, and then follow the steps on the page.

Note: Keep your invoice handy. Purchases made directly from Packt don't require an invoice.

Part 2

The Wizard's Grimoire — Mastering the Fundamentals of REST

Having completed your apprenticeship, you now open the wizard's grimoire to master the fundamental arts of REST API design. This sacred tome contains the essential knowledge that transforms you from someone who understands APIs conceptually to a skilled practitioner able to craft elegant and powerful REST APIs.

Within these pages, you'll study the ancient wisdom of different API styles and learn the divination arts needed to choose the right approach for any magical challenge. We'll delve deep into the mystical constraints and maturity models that govern REST, moving beyond simple incantations to understand the deeper principles that make an API truly RESTful. Through careful study of domain modeling and contract crafting, you'll learn to weave business requirements into robust API designs.

This grimoire contains the fundamental spells, patterns, and techniques that master API wizards use to create maintainable, scalable, and enchanting APIs. By mastering these teachings, you'll possess the core competencies needed to design REST APIs that serve both the technical realm and the business domain with equal grace.

This part includes the following chapters:

- Chapter 5, Comparing and Choosing the right API Style
- Chapter 6, REST Design Constraints and Maturity Models
- Chapter 7, Constructing an API Design Domain Model
- Chapter 8, Designing and Managing Effective API Contracts

5

Comparing and Choosing the Right API Style

This chapter delves into the critical concept of **application programming interface (API)** styles, providing a comprehensive understanding of how architectural principles influence API design. API styles dictate not only the structure and interaction patterns of an API but also how data is modeled, communicated, and managed. The choice of API style is pivotal to a project's success, as it directly impacts scalability, flexibility, and overall performance.

We'll explore the four major API style families—function-based, resource-based, query-based, and event-based—each of which is tailored to different use cases. A key focus will be on **resource-based APIs**, particularly the **Representational State Transfer (REST)** architectural style, which has gained popularity due to its simplicity, scalability, and alignment with web standards. REST APIs use standard HTTP methods to interact with resources and offer benefits such as statelessness, cacheable responses, and ease of use, making them an ideal choice for scalable web applications.

By reading this chapter, you will learn the following:

- What API styles are and how they guide the design and implementation of APIs
- The key features of function-based, resource-based, query-based, and event-based API styles, and how they differ
- The advantages of REST and how it fits into the resource-based API family
- When and why to choose specific API styles based on your system's needs, from synchronous operations to real-time event handling
- How API style impacts scalability, flexibility, and performance, enabling you to make well-informed design decisions for your project

By the end of this chapter, you will have a clearer understanding of how to select the appropriate API style to optimize for factors such as performance, scalability, and developer experience, ensuring that your architecture is built to handle the unique challenges of your system.

What's an API style?

An **API style** is a set of architectural principles and conventions that guide the design and implementation of an API. It defines how the API is structured, how clients interact with it, how data is communicated, and the protocols or standards used for communication. An API style encompasses the overall approach to exposing functionality and data to clients, including the following aspects:

- **Interaction patterns**: Whether the communication is synchronous or asynchronous, request-response, or event-driven

- **Data modeling**: How resources or services are represented and manipulated, such as through resources, functions, or queries

- **Communication protocols**: The underlying protocols used, such as HTTP for RESTful APIs or binary protocols for gRPC

- **Data formats**: The formats in which data is serialized and transmitted, such as JSON, XML, or Protocol Buffers

- **State management**: How the API handles state, whether it's stateless, such as REST, or maintains stateful sessions

Different API styles address different needs and use cases, influencing factors such as scalability, flexibility, performance, and ease of use. Common API styles include the following:

- **Function-based APIs** (e.g., **Remote Procedure Call (RPC)**, **Simple Object Access Protocol (SOAP)**, gRPC): Focus on executing remote procedures or functions as if they were local calls

- **Resource-based APIs** (e.g., REST): Interact with resources identified by URIs using standard HTTP methods such as GET, POST, PUT, and DELETE

- **Query-based APIs** (e.g., GraphQL): Allow clients to request exactly the data they need through structured queries, reducing over-fetching and under-fetching

- **Event-based APIs** (e.g., Webhooks, WebSockets): Handle real-time or asynchronous communication by sending or receiving events triggered by specific actions

Choosing the appropriate API style is crucial for aligning with the specific requirements of a project, such as performance needs, client flexibility, development resources, and scalability considerations. It affects how easily clients can consume the API, how the system scales under load, and how future-proof the API will be as requirements evolve.

Now that we have defined an API style, let's see why choosing the right one is critical to your project architecture.

Importance of choosing the right API style

Choosing the appropriate API architecture style is critical because it profoundly affects scalability, flexibility, maintenance, and the overall developer experience. **Scalability** is a crucial consideration for applications expected to handle a growing number of users or requests. Stateless API styles, such as REST, are inherently scalable because each request from a client to the server contains all the information needed to understand and process the request, allowing for easier load balancing across multiple servers.

Building upon scalability, **flexibility** refers to the ability of an API to accommodate varying client needs without requiring changes to the server-side implementation. **GraphQL** excels in this aspect by allowing clients to specify exactly what data they require, thereby reducing over-fetching and under-fetching issues common with REST. This flexibility is particularly beneficial for applications with diverse frontend requirements.

In addition to flexibility, maintenance involves the ease with which an API can be updated, extended, and debugged over time. Selecting an API style that aligns with the project's needs can significantly reduce the complexity of maintaining and evolving the API. For example, using a widely adopted and straightforward API style, such as REST, can simplify maintenance due to its simplicity and the vast ecosystem of tools and best practices available.

Furthermore, the developer experience is shaped by how intuitive and efficient it is to work with an API. While API styles such as gRPC offer high performance and are suitable for microservices architectures, they may require developers to learn new tools and protocols such as **Protocol Buffers**, introducing a learning curve and necessitating more sophisticated development environments. This can impact the overall productivity and satisfaction of the development team.

Therefore, evaluating the trade-offs and aligning the API architecture style with your project's unique requirements is essential for building efficient and effective software solutions. The requirements for choosing the right API style can vary significantly depending on your specific context and challenges, making it important to consider all these factors in your decision-making process.

To better understand the various options and how they fit different needs, it is helpful to categorize API styles into distinct families. This categorization can simplify the selection process by highlighting the core principles and typical use cases associated with each group.

API style families

To simplify the landscape of API styles, we can categorize them into four distinct families. Let's take a look at each one in detail.

Function-based APIs

Function-based APIs, such as RPC, SOAP, and gRPC, are designed to allow clients to execute commands on remote servers as if they were invoking local function calls. The primary goal of these APIs is to abstract the complexities of network communication, enabling developers to interact with remote services using familiar programming paradigms. This approach simplifies distributed computing by making remote method invocations resemble local code execution, thereby reducing the effort required to build networked applications.

Figure 5.1 illustrates the key components of function-based APIs such as gRPC and SOAP.

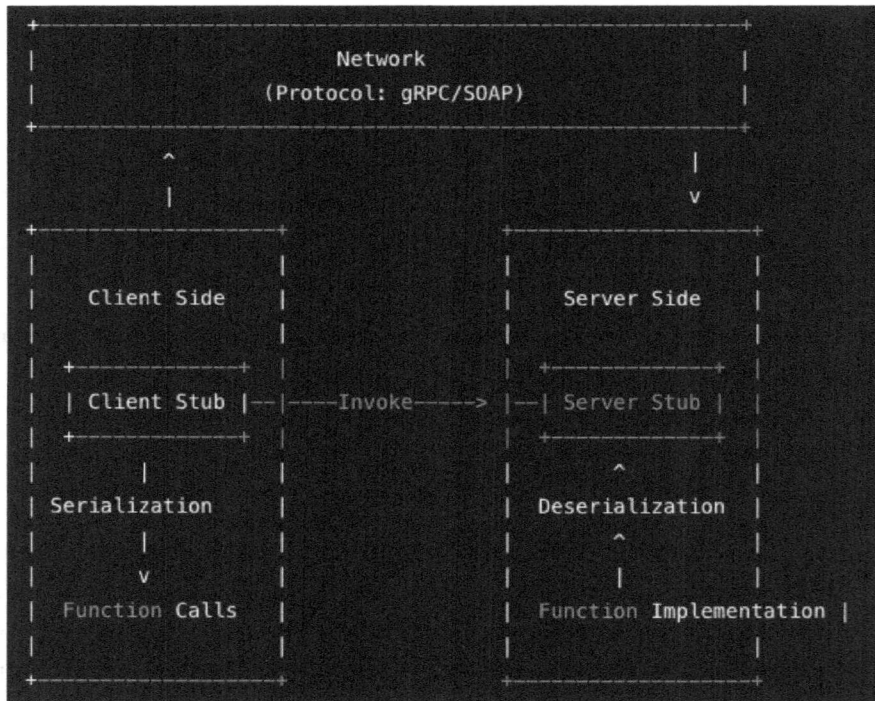

```
+-------------------------------------------------+
|                    Network                      |
|              (Protocol: gRPC/SOAP)              |
+-------------------------------------------------+

        ^                              |
        |                              v
+---------------------+      +---------------------+
|                     |      |                     |
|    Client Side      |      |     Server Side     |
|                     |      |                     |
|  +---------------+  |      |  +---------------+   |
|  | Client Stub |--|-----Invoke----->|--| Server Stub |   |
|  +---------------+  |      |  +---------------+   |
|        |            |      |         ^           |
| Serialization       |      | Deserialization     |
|        |            |      |         ^           |
|        v            |      |         |           |
| Function Calls      |      | Function Implementation |
|                     |      |                     |
+---------------------+      +---------------------+
```

Figure 5.1: Components of function-based APIs

🔍 **Quick tip**: Need to see a high-resolution version of this image? Open this book in the next-gen Packt Reader or view it in the PDF/ePub copy.

📖 **The next-gen Packt Reader** is included for free with the purchase of this book. Scan the QR code OR go to `https://packtpub.com/unlock`, then use the search bar to find this book by name. Double-check the edition shown to make sure you get the right one.

In these APIs, the client invokes functions or methods on a remote server, which processes the request and returns the results. This mechanism typically involves serializing function parameters, transmitting them over the network, and deserializing them on the server side for execution. The server then performs the requested action and sends the response back to the client in a similar serialized format. This process creates a tight coupling between the client and server, as both must agree on the function signatures and data formats used for communication.

Function-based APIs are characterized by their focus on actions, such as performing calculations, processing data, or triggering specific operations. They are well-suited for scenarios where procedural interactions are predominant and there is a need for precise control over remote executions. However, this tight coupling can lead to challenges in scalability and flexibility, as changes to the server-side functions often require corresponding updates on the client side. This can make it harder to adapt to evolving requirements without significant coordination between clients and servers.

Examples of function-based APIs include SOAP and gRPC:

* SOAP is a protocol that emphasizes strict contracts and formal methods, using XML for message formatting and relying on established standards for security and transaction management. While robust and feature-rich, SOAP is often considered heavy due to its verbosity and complexity.

- gRPC, developed by Google, is a high-performance, open source framework that uses Protocol Buffers for efficient binary serialization. It is commonly used in microservices architectures for its speed and scalability, but requires developers to become familiar with specific tooling and interface definition languages, potentially increasing the learning curve.

Function-based APIs, such as RPC, SOAP, and gRPC, typically demonstrate a lower level of maturity in API maturity models such as the **Richardson Maturity Model** and **Mike Amundsen's Maturity Model**. These maturity models assess APIs based on their adherence to RESTful principles and their ability to support scalable and flexible client-server interactions. In *Chapter 6*, we will delve into these maturity models as they can support you during API style selection decision-making.

Resource-based APIs

Resource-based APIs, such as REST and **OData**, are designed to interact with resources over the web using standard HTTP protocols. The primary goal of these APIs is to manipulate resources—such as objects or entities—identified by **Uniform Resource Identifiers (URIs)**. This approach aligns closely with the principles of the web, leveraging HTTP methods to perform operations on resources in a standardized and scalable manner.

In resource-based APIs, clients use standard HTTP methods such as GET, POST, PUT, and DELETE to perform **Create, Read, Update, Delete (CRUD)** operations on resources. Each resource is identified by a specific URI, and the HTTP methods define the action to be taken on that resource. For example, a GET request retrieves the current state of a resource, while a POST request might create a new resource. This uniform interface simplifies client-server interactions, making APIs more intuitive and easier to consume.

A key characteristic of resource-based APIs is stateless communication. This means that each request from the client to the server must contain all the information needed to understand and process the request, without relying on any stored context on the server. Statelessness enhances scalability and reliability, as servers do not need to maintain session information, allowing for easier load balancing across multiple servers. Additionally, responses in resource-based APIs are often cacheable, enabling clients and intermediaries to store responses for a certain period, which improves performance and reduces server load.

Examples of resource-based APIs include REST, which is widely adopted due to its simplicity and flexibility, focusing on resource CRUD operations. RESTful APIs are prevalent in web services, enabling interoperability between different systems on the internet. OData is another example that builds upon REST principles, providing a standardized protocol for querying and updating data.

It extends the REST model by adding powerful querying capabilities and metadata descriptions, making it easier to work with data-driven applications.

In addition, resource-based APIs can incorporate hypermedia and links to further enhance client-server interactions. This concept, known as **Hypermedia as the Engine of Application State (HATEOAS)**, allows clients to dynamically discover available actions and navigate through resources via hyperlinks embedded in API responses. Rather than hardcoding URI paths or resource relationships in the client, hypermedia enables clients to follow links provided by the server, making the API more flexible and self-descriptive. This approach helps decouple the client and server, allowing the server to evolve without breaking client integrations and making the API more adaptable to changing requirements.

Resource-based APIs, such as REST and OData, generally demonstrate higher maturity levels in API maturity models, such as the Richardson Maturity Model and Mike Amundsen's Maturity Model, compared to function-based APIs.

Furthermore, REST's popularity is evident in the industry. Based on Postman's *State of the API Report 2023*, REST is used by 86% of respondents. This high level of adoption underscores REST's widespread acceptance and effectiveness in modern API design, solidifying its position as the dominant API architectural style in use today.

Query-based APIs

Query-based APIs, such as GraphQL, are designed to enable clients to request exactly the data they need in a structured and flexible format. Unlike traditional APIs, where the structure of the data is predefined, query-based APIs empower clients to specify which fields and relationships they want in the response. This approach minimizes the issues of over-fetching (receiving more data than necessary) and under-fetching (not receiving enough data), thus optimizing the efficiency of data retrieval and network usage.

These APIs work by allowing clients to send structured queries to the server, which interprets the request and responds with the precise data requested using a resolver or data loaders. The server processes the query, retrieves the relevant information, and returns it in the format requested by the client. This decoupling of request and response structure gives the client greater control over the interaction and allows for more efficient communication, especially in cases where different clients (such as mobile apps and web apps) have different data requirements.

A key characteristic of query-based APIs is their flexibility in query structure. Clients can define not only what data they need, but also how deeply they want to explore relationships between resources. This eliminates the need for multiple API calls to gather related data and allows clients to retrieve complex, nested data structures in a single request. As a result, developers can create more efficient applications that avoid unnecessary round-trips to the server, enhancing performance and reducing latency.

A prime example of a query-based API is GraphQL, which allows clients to precisely define the structure of their responses. In GraphQL, clients can request only the fields they need, specify relationships between entities, and even perform mutations to modify data. This reduces the need for multiple API endpoints and minimizes the number of API calls required to fulfill the client's needs. By granting clients such control, GraphQL improves efficiency, reduces bandwidth usage, and provides a powerful tool for managing complex data interactions. According to Postman's *State of the API Report 2023*, 29% of respondents use GraphQL, demonstrating its increasing popularity due to its flexibility and efficient data retrieval capabilities, especially for applications requiring fine-tuned control over data fetching.

The following code shows an example of a GraphQL query:

```
{
  product(id: "12345") {
    name
    price
    reviews {
      rating
      comment
    }
  }
}
```

However, when it comes to scalability, query-based APIs introduce a layer of complexity compared to resource-based APIs such as REST. Unlike REST, which works hand-in-hand with the HTTP protocol and benefits from built-in caching mechanisms such as cache-control headers, query-based APIs require more complex caching strategies. Since each query is highly customizable and can vary from one client to another, caching at the HTTP level becomes less straightforward. This can lead to increased overhead in implementing application-level caching strategies, especially when managing frequently changing or large datasets. Additionally, the flexible nature of query-based APIs can complicate security, as it requires careful consideration of query permissions and rate-limiting strategies to prevent abuse, such as overly complex or expensive queries that could strain server resources.

When considering typical use cases, query-based APIs excel in scenarios where clients need fine-grained control over the data they retrieve. They are ideal for applications that require highly dynamic interactions, such as social media platforms where different clients (mobile, web, etc.) need to retrieve various subsets of user data. E-commerce platforms also benefit from query-based APIs, allowing clients to request specific product details, images, reviews, or prices based on the user's preferences. Furthermore, applications that involve complex, nested relationships between data entities, such as **content management systems** (**CMSs**), are well-suited for query-based APIs because they can retrieve deeply related content (e.g., articles, authors, comments) in a single request. These APIs are also widely adopted in mobile and **single-page applications** (**SPAs**), where reducing network traffic and optimizing the amount of data transferred is crucial for performance and user experience.

While query-based APIs offer significant flexibility and efficiency, they don't fully align with the highest levels of API maturity described in models such as the Richardson Maturity Model and Mike Amundsen's Maturity Model. Query-based APIs excel at reducing over-fetching and under-fetching (typical of *Level 1 and 2* in the maturity models), but they do not generally incorporate hypermedia controls. This absence of hypermedia, which allows clients to discover and navigate the API dynamically, means query-based APIs are less loosely coupled than hypermedia-driven APIs. Therefore, while query-based APIs are highly efficient for managing complex data retrieval, they may not achieve the same level of evolvability, scalability, and decoupling as fully RESTful APIs that leverage HTTP's native capabilities for caching and security.

Event-based APIs

Event-based APIs are designed to manage real-time or asynchronous communication between a server and clients, triggered by specific events. The goal of these APIs is to provide a mechanism where events, such as data changes and specific actions on the server, can immediately notify the client, allowing them to react in real time without continuously polling the server. This approach is essential in modern applications that require live updates or instant feedback, such as notifications, messaging systems, and financial market data streams.

These APIs operate by establishing communication channels where the server pushes updates or notifications to clients as events occur. Rather than the client continuously requesting new data, the server triggers notifications when necessary. Examples of event-based APIs include **Webhooks**, which use HTTP requests to notify clients when specific events occur, and **WebSockets**, which establish persistent, full-duplex communication between the client and server. This allows for re-al-time, two-way data transfer, making it ideal for applications such as live chat and collaborative tools. The asynchronous nature of event-based APIs ensures that clients stay updated in real time.

A defining feature of event-based APIs is their asynchronous communication, where the server independently sends updates without waiting for explicit client requests. This allows for more efficient data transfer and real-time interaction. In contrast to traditional APIs that rely on client polling, event-driven communication reduces latency and provides a more responsive experience. For example, Webhooks can notify an e-commerce system when an order's status changes, while WebSockets enable real-time experiences such as live sports updates and messaging.

In addition to Webhooks and WebSockets, event-based APIs often incorporate powerful messaging systems and **event-driven architectures** (**EDAs**), leveraging technologies such as **Apache Kafka**, **RabbitMQ**, and **AWS SNS/SQS**. These systems rely on **event brokers**, which act as intermediaries, routing events between producers and consumers. Event brokers ensure that events are delivered efficiently and reliably, allowing for scalable and decoupled architectures. For instance, Kafka allows services to publish and subscribe to topics, handling high volumes of real-time data with low latency, making it an ideal solution for streaming, real-time analytics, and event-driven microservices.

To standardize the way event-driven systems are described and documented, **AsyncAPI** is commonly used. Similar to OpenAPI for REST, AsyncAPI provides a structured format for defining event-driven APIs.

Here's an example of an AsyncAPI document for an Account Service responsible for processing user signups:

```
asyncapi: 3.0.0
info:
  title: Account Service
  version: 1.0.0
  description: This service is in charge of processing user signups
channels:
  userSignedup:
    address: user/signedup
    messages:
      UserSignedUp:
        $ref: '#/components/messages/UserSignedUp'
operations:
  sendUserSignedup:
```

```
      action: send
      channel:
        $ref: '#/channels/userSignedup'
      messages:
        - $ref: '#/channels/userSignedup/messages/UserSignedUp'
  components:
    messages:
      UserSignedUp:
        payload:
          type: object
          properties:
            displayName:
              type: string
              description: Name of the user
            email:
              type: string
              format: email
              description: Email of the user
```

In this example, the Account Service sends an event via the user/signed-up channel when a user registers, providing a clear structure for developers to understand how events flow through the system. The AsyncAPI format enables easy documentation and integration, ensuring that services can communicate efficiently in an event-driven ecosystem.

In conclusion, event-based APIs are foundational for building responsive, real-time systems. By using technologies such as Kafka for event brokering and leveraging standards such as AsyncAPI, developers can create scalable, efficient, and easily maintainable systems. This EDA allows services to decouple from each other, making the overall system more resilient, flexible, and capable of handling real-time communication at scale.

The true value in mastering these diverse API styles—whether function-based, resource-based, query-based, or event-based—lies not just in technical implementation but also in strategic selection. Each style is designed to address specific challenges, and understanding the nuances of each empowers you to *choose the right tool for the job*. It's not about adopting the most popular style; it's about making informed decisions that align with your project's unique needs. With a deep grasp of these styles, you'll be able to craft APIs that optimize performance, enhance scalability, and support long-term system evolution, ensuring that your architecture can adapt to changing business requirements.

Now that we've explored the distinct characteristics of each API style family, it's time to see how we can choose the right API style.

How to choose the right API style

Choosing the right API style for a system requires carefully considering the system's unique requirements and technical constraints and the nature of its interactions with your API consumers. This decision-making framework provides a guide for selecting between function-based, resource-based, query-based, and event-based API families. By understanding the system's goals and addressing key factors, you can make informed choices to align the API with both technical and business objectives.

Understanding the core requirements

The first step in selecting the most suitable API style is to thoroughly understand the system's core requirements. You can ensure that the API design aligns with the overall goals and use cases of the project by addressing the following questions:

- **What is the API's primary function?**

  In addition to what you've learned in *Chapter 1* about the *why* of API development, you need to determine whether the API is primarily designed to trigger actions, manipulate resources, retrieve specific data, or enable real-time communication. For example, a system focused on initiating transactions or processing calculations may benefit from a function-based API, whereas an e-commerce platform managing products and orders may lean toward a resource-based API. If the goal is to offer flexible data retrieval for different users or apps, a query-based API might be more appropriate. Similarly, for systems that push real-time updates—such as stock prices and chat notifications—an event-based API is likely the best fit.

- **Who are the consumers of the API?**

  Understanding the primary consumers of the API is critical to designing an architecture that meets their needs. The consumers may include internal teams, third-party developers, mobile and web applications, or real-time systems that rely on timely data. Additionally, **intelligent agents (IAs)**, such as AI-driven systems and bots, are increasingly becoming consumers of APIs. IA agents may need access to dynamic, real-time data to make automated decisions, as well as the ability to trigger actions based on predefined conditions. This could influence the API style; for example, IA agents often benefit from query-based APIs for precise data retrieval or event-based APIs for real-time updates.

- **What are the performance requirements?**

  Performance is a key consideration when choosing an API style. Does the system demand sub-millisecond low-latency communication, as is often the case with real-time apps and gaming systems, or can traditional request-response interactions suffice? If low latency is critical, an event-based API or high-performance function-based API such as gRPC might be necessary, especially in a closed (micro)service environment. Otherwise, a well-architected resource-based API such as REST could be ideal in most scenarios.

- **How dynamic is the data?**

  Consider whether the data returned by the API needs to be highly customizable for different consumers, such as mobile apps and desktop apps, or whether a standardized data structure can be used across the board. If precise and customizable data is needed—especially to avoid over-fetching or under-fetching—then a query-based API such as GraphQL would be appropriate. On the other hand, if the data structure is consistent across clients and can be easily standardized, resource-based APIs can provide a simpler, more uniform interface.

Now that we have listed the core requirements, let's dive deep into synchronous and asynchronous communication modes.

Synchronous versus asynchronous communication

Deciding between synchronous and asynchronous communication is another crucial factor:

- **Synchronous communication:** If the system primarily requires immediate responses (e.g., CRUD operations or executing commands), function-based or resource-based APIs are typically the best fit. These APIs are designed for real-time interaction where clients expect immediate feedback after making a request. For example, RESTful APIs are widely used for synchronous, resource-based operations, while gRPC is often employed for high-performance, function-based calls.

- **Asynchronous communication:** When the system needs to handle real-time updates or events that happen outside the direct control of the client, event-based APIs are a better fit. These APIs can notify clients of changes as they occur, without the need for continuous polling. Systems that push updates based on events—such as messaging apps, IoT devices, and financial data feeds—are prime candidates for event-based APIs such as WebSockets and Webhooks.

- **Mixed models**: Some systems may require a mix of both synchronous and asynchronous communication. For example, an application might use resource-based APIs for standard operations such as retrieving data, but switch to event-based APIs for real-time notifications or updates (e.g., a weather app that periodically fetches data but uses WebSockets for real-time alerts). In this case, the API design would need to accommodate both interaction models.

Mastering this balance between synchronous and asynchronous communication is pivotal in API design. Selecting the right communication model not only enhances performance and responsiveness but also ensures the scalability and efficiency of your system. By understanding when to leverage real-time interactions versus immediate responses, you can align your API style with the specific needs of your application.

Now, let's explore another important factor to consider when selecting an API style.

Data complexity and flexibility

The complexity and flexibility of data handling are important factors in choosing an API style:

- **High flexibility** (customizable data): If the API needs to allow clients to request specific fields or data relationships, query-based APIs such as GraphQL are an ideal choice. These APIs empower clients to request precisely the data they need, which is particularly useful when different clients require varying amounts of data or when over-fetching data would impact performance. GraphQL allows frontend teams to optimize data retrieval, making it well-suited for dynamic, data-driven applications such as analytics platforms and personalized content services. However, you can also achieve a similar level of flexibility using resource-based APIs with proper API design practices. By implementing filtering, sparse field sets, or embedding resources at the application level, clients can still retrieve only the data they need, minimizing over-fetching and optimizing performance. This approach works well when designing RESTful APIs for systems that value simplicity while maintaining flexible data retrieval.

- **Standardized data**: For APIs that manage consistent data structures across all clients, resource-based APIs such as REST offer a simpler and more efficient solution. RESTful APIs can handle CRUD operations with standardized endpoints and are a good fit when the data being retrieved or modified doesn't require customization for different consumers. Moreover, REST supports **content negotiation**, which allows the server to provide different representations of the same resource depending on the client's preferences or capabilities. Through **proactive content negotiation**, the server selects the most appropriate format, language, or encoding based on the user agent's stated preferences. Alternatively, **reactive negotiation** lets the server offer multiple representations for the client to choose from. This flexibility ensures that even with standardized data structures, a REST API can deliver responses tailored to the specific needs of clients, enhancing usability across diverse environments.

The choice between flexibility and standardization in data handling is critical to ensuring your API is fit for purpose. Whether you prioritize flexible, client-specific data retrieval or rely on standardized interactions, aligning the API style with your system's needs will optimize performance, scalability, and user experience.

Now, let's dive into another vital consideration—coupling. How tightly or loosely coupled your API is to its clients and servers plays a significant role in its flexibility, scalability, and ease of maintenance.

Coupling: tight versus loose

The level of coupling between the client and server impacts not only the API design but also the API's maturity level:

- **Tight coupling**: When clients need to perform highly specific and predefined actions—such as initiating transactions, executing calculations, and running complex commands—a function-based API (e.g., RPC or gRPC) is ideal. These APIs are designed for well-defined, action-oriented interactions where the server's functionality is closely tied to the client's requests. Tight coupling often aligns with lower levels of API maturity in models such as the Richardson Maturity Model, where APIs focus on RPC-style actions and are less flexible in terms of evolvability.

- **Loose coupling**: For systems where flexibility and adaptability are important, resource-based or event-based APIs are more appropriate. These APIs enable clients to interact with resources or subscribe to events without tightly coupling to the server's internal implementation. Loose coupling aligns with higher levels of API maturity, as seen in models such as Mike Amundsen's Maturity Model or the Richardson Maturity Model, where APIs evolve toward stateless interactions and hypermedia controls, allowing clients to dynamically navigate resources and decouple from the server's internal changes.

Mastering the balance between tight and loose coupling is essential for designing APIs that are both scalable and maintainable. Whether your system requires precise, predefined actions or flexible, adaptive interactions, understanding coupling will help guide your API strategy toward the most suitable design approach.

Next, we turn to another critical consideration: scalability and performance. As your system grows, the API must efficiently handle increasing loads while maintaining responsiveness.

Scalability and performance

Performance and scalability are key drivers in API selection:

- **High throughput and low latency**: For applications with stringent performance requirements, such as real-time data processing and gaming, event-based APIs such as WebSockets and event brokers (e.g., Kafka) are optimal. These APIs are designed to handle large volumes of data with minimal latency, enabling seamless real-time interactions.

- **Statelessness and scalability**: Resource-based APIs such as REST are ideal for scalable, stateless systems. These APIs take advantage of HTTP's statelessness, allowing requests to be easily distributed across multiple servers. This makes RESTful APIs a great choice for applications that need to scale horizontally, such as cloud-based services and e-commerce platforms.

- **Complex query requirements**: If clients need to retrieve complex, aggregated data (e.g., combining data from multiple sources), query-based APIs such as GraphQL excel. These APIs allow clients to retrieve multiple resources in a single request, which can greatly reduce API calls and improve performance.

Performance and scalability are central to API success. By aligning your API style with the specific demands of throughput, statelessness, and data retrieval complexity, you ensure that your system can scale efficiently and perform optimally under various loads.

Next, we'll explore how business needs and specific use cases should guide your API style selection.

Business and use case considerations

Selecting the right API style often depends on the specific business use case:

- **Transactional systems** (e.g., banking, financial apps): For applications requiring precise, action-oriented interactions, function-based APIs such as gRPC and SOAP provide the necessary security and reliability. These APIs excel in scenarios where well-defined procedures and stateful interactions are critical.

- **Data-centric applications** (e.g., e-commerce, content delivery): Resource-based APIs such as REST are the most suitable choice for systems focused on managing and manipulating resources, such as product catalogs and user profiles. Their simplicity and standardization make them easy to implement and maintain.

- **Data query flexibility** (e.g., CMS, analytics dashboards): Query-based APIs such as Graph-QL are ideal when clients need to customize data queries for different use cases. This makes them particularly effective for content management systems, where users may need to retrieve related data (e.g., articles, authors, and comments) in a single request.

- **Real-time updates** (e.g., IoT, stock market, messaging): Systems that require real-time updates, such as IoT devices and stock trading platforms, benefit most from event-based APIs. These APIs ensure that updates are pushed to clients as soon as they happen, enabling responsive and timely interactions.

Aligning your API style with your business use case ensures that the system not only functions effectively but also supports your specific operational and performance goals. Choosing the right approach based on your business needs can enhance scalability, maintainability, and user satisfaction.

Now, let's explore how developer experience can influence your API style selection.

Developer experience and integration

The ease of integration and developer experience can also significantly influence the choice of API style. The right API style should align with both the technical requirements and the skills or preferences of the development team. Factors such as familiarity, simplicity, control, and flexibility play a major role:

- **Familiarity and simplicity**: If ease of adoption is a priority, resource-based APIs such as REST are advantageous due to their simplicity and adherence to standard HTTP protocols. REST is widely known and understood across the developer community, making it easier to onboard developers and integrate with existing infrastructure, tools, and services. REST's well-defined principles around URIs, HTTP methods, and status codes contribute to a smooth development experience, particularly when building CRUD-based applications. Its simplicity also makes it ideal for smaller teams or projects where speed of development and ease of use are critical.

- **Control and flexibility**: Query-based APIs such as GraphQL offer more control to developers who need to tailor responses to specific needs. With GraphQL, developers can specify exactly which fields they want in a response, avoiding over-fetching or under-fetching data. This flexibility is especially beneficial for frontend developers working on dynamic, data-driven applications that may require varying data structures depending on the client or user. GraphQL improves the developer experience by reducing the need for multiple API calls and enabling more efficient data management. However, it does require a steeper learning curve and more careful design to manage complexity.

- **Developer efficiency and tooling:** The ease with which developers can use available tooling also plays a role in choosing an API style. REST-based APIs benefit from a rich ecosystem of tools, frameworks, and libraries that streamline API development, testing, and documentation. Tools such as Postman and SwaggerHub are widely used to create, consume, and document REST APIs. Conversely, GraphQL comes with its own robust ecosystem, including tools such as Apollo, GraphiQL, and code generators that enhance developer productivity but may require more specialized knowledge. For EDAs, AsyncAPI offers powerful tooling for designing and documenting asynchronous APIs. Similar to OpenAPI for REST, AsyncAPI provides a standard specification that helps developers work efficiently with event-driven systems, such as those using WebSockets, Kafka, or MQTT. Tools such as the AsyncAPI Generator and AsyncAPI Studio simplify the process of creating, testing, and maintaining event-driven APIs, making it easier for developers to work with systems that rely on real-time communication or asynchronous messaging.

- **Error handling and debugging:** REST APIs generally provide clearer and more standardized error handling using HTTP status codes, which are familiar to most developers. Errors such as **404 (Not Found)** and **500 (Internal Server Error)** are easy to understand and handle. In contrast, while GraphQL offers powerful error-handling capabilities, understanding and debugging complex queries can be more challenging due to the flexibility it offers, as errors can occur both at the network and query levels. Teams should weigh the complexity of their API consumers when choosing between these styles. For EDAs, error handling mechanisms are different and typically managed by the underlying message broker. Unlike REST and GraphQL, event-driven systems often rely on **dead-letter queues (DLQs)** to capture and manage messages that fail to be processed. This allows for better tracking of failed events without losing data, enabling more reliable error recovery. Additionally, various brokers such as Kafka, RabbitMQ, and MQTT support custom error formats and can provide more granular control over error handling. These systems may include retries, timeouts, and circuit breakers to handle transient errors, offering resilience in environments where message loss or failure is critical.

- **Scalability of API changes:** When an API is expected to evolve over time, GraphQL's ability to add fields without breaking clients ensures backward compatibility, making it easier to extend the API without versioning. On the other hand, REST APIs may require versioning strategies to manage breaking changes, though this can be mitigated with careful design.

In conclusion, the ease of integration and developer experience must be balanced with the needs of the application. While REST offers familiarity, simplicity, and a vast ecosystem of tools, GraphQL provides control, flexibility, and a more fine-tuned data retrieval process, which can lead to more efficient applications at scale. The choice between these API styles depends on the specific needs of the developers, the type of application being built, and the expected complexity of the data interactions.

Mixing API styles

In complex systems, using multiple API styles within a single architecture is often required to meet varying functional and non-functional requirements. Each API style has strengths suited to different scenarios, and it's often necessary to combine them to achieve the best results. Depending on the system's needs, you might not rely on just one API style but instead choose multiple styles that complement each other. This approach ensures flexibility, scalability, and efficiency.

For example, a web application might require the following:

- **REST** for general resource management, such as CRUD operations, where clients need structured and standardized access to resources
- **GraphQL** for customizable data retrieval, especially when clients need specific subsets of data without over-fetching
- **Webhooks** to notify third-party services asynchronously when events occur, such as order fulfillment and shipment status updates

By leveraging different API styles based on specific requirements, the architecture can handle synchronous data requests, dynamic queries, and real-time event-driven notifications.

Let's take a look at the use cases for each:

- **REST**: In a public e-commerce API, REST might be used to expose products and orders to clients, allowing them to browse product listings or submit new orders via standard endpoints
- **GraphQL**: For more dynamic data retrieval, such as displaying customized product data for specific customers or regions, GraphQL could be used to allow clients to request precisely the data they need
- **Webhooks**: Meanwhile, Webhooks would notify third-party logistics systems about order status updates, such as when an order is fulfilled or shipped

Depending on your system's requirements, you may need to mix and match API styles to meet various technical challenges, such as performance optimization, data customization, and real-time communication. By choosing multiple API styles strategically, you ensure that each part of your architecture is optimized for the task at hand, leading to a more resilient and efficient system.

In summary, selecting the right API style depends on several critical factors, including the system's core requirements, the interaction model, data complexity, coupling flexibility, scalability, and the use case. Each API style—whether function-based, resource-based, query-based, or event-based—has its own strengths and trade-offs. Systems that require precise actions or real-time event handling will benefit from function-based or event-based APIs, while systems with complex data interactions and varied client needs might favor query-based APIs. Resource-based APIs provide a strong foundation for simpler, CRUD-focused applications that prioritize scalability and ease of adoption.

By carefully considering API style trade-offs, architects and developers can make informed decisions that not only meet the technical demands of the system but also ensure smooth integrations, optimal performance, and an excellent developer experience. Ultimately, the goal is to create an API architecture that evolves with your project, enabling flexibility, scalability, and long-term success.

Summary

In this chapter, we explored the core concept of API styles, which shape how an API is structured, interacts with clients, and communicates data. We delved into the four major API style families—function-based, resource-based, query-based, and event-based—each designed to meet specific system requirements and use cases. The chapter emphasized the resource-based API style, particularly REST, highlighting its scalability, simplicity, and alignment with web standards, making it one of the most popular choices in modern web applications.

We discussed how choosing the right API style can have a profound impact on factors such as scalability, flexibility, and developer experience. Whether building APIs for real-time systems, highly dynamic data interactions, or simple resource management, understanding these styles will help developers and architects make well-informed decisions for their projects.

By now, you should have a clear understanding of the following:

- The different API style families and how they align with specific technical and business needs
- The benefits and use cases of each API style, including REST's advantages in scalability and flexibility
- How API styles impact performance, maintainability, and scalability, allowing you to select the most appropriate style for your system architecture

In the next chapter, we'll dive deeper into the core principles of RESTful API design, covering key REST constraints such as statelessness, cacheability, and the uniform interface. We'll also introduce the Richardson Maturity Model and Web API Design Maturity Model, providing frameworks to assess and improve the maturity of your API designs. This next chapter will help you create APIs that are scalable, robust, and future-proof.

Get This Book's PDF Version and Exclusive Extras

UNLOCK NOW

Scan the QR code (or go to packtpub.com/unlock). Search for this book by name, confirm the edition, and then follow the steps on the page.

Note: Keep your invoice handy. Purchases made directly from Packt don't require an invoice.

6

REST Design Constraints and Maturity Models

This chapter dives into API design specifics, delving into the core principles that guide RESTful API design as originally introduced by Roy Fielding. Here, we will explore the main REST design constraints that shape effective APIs nowadays and for years to come. This chapter will also introduce the **Richardson Maturity Model** (**RMM**) and the **Web API Design Maturity Model** (**WADMM**), providing a roadmap for assessing and improving the maturity of their API designs. It's a must-read for anyone aiming to create APIs that are robust, scalable, and easy to maintain.

In this chapter, we're going to cover the following main topics:

- The HTTP protocol
- REST API design constraints
- API design maturity models
- How to assess and improve your API's maturity

By the end of this chapter, you will be able to determine the set of constraints that will help ensure you design a mature API.

Technical requirements

To get the most out of this chapter, you must be familiar with the HTTP protocol and **JavaScript Object Notation** (**JSON**).

The HTTP protocol

The HTTP protocol serves as the foundation for data communication on the World Wide Web. It is the most prevalent protocol used today for data exchange. Although not formally required for REST APIs, nearly all of them utilize HTTP as the exchange protocol. In this book, we will continue with this approach. Understanding the basics of HTTP is crucial for reasoning about REST design constraints and maturity models. While we assume you are familiar with the basics of the HTTP protocol in this book, let's briefly recap its most important aspects.

Characteristics of the HTTP protocol

Let's take a closer look at the HTTP protocol's characteristics:

- **Client-server communication**: HTTP operates as a client-server protocol. Requests are initiated by the client, typically a web browser or an application—and sent to a server. The server then processes the request and responds to the client. This characteristic emphasizes the client's independence from the server, allowing them to evolve separately.

- **Statelessness**: Each client-to-server request contains all the necessary information to complete the request. No session information is stored by the server or required for processing.

- **Caching**: Requests and responses can be cached by the client to improve performance. Cached responses can be reused when identical requests are made, enhancing overall system performance.

- **Uniform interface**: HTTP relies on a uniform interface, simplifying the architecture. Each HTTP request includes a resource identifier, a method, and metadata. It may also contain other elements, such as query parameters.

- **Layered system**: Clients are unaware of the source of the response—whether it came directly from the end server, a reverse proxy, or another intermediary element. This layered approach enables flexibility and scalability.

- **Extensibility**: HTTP is an extensible protocol that has evolved multiple times. It serves various purposes, including retrieving HTML documents (websites), images, and videos, and enabling content manipulation on servers. Currently, multiple iterations of HTTP work in parallel, such as HTTP 1.1, HTTP/2, and HTTP/3. Later in this chapter, we'll discuss the pros and cons of these newer versions.

In the *REST API design constraints* section, we'll explore how closely these characteristics align. Next, we'll delve into the structure of an HTTP request, highlighting its main elements.

The structure of an HTTP request and response

The communication pattern in HTTP is composed of a request coming from the client, followed by a response from the server, as detailed in *Figure 6.1*. They always follow the same structure, and in this section, we will go through each of them and focus on the most important details regarding REST.

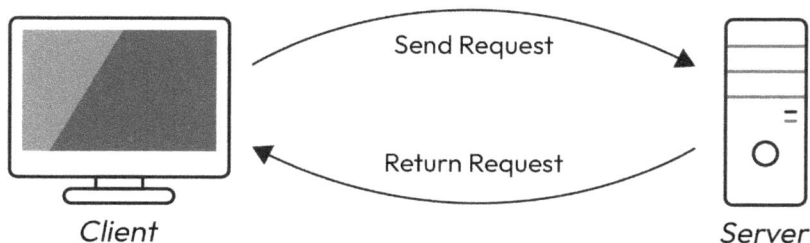

Figure 6.1 – Elements of the HTTP protocol

If we look back at the **uniform interface** characteristic of the HTTP protocol, we can see that HTTP requests and responses relate to it. We can distinguish the following elements of HTTP requests and responses:

- A URI, the resource identifier, which may also contain query parameters
- An HTTP method specifying the type of operation performed over the resource
- Request headers containing request metadata
- A payload, which is the data object we send to the server
- Response codes indicating the result of the request

The following is an example of a request:

```
POST
https:// api.magicstore.com/products
Content-Type: application/json
Authorization: Bearer your_access_token

{
  "name": "Magic Wand",
  "price": 29.99,
  "category": "Wands"
}
```

Here's the response:

```
HTTP/1.1 201 Created
Content-Type: application/json
Location: https://api.magicstore.com/products/12345

{
  "id": "12345",
  "name": "Magic Wand",
  "price": 29.99,
  "category": "Wands",
  "available": true
}
```

💡 **Quick tip:** Enhance your coding experience with the **AI Code Explainer** and **Quick Copy** features. Open this book in the next-gen Packt Reader. Click the **Copy** button (1) to quickly copy code into your coding environment, or click the **Explain** button (2) to get the AI assistant to explain a block of code to you.

```
                                              Copy      Explain
function calculate(a, b) {
  return {sum: a + b};                          1          2
};
```

📖 **The next-gen Packt Reader** is included for free with the purchase of this book. Scan the QR code OR go to https://packtpub.com/unlock, then use the search bar to find this book by name. Double-check the edition shown to make sure you get the right one.

URI

The **Universal Resource Identifier (URI)** is the network location of the resource. It consists of five elements:

- The scheme, which identifies the protocol used to access the resource. In our case, it will be HTTPS, which is the secure version of the HTTP protocol that uses SSL or TLS to encrypt the transferred data. HTTPS also uses a different default port for communication (443 instead of 80).

- The authority, which specifies the host under which our resource is available. The authority may also contain user information (followed by @), but this is not used in REST APIs.

- Another element of the authority is the port (preceded by :). This is also optional, as the HTTP and HTTPS protocols use a default port number. Custom port numbers are mostly relevant in pre-production and local environments.

- A path identifying the specific resource the URI is pointing to. This is always relative to the host.

- Query parameters, preceded by a ? character. This is usually used to pass parameters in the request, such as filters.

HTTP methods

HTTP methods are used in the interaction between a client and a server. They specify what kind of action is going to be performed on the server. For example, GET `https://api.magicstore.com/wizards` will request to retrieve the set of wizards (the resource) from the `api.magicstore.com` host.

> Idempotency
>
> Before going through each HTTP method, we should introduce an important concept: **idempotency**. This concept is important in the context of APIs, especially regarding their methods. In short, idempotent requests can be made multiple times and will give the same results each time. They do not affect the server in a way that would result in a different result for a request. This is especially important in the context of security as it improves fault tolerance. It also ensures alignment between systems—we know that the same requests will give us the same results.

The following are the primary HTTP methods that are used in the context of a REST API:

- GET: This method is used to retrieve data from a server. It is a read-only operation, so it does not change anything on the server. GET is idempotent as it does not alter the state of the server in a way that it would give different results for the same data.

- HEAD: This method is very similar to GET, with one crucial difference: it does not request the payload and instead is used to retrieve only the metadata (headers) of the request. Like GET, it is also idempotent.

- POST: This method is used to send data to a server to create a new resource. It can create a new instance of a resource or initiate a process. POST is not an idempotent method, as creating a new resource will give a different result on the server each time (e.g., a new ID).

- PUT: This method is used to update or replace a resource on the server. The request must contain the entire object that is going to be updated, as the PUT payload will overwrite the existing resource with the data it sends. It is an idempotent method as it will always give the same results, despite the current state of the resource it overwrites.

- PATCH: Unlike PUT, which completely overwrites a resource object, this method is used to apply partial modifications to a resource on the server. The client sends just the changes to the server. In the context of APIs, there are two different ways to implement the PATCH method, both of which will be explained shortly. This method is not idempotent by default, but it can be if it's implemented idempotently.

- DELETE: This method is used to delete a resource on the server. Once a resource is removed, it cannot be removed again. This means that the server will not change after the initial deletion, thus making DELETE idempotent.

- OPTIONS: This method, like GET, retrieves data from the server. However, unlike GET, which retrieves a representation of a resource, OPTIONS retrieves what kind of other HTTP methods can be performed over a resource. Because this operation does not change the server's state, it is also idempotent.

JSON Patch and JSON Merge Patch

These are two different standards regarding the implementation of the PATCH method. **JSON Patch (RFC 6902)** and **JSON Merge Patch (RFC 7396)** are commonly used in REST APIs to partially update resources in JSON format.

JSON Patch represents the update as a series of operations that should be applied to the source document. Each operation is represented as a JSON object, and the series of operations is represented as an array of these objects. Here's an example:

```
[
  {
    "op": "replace",
    "path": "/class",
    "value": "Wizard"
  },
  {
    "op": "remove",
    "path": "/hero/name"
  }
]
```

This approach is very flexible and can represent complex modifications, but it can also be more difficult to write and understand. It can also lead to very long request bodies in the case of large updates with many operations.

However, JSON Patch is not inherently idempotent for several operations. Using the add operation to add elements to arrays, without specifying indices, can cause duplication:

```
{"op": "add", "path": "/effects", "value": "healing"}
```

This transforms [] into ["healing"] the first time, then into ["healing", "healing"] when executed again.

Also, moving elements repeatedly can cause cascading changes:

```
{ "op": "move", "from": "/powers", "path": "/effects" }
```

This operation is not idempotent, as a second application would fail since the source no longer exists.

Despite these limitations, JSON Patch can be implemented idempotently. To do so, you can do the following:

- Use the test operation to verify the current state before applying modifications:

```
[
  { "op": "test", "path": "/powers", "value": "healing" },
```

```
    { "op": "move", "from": "/powers", "path": "/effects" }
]
```

This approach ensures that the move operation is performed only when the powers value is equal to healing, as stated in the precondition.

- Target specific indices when performing the add operation on an array:

```
{ "op": "add", "path": "/potions/0", "value": "Potion of Healing" }
```

This adds predictability to array operations and ensures they will always be idempotent.

JSON Merge Patch approaches the change differently. In this approach, the client only sends a part of the JSON body of the resource they want to update. This part only includes the updates the client wishes to make—modifications, additions, or deletions. Parameters that the client wants to delete are represented with a null value. Here's an example:

```
{
  "class": "Wizard",
  "hero": {
    "name": null
  }
}
```

This approach is simpler and more intuitive than JSON Patch. It is also a much more common approach. Moreover, JSON Merge Patch is naturally idempotent. However, it also has some limitations, such as the inability to modify values in an array.

In summary, JSON Patch is more powerful and flexible, while JSON Merge Patch is simpler, easier to use, and idempotent by default. The choice between the two depends on the specific requirements of your application, such as the need to operate on specific array elements.

HTTP headers

HTTP headers carry the metadata about both requests and responses. Their structure consists of key-value pairs. We can divide headers into the following areas:

- Request headers, which carry information regarding the resource to be fetched or the client.
- Response headers, which hold information such as the response's location and the server providing it, as well as the instance of the resource (e.g., ETag).

- Representation headers, which provide information about the body of the resource. They are used for content negotiation and similar purposes.

- Payload headers, which contain information about payload size, encoding, and more.

For REST APIs, the headers that are used for authorization and authentication are especially common. Note that content negotiation and cache control can also be specified using headers.

HTTP response codes

Response codes are responsible for indicating the result of the HTTP request in a simple and standardized way. They consist of a three-digit response code and a description of the code's nature. Response codes are grouped into five classes of responses:

- **1xx (informational)**: These responses communicate transfer-protocol-level information. They are not used in REST.

- **2xx (success)**: These responses indicate a successfully processed request.

- **3xx (redirection)**: These responses notify the client of additional actions that are required to complete the request—for example, a long-running process or a redirection to another host.

- **4xx (client error)**: These codes notify the client that there was an issue with the request on the client side. This could be a wrongly formed request, a lack of authorization rights, and so on.

- **5xx (server error)**: This code specifies that the error was caused by the server. Usually, it informs the client that the server-side application had an uncaught exception or there was a timeout on the server.

In general, these codes help us understand what has happened. Due to their standardized nature, they help with programming the client application accordingly so that it can react correctly, depending on what has happened to the request.

HTTP/2 and beyond

As mentioned earlier, HTTP is an extensible protocol, which means that it continues to evolve. Still, the most common version of the HTTP protocol, and the one that is the base for all subsequent versions nowadays, is HTTP/1.1. HTTP/2 and HTTP/3 are newer versions of the HTTP protocol that offer performance improvements over HTTP/1.1.

HTTP/2 introduces several performance enhancements, such as multiplexing, header compression, and server push. Multiplexing allows multiple requests to be sent in parallel over a single TCP connection, header compression reduces their size, and server push allows the server to send the client resources it has not requested yet. In certain scenarios, these features can lead to significant gains in performance. On top of that, HTTP/2 and HTTP/3 are binary protocols, which means they're binary instead of textual. This leads to higher reliability of data transfer.

Regarding HTTP/3, its main difference compared to HTTP/1.1 is its use of QUIC as its transport layer protocol. QUIC uses UDP instead of TCP. This can result in faster connection times and improved handling regarding packet loss, which can be beneficial for REST APIs, especially in mobile or high-latency environments.

It is important to note that adopting HTTP/2 or HTTP/3 does not require any additional work from an API design standpoint. This is handled by the application server and network instead.

In this section, we talked about the HTTP protocol and its importance for REST APIs. We also noted that an HTTP request and response consist of the following elements:

- The resource identifier (URI)
- The HTTP method, which specifies the action to take
- HTTP headers, which contain the metadata
- Request and response bodies, which carry the data
- HTTP response codes, which inform the client of the request's results

In the next section, we will focus on REST API design constraints. Here, we will see how similar most of these constraints are to the HTTP protocol's characteristics.

REST API design constraints

Having gone through the HTTP protocol's nuts and bolts, we can start to analyze the REST API's architectural style and constraints. This will act as a foundation for all further discussion on the design of REST APIs.

Out of all the API architectural styles available, REST and its derivatives are the most common. This means that it is also the most proven and battle-tested. A great example of a REST-like architecture that's implemented on a large scale is the World Wide Web. Being created in 1992, it predates REST. You can think of the World Wide Web as a large-scale implementation of REST principles, using HTTP as its protocol and web browsers as clients. REST was abstracted from the World Wide Web's architecture to describe a broader spectrum of applications, but using the World Wide Web as an example helps us reason about REST.

REST APIs were originally proposed by Roy Thomas Fielding in his 2000 doctoral dissertation titled *Architectural Styles and the Design of Network-based Software Architectures.* It was a foundational work that turned out to be the key architectural principle for the World Wide Web. In his paper, Fielding defines REST using the Null Style and builds a set of constraints on top of it that define the REST architectural style. As evidenced, REST's constraints are the same as the HTTP protocol's characteristics, all of which were listed earlier. However, because the context of REST APIs is more specific, let's look at each of these constraints one by one.

Client-server

Essentially, this constraint means that client and server applications must be able to evolve separately, without any dependency on each other. A client should only know the resource identifier (address). As an example, a client application, such as a mobile application, connects to a server to retrieve data. The only information it needs to initiate the retrieval process is the server's address and the location of the resource it is looking for within the server. This enables independent evolution of the server, as well as client applications. Clients can grow in terms of features while the server remains the same. Servers and clients may also be replaced and developed independently if the interface between them is not altered. This promotes flexibility and scalability in the system, thereby *supporting the internet-scale requirement of multiple organizational domains.*

Stateless

This constraint means that the requests from the clients must contain all the information necessary for them to be understood by the server, while not taking advantage of any kind of context on the server. This also implies that servers must include all the necessary information in their response so that clients can maintain the state on their side if needed. *"This constraint induces the properties of visibility, reliability, and scalability."* Monitoring systems do not have to retrieve any additional information about a single request since it is self-contained. Reliability is also improved because recovering from failures is easier. Additionally, stateless systems are easier to scale due to simplified state and resource management.

Cacheable

This constraint is added to improve the network efficiency of communication. It requires data, in response to a specific request, to be labelled as cacheable or non-cacheable. This can be either explicit or implicit. Explicit labeling relies on setting specific metadata headers, while implicit labeling relies on the characteristics of the HTTP protocol. Responses to GET requests are cacheable by default, while POST requests are not and require explicit labeling. PUT and DELETE requests are not cacheable at all. Cached data is stored in several places along the request-response path. When a client requests a resource representation, the request goes through a cache, or a series of caches (local cache, proxy cache, or reverse proxy), toward the service hosting the resource. If any of the caches along the request path contains a fresh copy of the requested representation, it uses that copy to satisfy the request. If none of the caches can satisfy the request, the request travels to the service (or origin server, as it is formally known). Leveraging caching has several benefits:

- Reduces bandwidth by utilizing the network's limited depth
- Reduces request-response latency by serving the data from the closest network element containing cached data
- Reduces load on servers by utilizing cached data; not all requests will reach the server
- Hides network failures by utilizing cached data instead

> Note
>
> Cacheable responses (whether to a GET or a POST request) should include a validator—either an ETag or a Last-Modified header. An ETag is a header that contains a token value that a server associates with a specific state of a resource. This means that if anything related to a requested resource changes, the value of the ETag also changes. Think of this as a unique stamp. Comparing the ETag's values will tell you whether two representations of the same resource are identical. The Last-Modified header plays the same role, but its value is a timestamp instead of a token.

In summary, the cacheable constraint promotes a decoupled and scalable design, which improves the usability and maintainability of APIs.

Uniform interface

This constraint simplifies and decouples the architecture. This, in turn, enables each part of the system architecture to evolve independently. There are four core principles of the uniform interface. Let's go through each of them:

- **Identifying resources**: Each resource is identified in requests using a unique identifier. In the case of HTTP, this is a URI. A resource can be any entity that the API can provide information about. For example, in an e-store, we could have a user, an order, and a product, and each of these entities would be a resource. We would identify them in the system as Users, Orders, and Products and store them under specific URIs, such as `https://api.e-store.com/users`, `https://api.e-store.com/orders`, and `https://api.e-store.com/products`. This constraint emphasizes that all interactions with the API are done via these URIs.

- **Manipulating resources through representations**: REST communicates by transferring a representation of a resource in a format that the client can understand. This means that the responses from the server will match the information included in the request's metadata format and the representation of the desired resource. This is usually provided through content negotiation and applies both to reading the data in a proper format and writing data to the server. The representation that's sent back to the client or saved on the server is virtually never the same as the data stored on the server (an exception to this could be retrieving or sending some specific log files). This is not only applicable to the data format (e.g., JSON, REST, CSV, etc.) or language, but also to the data itself. Representations aim to send only the subset of data that is required by the client and do not expose any internal or implementation-specific information.

  Content negotiation

  Content negotiation allows clients and servers to agree on the representation of the requested resource. It ensures that clients receive data in a format they can understand. Content negotiation is usually client-driven, where the request contains metadata that will determine the representation format. This is done through headers. For example, the **Accept** header specifies what kind of data format the client understands; based on that, the server will respond with the desired format, such as JSON or XML. Content negotiation is also used for specifying things such as the desired language of the response, date format, and so on. We will learn more about content negotiation in *Chapter 12*.

- **Self-descriptive messages**: Every message must include enough information to describe how to process the message. Such information should be included in the header metadata. This relates closely to the *stateless* constraint. A self-descriptive message typically includes the HTTP method describing the action to perform over the resource, the resource identifier, headers that provide metadata about the message, and a body that contains the representation of the resource (if applicable). We learned about the structure of HTTP requests and responses in the *HTTP protocol* section.

- **Hypermedia as the Engine of Application State (HATEOAS):** This principle ensures that a REST API provides hypermedia links to related resources and actions within the resource responses. This aims to make APIs more self-descriptive and discoverable. HATEOAS allows clients to navigate the API without any prior knowledge of it. This principle is the most divisive one and has caused a lot of issues regarding what can be called a real REST API and what can't. Most REST APIs we see do not include hypermedia controls. This is mostly due to two reasons. Firstly, it is harder to design hypermedia APIs as all the resource representations must provide relevant information about the related resources; at the same time, the API should provide full coverage of the API space. Even more complications come when we have more granular access control over the API and do not want to include information that certain clients should not be able to access. On top of that, creating clients that leverage HATEOAS controls well may be quite complicated. HATEOAS provides a lot of benefits, but this doesn't come without a cost. We encourage you to design your APIs with hypermedia in mind, but you should really build APIs for specific use cases, so be mindful of this. We have dedicated *Chapter 12* to hypermedia APIs and why they are fantastic tools nowadays.

  HATEOAS and AI

  Despite their troubled past, hypermedia APIs are going to be especially important in the coming years. Their biggest downside of being difficult to leverage by clients is quickly becoming irrelevant with the emergence of AIs that use **large language models (LLMs)**. What's more, because one of the core functionalities of those AI systems comes from connecting to various Web APIs, systems that are easily discoverable and navigable will play a much bigger role. Go to *Chapter 11* for more information.

Layered system

This constraint says that there can be multiple layers between the client and the server that hosts the resource. Those layers can be network elements such as the cache, load balancer, proxy, firewall, and so on. The client, however, can't tell whether the response comes directly from the server or has been delivered through any intermediary layers. This architectural approach provides the following benefits:

- **Modularity:** Layers can be added, removed, updated, or replaced independently without affecting traffic

- **Scalability**: Load balancers can distribute requests across multiple server instances, making it possible to scale horizontally
- **Security**: Firewalls can provide an additional layer of security
- **Caching**: The caching layer allows the *cacheable* constraint in the network layer to be fulfilled

However, having too many layers in your system can also have some consequences. Firstly, it can add additional latency, because most of the layers will be processing the request and thus adding to the system's performance. Another aspect is the added complexity of the system. Whenever you're adding another layer to your system, take the consequences into account and try to plan according to your needs. Most APIs nowadays have a reverse proxy layer in the form of an API gateway and a load balancer between your servers and the reverse proxy. We will dive deeper into API gateways and other topics related to the *layered system* constraint in *Chapter 13*.

Code on demand (optional)

This optional constraint may be controversial as it allows servers to extend or customize the client's functionality by responding with code. This code is usually sent in the form of scripts (e.g., JavaScript) to be executed by the client application. It can simplify the client by reducing the number of functionalities to be implemented. However, it can reduce the visibility on the client side by depending too much on the server. This, in turn, increases the coupling between the client and the server. This constraint is very rare in APIs nowadays, especially in public APIs. In summary, while code on demand can increase the flexibility and extensibility of a REST API, it is an optional constraint due to its potential drawbacks.

API maturity

When designing APIs, we adhere to a certain set of rules. Usually, these rules would be the design constraints specific to the architectural style we have chosen. In our case, that would be REST. Additionally, we aim to follow a set of guidelines, such as industry best practices or internal organization rules. This is a crucial step to ensure our API's quality as early as possible in the design stage of its life cycle.

In this section, we examine two models for assessing API design maturity. Maturity models provide a structured way to validate and score the quality of an API design. We begin with the Richardson Maturity Model (RMM), which evaluates how closely an API aligns with the constraints of the REST architectural style. Next, we turn to the Web API Design Maturity Model (WADMM), which focuses on assessing how client-centric an API is through the design of its document model. Let's explore each of these maturity models in more detail.

> Why does it matter?
>
> Having a set of rules that goes beyond merely the architectural constraints is very important for API design. REST design constraints may look specific at first glance; however, in real applications, they leave a lot of freedom regarding the approach to take. Following a stricter set of guidelines defined by the industry and by our organization's internal context will make our APIs not only more predictable and standardized but also provide a better **developer experience (DX)** to any consumer application. The design model impacts API stability and usability over time. The longer we maintain an API, the more effective it will become, and there will be more possibilities for our clients to be broken or the API's reliability being affected. In an ecosystem composed of multiple APIs, this is especially important—we are no longer talking about singular APIs but rather a distributed system of interdependent interfaces.
>
> API maturity models help us choose an already industry-proven set of design guidelines. Choosing the right level should align with your organization's needs and capabilities. A system's reliability relies not only on its technical aspects but also on predictability.

RMM

RMM is a model suggested by Leonard Richardson in 2008. It aims to assess APIs to ensure they conform to the REST style's design constraints. It does so by analyzing three core factors:

- Resource identifiers (URIs)
- HTTP methods
- Hypermedia controls

As shown in *Figure 6.2*, RMM classifies APIs into four maturity levels. As expressed by its creator, each of these levels corresponds to the adoption of a specific technology and focuses on the response documents. We will describe each of these levels with a simple example.

Glory of REST

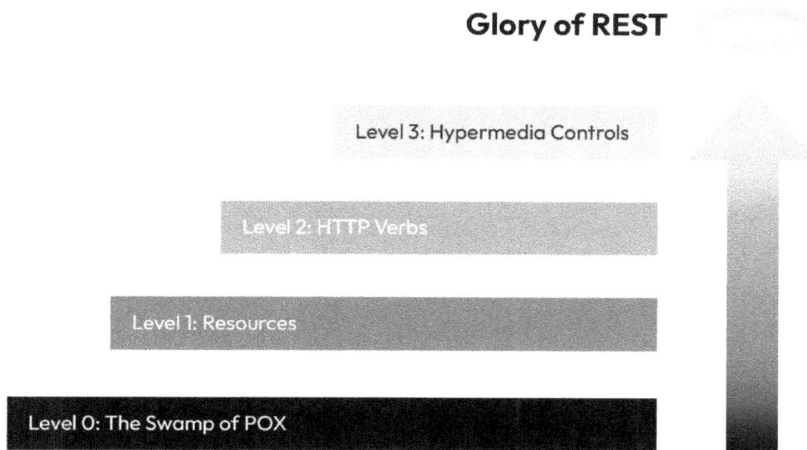

Figure 6.2 – RMM (https://martinfowler.com/articles/richardsonMaturityModel.html)

Level 0: The Swamp of POX

POX in this context doesn't mean a nasty disease, even though this level's placement at the very bottom of the maturity model could suggest that; it stands for **Plain Old XML** and refers to the class of APIs that operate on a single endpoint. Such APIs accept all the operations supported by the service on every resource in the API. For example, SOAP APIs fall under this category, and their operation, resource identification, and part of their metadata are sent in a so-called envelope within the XML payload. Another popular example of a Level 0 API could be a GraphQL API. They tend to have only one endpoint and provide a query language to request all the data stored. GraphQL and SOAP APIs only utilize the POST method to complete all operations, thus breaking the HTTP protocol, and always return a 200 OK response. Level 0 systems don't classify as RESTful.

The following is an example of a request:

```
POST https://api.magicstore.com/shop
{
    "function": "readProducts",
    "arguments": [
        "available"
    ]
}
```

Here's the response:

```
HTTP/1.1 200 OK
{
    "result": {
            "products": [
                    "wizard hat",
                    "magic weapon"
        ]
     }
}
```

In this example, we are making a POST request to fetch data about available products in our magic store. This, by itself, is breaking the HTTP protocol's semantics as POST requests should create records. The type of operation that's performed is defined in the payload by the "function" parameter. This happens because there is only a single entry point to the API via the /shop endpoint, and it does not use HTTP semantics. Note that even though Level 0 is called The Swamp of POX, we are operating on JSON files in this example. Having XML in the name refers to a class of APIs that typically utilize XML as the data format.

Level 1: Resources

At Level 1 of the maturity model, we start operating on resources. An API at this level introduces distinct URIs for individual resources but still violates HTTP protocol constraints by relying solely on POST for all actions and ignoring standard response codes. This approach is common in **Remote Procedure Call (RPC)** APIs, where all actions (read, write, etc.) use POST requests and return 200 OK regardless of the outcome. RPC APIs also favor action-oriented URIs such as /purchase-order/start, which breach REST's uniform interface principle. While Level 1 begins organizing resources, it does not meet REST's architectural constraints yet.

The following is an example of a request:

```
POST https://api.magicstore.com/products
Content-Type: application/json
{
  "op": "read",
  "arguments": ["available"]
```

Here's the response:

```
HTTP/1.1 200 OK
{
    "products": ["wizard hat", "magic weapon"]
}
```

In this example, the API has moved beyond a single entry point and now exposes multiple resource-specific endpoints. However, it still relies on an RPC-style approach by specifying the desired operation in the request payload using the op parameter, rather than leveraging the semantics of HTTP methods, such as GET, for retrieval. Additionally, the API responds with a 200 OK status to every POST request, regardless of the actual operation performed, which can obscure the true outcome of the request. Another issue is the absence of a Content-Type header in the response, which can lead to problems for clients, especially if the API supports multiple response formats. Properly utilizing HTTP methods, status codes, and headers would make the API more robust, predictable, and RESTful.

Level 2: HTTP Verbs

This is where we'll start to talk about APIs we typically call RESTful. RMM Level 2 APIs begin to leverage the structure of the HTTP protocol more fully by using resource-specific URIs, appropriate HTTP methods (GET for reading, PUT for replacing, etc.), and meaningful responses. This approach allows each operation to be clearly defined and mapped to standard HTTP semantics, improving clarity.

There is an ongoing debate in the industry about whether APIs at this level can be considered REST or not since they do not follow the HATEOAS design constraint, which is at the core of the original REST style's definition. The prevailing consensus is that RMM Level 2 APIs are commonly referred to as RESTful in practice, even though they do not fully adhere to all REST constraints.

The following is an example of a request:

```
GET https://api.magicstore.com/products?available=true
```

Here's the response:

```
HTTP/1.1 200 OK
Content-Type: application/json
{
    "products": [
            "wizard hat",
```

```
            "magic weapon"
     ]
   }
```

In this RMM Level 2 example, our API correctly utilizes the HTTP protocol's semantics. The client retrieves the available products from the magic store by sending a GET request to a resource-specific URI, using the available=true query parameter to filter the results. This approach leverages the standard meaning of HTTP methods—in this case, GET for data retrieval—making the API more intuitive and predictable. The server responds with a 200 OK status code to indicate a successful request and includes Content-Type: application/json as a header to communicate the format of the response body. By using GET, the response can be cached by browsers, proxies, and other intermediaries, which can help improve performance and reduce unnecessary server load.

However, while this API design is more RESTful than previous levels, it still lacks hypermedia controls. This means clients cannot discover related actions or navigation links dynamically in the response. Instead, they must rely on external documentation to understand how to interact with the API further. This limits the API's discoverability and self-descriptiveness, which are key aspects of full REST maturity.

Level 3: Hypermedia Controls (HATEOAS)

This is the holy grail level for REST APIs. An API at this level conforms to all REST API design constraints, including the use of hypermedia controls, as described earlier in this chapter.

In addition to the proper use of HTTP methods and resource URIs, which is provided at Level 2, Level 3 APIs embed links in their responses, enabling clients to discover related resources and available actions dynamically. Hypermedia controls, central to the HATEOAS constraint, make APIs more self-descriptive and reduce coupling between clients and servers. Clients can navigate the API by following links provided in responses, rather than relying on hardcoded URIs or external documentation. This approach increases flexibility and adaptability, allowing APIs to evolve without breaking clients.

Moreover, hypermedia enables advanced features such as discoverable pagination, state transitions, and richer interactions beyond basic CRUD operations. While implementing hypermedia can be more complex for API designers, it results in APIs that are more robust, maintainable, and user-friendly.

The following is an example of a request:

```
GET https://api.magicstore.com/products?available=true
```

Here's the response:

```
HTTP/1.1 200 OK
Content-Type: application/json
Link: <https://api.magicstore.com/products?available=true>; rel="self",
<https://api.magicstore.com/products?available=true&page=2>; rel="next"
{
  "products": [
    {
      "name": "wizard hat",
      "_links": {
        "self": {"href": "/products/wizardhat"},
        "reviews": {"href": "/products/wizardhat/reviews"}
      }
    }
  ]
}
```

In this example, we finally get a fully RESTful API at Level 3 of RMM. Like at Level 2, we are correctly leveraging the HTTP protocol's semantics for the request and response. Also, our response contains hypermedia controls that provide links to itself and any related resources. This allows for programmatic discovery of the API.

In this book, we aim to show you how important it is to design APIs as per the client's needs. It's not always easy to validate the quality of an API. Next, we'll introduce you to another maturity model that aims to build API documents that respond to clients' requirements.

WADMM

While RMM focuses on response documents and the adoption of specific elements of the HTTP protocol, it doesn't cover the design of the data models that are exposed. In 2016, Mike Amundsen introduced WADMM as a complement to RMM for RESTful services. His focus here was on the adoption of a specific model description to expose the API. Comparing this to the REST design constraints, we can see that it closely relates to the uniform interface's *Manipulating resources through representation* constraint:

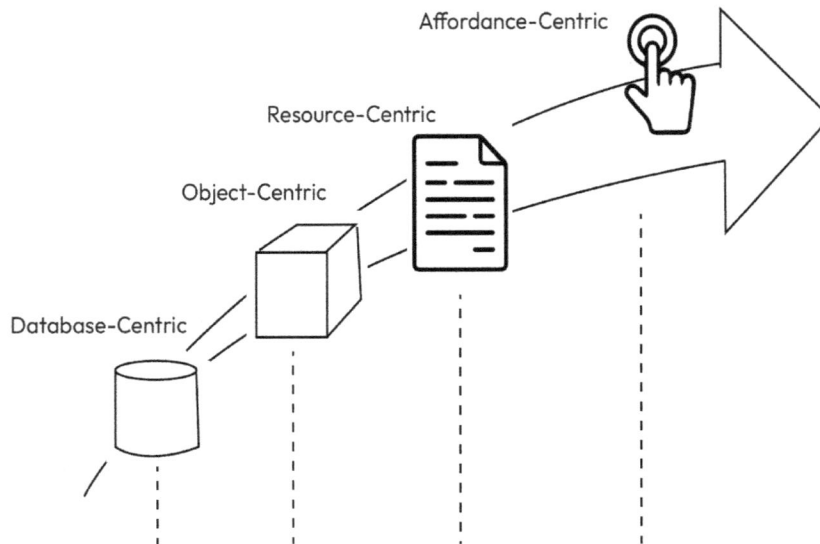

Figure 6.3 – WADMM (http://amundsen.com/talks/2016-11-apistrat-wadmm/2016-11-apist-rat-wadmm.pdf)

Similar to RMM, WADMM classifies REST APIs into four levels of maturity. The first two maturity levels expose the internal data models, while the latter two operate on external data models. Let's take a closer look at each of these levels.

Level 0: Database-centric

At this maturity level, your API is the exposed data model of your service. Effectively, no effort is put into the API-specific design of the data model. An API at this level of maturity would most probably expose raw data from your database, including internal information such as IDs, the internal business model, or security information. It is a quick and easy approach that's often provided by tools in your programming environment. However, besides exposing too much data, it also tightly couples your API with your internal data model. When your application evolves, so does its internal data model. At Level 0, that would affect your clients and possibly break their integration with your API. The cost of that is pushed to the clients instead of being held at the origin point. We have dedicated the majority of *Chapter 13* to the topic of API evolution.

The following is an example of a request:

```
GET https://api.magicstore.com/products?id=98765
```

Here's the response:

```
HTTP/1.1 200 OK
Content-Type: application/json
{
  "product_id": "98765",
  "name": "Wizard Hat",
  "price": 15.99,
  "category": "Accessories",
  "db_internal_id": "db12345",
  "business_model_id": "bm67890",
  "security_info": {
    "created_by": "admin",
    "last_modified": "2024-09-28T12:00:00Z"
  },
  "itemCreator": "Pierre O'Gui The Magnificent"
}
```

Breaking the data-centric approach is important both for consumers and providers. By putting more effort into your model design, you can make the API more resilient, reliable, and secure. The first step in this direction is to design your API for the business capabilities it offers.

Level 1: Object-centric

Similar to Level 0, this level still exposes the internal object model of your API. However, it does not expose your database directly but rather your object model, as defined in your programming environment of choice. Even though some database-specific information, like that at Level 0, is not exposed, we are still including implementation details. This level still suffers from the tight coupling between implementation and the API layer. Any changes to the internal models can leak out to the interface; there is rarely a consumer model. On the upside, we get good tooling support to expose data and have more control over the models compared to what we have at Level 0.

The following is an example of a request:

```
GET https://api.magicstore.com/products/98765
```

Here's the response:

```
HTTP/1.1 200 OK
Content-Type: application/json
{
```

```
    "product_id": "98765",
    "name": "Wizard Hat",
    "price": 15.99,
    "category": "Accessories",
    "createdBy": "Pierre O'Gui The Magnificent",
    "model": "Product",
    "schema_version": "1.0",
    "_type": "com.magicstore.Product"


}
```

To successfully step out of the internal model approach, we should focus on the idea of messaging instead of data objects.

Level 2: Resource-centric

This maturity level operates on an external interface design, decoupling the API from internal data models. This is beneficial as at this level, we are decoupling the internal data model from the actual interfaces, which leads to higher reliability and robustness of the data exchange. APIs at this level have an interface that operates on a set of HTTP resources. Because your resource model is an abstraction of the object or data model, changes to the implementation are less likely to break your clients.

The following is an example of a request:

```
GET https://api.magicstore.com/products/98765
```

Here's the response:

```
HTTP/1.1 200 OK
Content-Type: application/json
{
    "product_id": "98765",
    "name": "Wizard Hat",
    "price": 15.99,
    "category": "Accessories",
    "itemEnchanter": "Pierre O'Gui The Magnificent"
}
```

Level 2 is what we are used to associating with REST APIs. Most APIs are designed with resources in mind. There is a plethora of great tooling that helps with this kind of design, such as **OpenAPI**

Specification (OAS), which is used to describe resource-based APIs. *Chapters 9* and *10* cover OAS in more detail. However, we should note that there are some downsides to this design approach. APIs designed at this level usually only support the basic CRUD operations of the internal data model. And the biggest and most common issue is that resource-centric APIs are still created based on an implementation, replicating internal data models in the form of resources instead of being built based on an interface and the real-world use cases of the clients.

Level 3: Affordance-centric

Finally, we have the highest level of maturity in WADMM. Affordance-centric APIs are based on a completely external data model decoupled from any internal models. They focus on use cases, messages, and actions instead of just CRUD operations that are performed over resources. An affordance-centric API would serve its contents not only as the resources needed by the clients; it would also expose them in any format, protocol, or workflow convenient to the client application.

The following is an example of a request:

```
GET https://api.magicstore.com/itemEnchanter?product="wizardhat"
```

Here's the response:

```
HTTP/1.1 200 OK
Content-Type: application/json
{
  "name": "Pierre O'Gui The Magnificent",
  "occupation": "Magic Items Designer",
  …
  "itemsCreated": [
    "Wizard Hat": {
      "_link": "https://api.magicstore.com/products/98765",
      "name": "Wizard Hat"
    }
  ]
}
```

Level 3 APIs are what we have been advocating for since the beginning of this book. The highest value for an API will come from building it for specific use cases. An affordance-centric API builds its resources and the models of those resources according to the consumers' needs. In Level 3 WADMM APIs, *"the information becomes the affordance through which the user obtains choices and selects actions."* This may result in the creation of more endpoints and a generally more granular

API. Unfortunately, at the time of writing, there is a limited amount of tooling that supports designing Level 3 WADMM APIs. This is mostly because use-case-specific design is very contextual and requires a targeted approach.

Having covered the details of RMM and WADMM, let's focus on how to use them in a project. In the next section, we will focus on how to assess your API design and cover strategies you can use to bring it to the desired maturity level.

How to assess and improve your API's maturity

So far in this chapter, we have learned about REST API design constraints and the important aspects of API design regarding the HTTP protocol. We have also familiarized ourselves with two API design maturity models. This all may sound a little bit abstract. So, let's take all that knowledge and turn it into a process composed of a set of actionable steps.

When assessing your API, your approach will depend on whether it is already running in production or is still in the early stages of its life cycle. In the latter case, we have a much easier task, as no client depends on us yet. We can start designing with a specific maturity level in mind and express those maturity level constraints as a set of design rules. Later, those rules can be enforced automatically or semi-automatically in the design stage of the API's life cycle, and then as automatic validation in the CI/CD pipeline. We will cover this approach in more detail in *Chapter 10*.

For now, though, let's focus on the use case where we already have an API running in production with active clients. Assessing and improving the maturity of such an API involves several steps. Because the focus of this book is REST APIs, we will only consider that maturity levels 2 and 3 in both models are valid. As explained previously, anything below these levels is not considered REST:

1. **Assess your current state**: Evaluate your API against the maturity model. Consider the following aspects:

    *   **Resources and URI design**: Remember that we have to satisfy the *Manipulating resources through representations* constraint, so the resources should at least reflect the business case of the API and be decoupled from the internal data representation. That would satisfy at least Level 2 of both maturity models. However, to satisfy WADMM Level 3, we should design our resources and their identifiers according to our current and future consumers' use cases and what they can afford. Here's how we can do that:

        ```
        GET /checkout/cart
        ```

- This example shows a design for client use cases—in this case, a cart checkout, not database tables.

- **HTTP verbs**: The usage of HTTP methods must reflect their semantics. GET is responsible for reading data, POST for creating it, PUT for replacing it, PATCH for updating it, and DELETE for removing it. This will guarantee at least RMM Level 2:

```
DELETE /orders/98765  # Correct (RMM L2)
```

Avoid situations such as the following:

```
POST /deleteOrder      # Incorrect (RMM L0)
```

- **Response codes**: Just like HTTP verbs, be careful about the semantics of your responses. Focus on the correct usage of response codes, both for clarity of communication and observability. However, you don't have leverage all the defined response codes. Focus on what makes sense and is important for your consumers. Avoid using special response codes, such as those defined by WebDAV, or proprietary ones, as they require additional treatment by your consumers and do not support any external tooling. Good usage of response status codes will guarantee RMM Level 2:

```
POST /orders              # Creating a resource
HTTP/1.1 201 Created      # After resource creation
Location: /orders/98765
```

- This makes our API predictable for other users, but also for tools that enhance our work.

- **The use of hypermedia**: Check your APIs for hypermedia controls within their response bodies. They should contain related or embedded resources or pagination as hyperlinks. Some APIs may also contain a "Links" header, with related resources in the headers part of your message. Having well-designed hypermedia controls will bring your API to RMM Level 3 and will also help to do the same for WADMM:

```
{
  "_links": {
    "self": { "href": "/orders/98765" },
    "customer": { "href": "/customers/456" }
  }
}
```

- In the preceding example, we are using a structured approach to hypermedia controls, application/hal+json, and dynamically including related resources in the response body.

- **Affordance**: Validate not only whether your data model is decoupled from the implementation, but also that it fulfills consumers' needs. Do not forget about content negotiation, as data format is also part of your consumer's affordance. This step is what brings us to WADMM Level 3:

```
GET /products/98765 HTTP/1.1
Accept: application/xml
```

- In this example, even though our API uses JSON as the representation format by default, we are requesting that it respond to us with an XML body. This allows for greater interoperability regarding diverse client needs.

2. **Identify areas for improvement**: Based on your assessment, identify areas where your API could be more RESTful or could better meet the needs of its consumers. Compare your initial goals, such as which level of design maturity makes most sense in your organization, along with the results of step 1. This will be your baseline for all the updates you will be making.

3. **Create a plan**: Develop a roadmap for improving your API's maturity. This might involve redesigning parts of your API, refactoring code, or even rethinking your overall API strategy. Plan according to the overall life cycle model you have devised for your API; start by rethinking the strategy and then focus on each stage of the API lifecycle.

4. **Implement changes**: Start making the necessary changes to your API. This could be a gradual process, especially if you're maintaining a live API that's being used by clients. Start with the API design and the CI/CD pipelines between different stages of the life cycle. Then, go through the remaining stages until publishing occurs.

For example, in phase 1, we could add hypermedia links to high-traffic endpoints, like so:

```
{ "_links": { "next": "/orders?page=2" } }
```

In phase 2, we would deprecate non-RESTful endpoints, such as /getOrder.

5. **Monitor and iterate**: Continuously monitor your API's performance and usage. Gather feedback from your API's consumers and use this to make further improvements. Do not put untested updates directly into production, and do all the necessary testing beforehand. Reiterate through all the steps in case the results do not meet your expectations. It's important to monitor meaningful metrics for our maturity improvement effort. For example, we could track metrics such as the client's adoption of new endpoints or reduced errors from misused HTTP methods.

Remember, improving your API's maturity is not just about adhering to RESTful principles. It's also about making your API more useful, reliable, and developer-friendly. You are not building your APIs for perfection or to satisfy the authors of this book, but rather to fulfill internal and external business needs.

Summary

This chapter acted as a foundation to help you understand the principles of REST API design. To do so, we focused on the HTTP protocol, which is the basis for virtually all REST API communication. We then covered the REST API design constraints, setting the stage for what it means to create a RESTful API. With this groundwork, we walked through RMM and WADMM to assess whether our designs meet REST design constraints and to what degree. Finally, we proposed an approach for updating your API so that it meets the required maturity level and is more reliable and consumer-friendly. In the next chapter, we'll discuss constructing an API design domain model and how it shapes the foundation of effective API design. We'll explore the role of API modeling, take a closer look at JSON Schema as a modeling tool, and highlight the importance of adopting the minimal API surface principle. Finally, we'll bring these ideas together by constructing an API design domain model based on a ubiquitous language.

Get This Book's PDF Version and Exclusive Extras

UNLOCK NOW

Scan the QR code (or go to `packtpub.com/unlock`). Search for this book by name, confirm the edition, and then follow the steps on the page.

Note: Keep your invoice handy. Purchases made directly from Packt don't require an invoice.

7

Constructing an API Design Domain Model

Designing an effective REST API begins with a well-thought-out API design domain model. This chapter explores how to approach API modeling strategically, emphasizing its role as a foundational step in crafting APIs that align with business goals and deliver meaningful value to consumers. Instead of treating API modeling as a mere technical exercise, this chapter highlights the importance of understanding your business domain, identifying key entities, and defining their relationships to create APIs that go beyond basic **Create, Read, Update, Delete** (**CRUD**) operations.

We'll distinguish API modeling from database modeling, addressing common pitfalls such as over-reliance on database-first design, which often results in APIs that are disconnected from real business needs. Additionally, the chapter introduces principles such as the **minimal API surface principle**, demonstrating how these approaches lead to APIs that are more secure, maintainable, and user friendly. By the end, you'll have the tools and insights needed to build APIs that are not just functional but also strategically aligned with your organization's goals.

In this chapter, we're going to cover the following main topics:

- Understanding the role of API modeling in API design
- Diving into JSON Schema for API modeling
- Adopting the minimal API surface principle
- Constructing an API design domain model from a ubiquitous language

By the end of this chapter, you'll have a solid understanding of how to build an effective API model that aligns with your business goals and meets high-quality design standards.

Technical requirements

To fully benefit from this chapter, readers should have the following technical background:

- Knowledge of HTTP methods and status codes
- Knowledge of JSON Schema
- Familiarity with **domain-driven design** (DDD)
- Basic knowledge of the OpenAPI Specification

Magic Items Store example

Throughout this chapter, we'll continue using the Magic Items Store as a practical example to demonstrate how effective API modeling leads to better REST API design. As a fictional online retailer offering magical items — enchanted artifacts, spellbooks, and mystical potions — the Magic Items Store provides a straightforward yet rich domain for exploring key API design concepts.

We'll focus on modeling APIs that align with business objectives and deliver a seamless experience for users. This chapter will guide you through defining resources, designing intuitive endpoints, and structuring data models — all rooted in REST principles. The Magic Items Store will help illustrate how thoughtful API modeling can enhance functionality, scalability, and maintainability in real-world applications.

Understanding the role of API modeling in API design

In the realm of software development, API modeling serves as the blueprint for crafting APIs that are both efficient and aligned with business objectives. But what exactly is API modeling, and why is it crucial?

What is API modeling?

API modeling is the systematic process of designing and defining the structure of an API before any code is written. It involves more than just outlining technical components; it requires the abstraction and specification of key elements such as data structures, endpoints, operations, and relationships that constitute the API.

This approach ensures that the API is not only functional but also robust, user friendly, and aligned with the business's overall objectives. By focusing on the structure before implementation, API modeling enables developers to create more effective and efficient interfaces that meet both technical and business requirements.

API modeling components

Let's explore the key components involved in API modeling: data structures, endpoints, operations, and relationships.

Data structures

The first crucial component of API modeling is **data structures**, often referred to as **models**. These represent the core entities and resources within a business domain. In most domains, common key entities might include users, products, orders, invoices, and services. Each of these entities should have clearly defined attributes and validation rules to ensure that the data adheres to expected types, formats, and constraints.

Tools such as JSON Schema are commonly used to define and validate these data structures, enabling consistency and integrity across the API.

In a hypothetical e-commerce platform such as a Magic Items Store, the data structures represent the core entities. For this example, let's consider three key entities: **Product**, **Order**, and **Customer**. Each of these entities has attributes that define their characteristics, and validation rules ensure the data conforms to expected types and formats.

For example, we could define a product entity with the following attributes:

- `productId` (string, UUID): A unique identifier for each product
- `name` (string): The name of the product
- `description` (string): A brief description of the product
- `price` (number, positive): The price of the product; must be a non-negative value
- `stock` (integer, non-negative): The quantity of the product available in stock
- `category` (string): The category to which the product belongs (e.g., "Illusions" or "Accessories")

And we can define a product entity with the following validation rules:

- `productId`: Must be in UUID format
- `price`: Must be a non-negative number
- `stock`: Must be a non-negative integer

This can be represented using JSON Schema (we will explore JSON Scheme in depth in *Chapter 11*), as shown here:"

```json
{
  "$schema": "http://json-schema.org/draft-07/schema#",
  "title": "Product",
  "type": "object",
  "properties": {
    "productId": {
      "type": "string",
      "format": "uuid"
    },
    "name": {
      "type": "string"
    },
    "description": {
      "type": "string"
    },
    "price": {
      "type": "number",
      "minimum": 0
    },
    "stock": {
      "type": "integer",
      "minimum": 0
    },
    "category": {
      "type": "string"
    }
  },
  "required": ["productId", "name", "price"]
}
```

Defining your data structures and validation rules early in the modeling process ensures that your API is robust, consistent, and easy to maintain. A well-structured data model improves API usability and helps consumers better understand how to interact with it. By enforcing validation at the schema level, you can prevent invalid data from propagating through your system, ultimately reducing errors and improving data integrity.

Endpoints

Next, we must consider **endpoints**, which define the routes through which clients access resources in the API. This involves designing a URI structure that is consistent and intuitive, making it easy for API consumers to interact with the system.

Each endpoint corresponds to a specific resource and is paired with HTTP methods such as GET, POST, PUT, and DELETE, depending on the desired operation. For instance, retrieving a product list might be handled with a GET request to `/products`, while updating an existing order would require a PUT request to `/orders/{id}`.

Operations

The **operations** an API supports are another key aspect of API modeling. These can be broadly categorized into CRUD operations, which deal with the manipulation of data, and more complex business logic operations that represent domain-specific actions. For instance, in an e-commerce platform, operations such as placing an order, processing a payment, and sending notifications are examples of business logic operations that go beyond standard CRUD functionality.

Example: Placing an order

When a customer places an order in the Magic Items Store, the API must handle multiple steps to ensure a successful process. This operation typically involves validating the inventory, calculating the total price (including taxes and discounts), and reserving items in stock. The following is an example request for placing an order:

Request: POST /orders

```json
{
    "customerId": "123",
    "items": [
      {
        "productId": "32121",
        "quantity": 3
      },
      {
        "productId": "3454354",
        "quantity": 1
      }
    ],
    "paymentMethod": "credit_card"
}
```

Moreover, API operations can also include batch processes, where multiple resources are handled in a single request, increasing efficiency for certain use cases. Properly defining these operations ensures that the API caters to both basic and advanced business needs.

Relationships

Lastly, **relationships** between entities are an integral part of API modeling, as they define how resources are connected and interact with each other. These relationships may take different forms, such as one-to-one, one-to-many, or many-to-many associations. For example, in the Magic Items Store, a customer may have many orders, and each order may contain multiple products. Modeling these relationships allows the API to reflect real-world connections between data entities.

Additionally, techniques such as hypermedia controls **Hypermedia as the Engine of Application State (HATEOAS)** can be employed to help navigate between related resources, offering clients a seamless way to traverse the API. Deciding whether to embed related resources in responses or provide links to them is another important design consideration, affecting both API efficiency and usability.

In conclusion, API modeling is a foundational process that helps in designing a well-structured API by defining its core components—data structures, endpoints, operations, and relationships. By thoroughly modeling these aspects, developers can create APIs that are both easy to use and aligned with business goals. This approach leads to APIs that are scalable, maintainable, and capable of meeting the diverse needs of their consumers, ultimately enhancing the overall API experience.

Now that we've covered the definition of API modeling, let's dive deeper into the relationship between API modeling and API design.

API modeling and API design

API modeling and API design are closely related yet distinct activities that together ensure the development of an effective and high-quality API. API modeling involves defining the structure of an API, including its resources, relationships, and data models, while API design focuses on the decision-making process that guides how those models are exposed to and interact with clients, emphasizing usability, best practices, and user experience.

API modeling lays the foundation for API design by defining the building blocks—the resources, relationships, and operations—that need to be represented. Once these elements are well-defined through modeling, the design phase focuses on how to effectively and elegantly present them to developers who will be using the API.

Further, API modeling serves API design in the following aspects:

- **Establishing the blueprint for API design**: API modeling serves as the blueprint for API design by providing a conceptual representation of what the API should contain and how different resources should interact. The design process then uses this blueprint to create endpoints, choose naming conventions, and apply RESTful principles or other architectural styles.

- **Ensuring consistency across the API**: A well-modeled API leads to a more consistent design. When resources, fields, and relationships are properly modeled, it becomes easier to apply a uniform design across all endpoints, making the API more predictable for its users.

- **Defining the boundaries of operations**: API modeling defines the boundaries and roles of different resources, which directly informs the design of operations and endpoints. Modeling provides clarity on what data should be available for each resource and how these resources should be accessed or manipulated.

- **Improving user experience and discoverability**: API modeling often includes defining relationships and behaviors of resources, which informs the design of features such as hypermedia controls. These controls guide users through the API in a discoverable manner, making the overall user experience more intuitive.

- **Bridging technical and business requirements**: API modeling focuses on aligning the API's structure with the domain's business needs by accurately representing resources and their relationships. API design bridges this model with usability requirements, ensuring that the API is easy to understand and use by developers.

API modeling and API design are interdependent processes that work together to create high-quality APIs. API modeling provides the conceptual framework—the definition of resources, relationships, and operations—that underpins the API. API design takes this framework and determines how best to expose it to clients, focusing on usability, consistency, and adherence to best practices.

Now that you have grasped the role of API modeling in API design practice, let's uncover other flavors of API modeling.

Beyond physical API modeling

API modeling involves more than just defining the physical model of data structures, endpoints, operations, and relationships. It encompasses a broader context, which includes capturing essential metadata and configurations that influence how the API is consumed, secured, and managed. This extended scope of API modeling leads to a more comprehensive approach, ensuring the API is suitable for its intended audience, scalable, and capable of evolving as requirements change.

Let's explore some concepts beyond the physical model, focusing on the importance of API profiles and their applications.

API profiles: Capturing broader context

API profiles capture the necessary information about an API beyond its core data structures and operations, independent of the specific API style or styles (e.g., REST, GraphQL) it may support. An API profile includes details such as **service-level agreements (SLAs)**, security requirements, and the scope of the API—whether it is public, internal, or meant for partners. This allows API designers to create well-rounded APIs that cater to different user groups and use cases effectively.

In the context of the Magic Items Store, the Merchant Public API can have a profile that includes the following:

- **SLA**: Defining a guaranteed uptime of 99.9%, which is crucial for merchants who rely on the API for integrating their product catalog and managing orders in real time.
- **Security**: Specifying OAuth 2.0 as the authentication mechanism, with different scopes for reading product information (`scope: products:read`) versus creating orders (`scope: orders:create`). These security details ensure that the API is used safely and that sensitive actions require explicit permissions.
- **API scope**: Indicating that this API is a public-facing one, available to all registered merchants, whereas other APIs (such as internal inventory management APIs) may have limited access.

API profiling, thus, extends the API model to include these essential non-functional requirements, ensuring that the API is secure, reliable, and appropriately targeted.

Logical versus physical models

API modeling also involves differentiating between logical and physical models. A logical model represents the abstract definition of entities and relationships, independent of any specific implementation details. On the other hand, a physical model details the concrete representation—such as the exact endpoints, field formats, and data types used in the API.

In the context of our Magic Items Store example:

- **Logical model**: The logical model for the Magic Items Store might define entities such as Product, Order, and Merchant, along with their relationships. For example, each Merchant may have multiple Products, and each Order is associated with a specific Product and Customer.

- **Physical model**: The physical model takes these abstract concepts and translates them into API endpoints, such as `GET /merchants/{merchantId}/products` to retrieve all products for a merchant, or `POST /orders` to create a new order.

By distinguishing between these models, API designers can first focus on capturing business requirements and relationships at a high level before diving into the specifics of implementation.

Extending the model with business rules

Beyond defining resources and endpoints, API modeling also involves capturing the rules and constraints governing how the API can be used. These business rules ensure that the API aligns with the domain requirements and operational policies of the business.

In the context of the Magic Items Store, the Merchant Public API represents an external-facing API that allows third-party merchants to manage their product listings, inventory, and orders within the Magic Items Store platform. This API enables merchants to integrate their systems with the Magic Items Store, giving them programmatic access to manage their business operations.

Examples of business rules for the Merchant Public API might include the following:

- **Product inventory limits**: Merchants cannot list more than 1,000 active products at a time. This rule ensures the efficient use of resources and keeps the product catalog manageable.
- **Order processing**: Orders placed through the API must include valid payment information, and the status must be updated within a specific timeframe. These rules enforce the integrity of the order process and ensure timely fulfillment.

These rules go beyond the basic physical structure of the API to ensure it operates according to business logic, maintaining consistency and preventing misuse.

Addressing multiple API styles

Another crucial element of extended API modeling is planning for different API styles. The same underlying model may need to support different interaction patterns based on the client requirements—for example, REST for a traditional web application and GraphQL for a modern front-end needing flexible queries.

In our Magic Items Store example, the `GET /products/{productId}` REST endpoint is used to retrieve detailed information about a specific product, identified by its unique `productId`. This approach provides a predefined response structure that delivers comprehensive product details.

In contrast, the GraphQL query allows clients to request only the specific fields they need, such as name and price, through a flexible endpoint such as /graphql. This enables clients with different requirements to interact with the product resource in a more customized and efficient manner, reducing unnecessary data transfer and improving performance.

Having a unified logical model that can be exposed through multiple API styles ensures flexibility while maintaining consistency across the API's offerings.

API modeling goes beyond defining the physical aspects of an API, such as data structures, endpoints, operations, and relationships. It also involves capturing the broader context through API profiles, which detail SLAs, security measures, and the intended scope of the API. Additionally, differentiating between logical and physical models, defining business rules, and accommodating multiple API styles all contribute to a more comprehensive approach to API modeling.

In the case of the Magic Items Store, these extended modeling concepts help create an API that is not only functional and efficient but also aligned with the business's strategic goals, capable of supporting various client needs, and resilient in the face of future changes. By incorporating both the physical and logical aspects, along with the broader profile information, the Magic Items Store's Merchant Public API can meet diverse needs effectively while maintaining consistency and scalability.

To bring these concepts to life, we'll now dive into **JSON Schema**—a powerful tool for defining and validating data structures in APIs. JSON Schema provides a standard way to describe the shape of your API's data, ensuring consistency and improving developer experience. In this next section, we'll explore how JSON Schema can enhance your API design by enabling robust data validation, clear documentation, and support for multiple API styles.

Diving into JSON Schema for API modeling

JSON Schema is a powerful tool that facilitates the description and validation of JSON documents, making it invaluable in API modeling. This deep dive explores how JSON Schema can enhance REST API design and how its principles can be applied across different API styles, making your API more robust and developer friendly.

What is JSON Schema?

JSON Schema is a vocabulary that allows you to define the expected structure, constraints, and validation rules for JSON documents. In essence, it acts as a blueprint, ensuring that JSON data adheres to a predictable format. By providing a formal contract for the data, JSON Schema not only helps in validation but also in communicating the structure of data between different systems and teams.

The core concepts of JSON Schema include specifying data types, properties, validation rules, and relationships between data. This ensures consistency and helps to catch errors early, especially when different parts of an application or different applications are interacting with the same data.

The importance of JSON Schema in REST APIs

In the context of REST APIs, JSON Schema plays several crucial roles that enhance both the development and consumption of APIs:

- **Data validation**: JSON Schema acts as a gatekeeper, ensuring that data sent and received conforms to predefined formats and rules. This validation is critical to maintain data integrity and helps prevent malformed data from causing issues downstream.

- **Documentation**: JSON Schema serves as living documentation for your API. Unlike static docs, the schema evolves with the API, providing developers with an accurate representation of what to expect. This helps in reducing confusion and ensures that consumers of the API know precisely what data to send or expect in return.

- **Automation and code generation**: JSON Schema also facilitates automation in the API lifecycle. Many tools can utilize JSON Schema to automatically generate client libraries, perform data validation, and even create mock servers for testing purposes. This boosts productivity and allows developers to focus more on building features rather than manually writing validation code or maintaining redundant documentation.

Consider the following JSON Schema for a product entity:

```
{
  "$schema": "http://json-schema.org/draft-07/schema#",
  "title": "Product",
  "type": "object",
  "properties": {
    "id": {
      "type": "string",
      "format": "uuid"
    },
    "name": {
      "type": "string"
    },
    "price": {
      "type": "number",
      "minimum": 0
```

```
    }
  },
  "required": ["id", "name", "price"]
}
```

In this schema, a product object is defined with three properties: id, name, and price. Each property has constraints that dictate the data type and acceptable values. For instance, price must be a non-negative number, ensuring invalid data such as negative pricing cannot be introduced.

JSON Schema beyond REST: other API styles

While JSON Schema is primarily associated with REST APIs, its utility extends to other API styles and paradigms, showcasing its flexibility:

- **AsyncAPI and event-driven architectures**: In event-driven systems, JSON Schema is used to define the payloads of messages. This helps standardize communication in publish-subscribe models, ensuring that events emitted by producers are correctly interpreted by consumers.

- **GraphQL**: Although GraphQL uses its own schema definition language, the core idea of specifying data structures aligns closely with JSON Schema. This similarity makes transitioning between different API styles easier for teams, as the concept of defining and enforcing structured data remains consistent.

- **gRPC and Protobuf**: JSON Schema concepts can be compared to Protobuf in gRPC, where defining strict message formats ensures clear contracts between client and server. JSON Schema's flexibility to handle rich validation makes it a valuable reference, even when working with binary protocols such as gRPC.

Best practices for using JSON Schema in API modeling

To leverage JSON Schema effectively in API design, consider the following best practices:

- **Keep it simple**: Avoid overly complex schemas that become difficult to maintain. Strive for simplicity and clarity to make it easier for developers to understand the expected data structure.

- **Modular schema design**: Break down large schemas into reusable components. This helps in managing schemas more effectively and promotes consistency across different parts of the API.

- **Documentation integration**: Integrate JSON Schema into your API documentation. Tools such as **Swagger** and **OpenAPI** can use JSON Schema to provide interactive documentation, allowing developers to experiment with their APIs without needing extensive explanations.
- **Validation and testing**: Make JSON Schema validation a part of your testing pipeline. This ensures that any changes in data structures are caught early, reducing potential integration issues.

JSON Schema is more than just a validation tool—it provides a formal contract, improves documentation, and supports automation in API modeling. Whether you are designing REST APIs or event-driven architectures, or working with other API styles, understanding and leveraging JSON Schema will lead to more reliable, maintainable, and user-friendly APIs.

Next, we will explore the concept of the minimal API surface principle, focusing on how to avoid over-engineering and keep your APIs efficient and easy to use.

Adopting the minimal API surface principle

In API design, less is often more. Striving for simplicity and focusing on the essential aspects of an API can lead to a more robust, scalable, and user-friendly interface. This is the core idea behind the minimal API surface principle—a design philosophy that encourages limiting the exposed surface of an API to what is absolutely necessary to achieve its intended purpose. By applying this principle, API designers can reduce complexity, improve security, and enhance the developer experience.

This principle serves as a counterbalance to over-engineering, where APIs become bloated with unnecessary features in an effort to address every conceivable use case. Instead, minimizing the API surface forces designers to focus on the most critical business operations and data, making the API easier to use and maintain.

In the following sections, we'll explore the common pitfalls of over-engineering and how adopting the minimal API surface principle can address these challenges.

The problem of over-engineering

Over-engineering in API design often stems from a desire to create a comprehensive solution that anticipates all potential use cases, leading to the inclusion of unnecessary features. While this may seem like a proactive approach, it introduces accidental complexity that can undermine the utility and maintainability of the API. Over-engineered APIs tend to expose excessive properties, resulting in a convoluted interface that is harder for developers to understand and work with.

By attempting to serve every possible requirement upfront, the API becomes bloated, making it less accessible and efficient for clients.

One of the most significant risks of over-engineering is poor API design, especially when driven by a simplistic CRUD approach. When developers think solely in terms of database fields and attempt to expose all data properties, the resulting API lacks a meaningful representation of business logic. It becomes a mere reflection of the internal data structure, rather than a thoughtful interface designed to solve specific business problems. This kind of design typically results in poor usability, where the API neither effectively communicates its purpose nor empowers clients to achieve their goals with ease.

Another major consequence of over-engineering is the increased security risks associated with excessive data exposure. By including all properties in an API response, developers may inadvertently expose sensitive information that should remain internal. This exposure makes the API a larger target for security vulnerabilities, as attackers have more data to exploit. Minimizing the API surface by carefully selecting which properties and endpoints are necessary can significantly reduce these risks, leading to a safer and more secure implementation.

The minimal API surface principle

When designing APIs, it's tempting to include every possible property and endpoint to cover future needs. However, this approach often leads to bloated and inefficient APIs. The minimal API surface principle encourages designing APIs with only the necessary components to fulfill the current product requirements without over-committing to future features that may never be needed.

As highlighted in the Adidas API guidelines: *"Every API design MUST aim for a minimal API surface without sacrificing on product requirements. API design SHOULD NOT include unnecessary resources, relations, actions, or data. API design SHOULD NOT add functionality until deemed necessary (YAGNI principle)"* (`https://adidas.gitbook.io/api-guidelines`).

This principle emphasizes focusing on the essential features, keeping the API lean, and avoiding unnecessary complexity that can hinder its usability and maintainability.

A key strategy for achieving this is by adopting the **you aren't gonna need it (YAGNI)** principle. This principle encourages developers to resist the urge to add features or functionality until they are genuinely required. By focusing only on the current requirements, YAGNI helps keep the API lean and straightforward, making it easier to understand and use. Adhering to YAGNI often results in APIs that are more robust and less prone to issues caused by unnecessary complexity, as the scope is limited to solving the immediate problem effectively.

Following the YAGNI principle not only simplifies the API but also leads to faster development and reduced maintenance overhead. Developers can spend their time addressing real, tangible needs instead of building features based on assumptions about future requirements. This approach minimizes the risk of wasted effort on functionality that might never be used, while also ensuring that the API evolves naturally alongside the product. By keeping the focus on what is needed today, YAGNI helps teams deliver value more efficiently and avoid the pitfalls of speculative development.

Now that we've grasped the concept of a minimal API surface, let's deep dive into an example.

Examples of a minimal API surface versus an over-engineered API

Consider the following two payloads for a product object in an e-commerce API.

Example 1: Minimal API surface

```
{
  "id": "123e4567-e89b-12d3-a456-426614174000",
  "name": "Running Shoes",
  "price": 99.99,
  "url": "https://example.com/products/123e4567-e89b-
12d3-a456-426614174000"
}
```

In this example, the payload contains only the essential properties: id, name, price, and url. These are the key attributes needed for a product, providing a lean and efficient response suitable for clients that require only basic product details. This aligns perfectly with the minimal API surface principle, ensuring the API is simple, secure, and easy to maintain.

Example 2: Over-engineered API

```
{
  "id": "123e4567-e89b-12d3-a456-426614174000",
  "name": "Running Shoes",
  "description": "High-performance running shoes for all terrains.",
  "price": 99.99,
  "currency": "USD",
  "stock_quantity": 50,
  "supplier": {
    "id": "supplier-7890",
```

```
    "name": "Sports Gear Inc."
  },
  "relatedProducts": [
    {
      "id": "related-4567",
      "name": "Running Socks",
  ....
      }
  ]
  ....
}
```

Here, the response is overloaded with additional details—such as the product description, stock quantity, supplier information, and related products—that may not be relevant to most clients. While these properties could be useful in specific contexts, exposing all of them in a single API response adds unnecessary complexity. This bloated response increases payload size, reduces efficiency, and introduces potential security risks by exposing sensitive information.

The minimal API surface principle highlights the balance between functionality and simplicity. By focusing on essential properties and avoiding unnecessary elements, APIs become leaner, more secure, and easier to maintain. This minimalist approach enhances usability and allows APIs to evolve with real needs, avoiding the burden of speculative features. With these principles in mind, let's apply them step-by-step to construct an API design domain model using our Magic Items Store example.

Constructing an API design domain model from a ubiquitous language

In this section, we will guide you through the process of building an API model for the Magic Items Store using domain-driven design principles. This approach ensures that the technical implementation aligns closely with the business domain, facilitating clear communication between developers and stakeholders.

Step 1: Define the ubiquitous language

The first step in domain-driven design is to establish a ubiquitous language—a common vocabulary shared between developers and domain experts. This shared language eliminates misunderstandings and ensures that everyone involved has a consistent understanding of the key concepts and entities within the domain.

Begin by collecting and defining key domain terms used in the context of the Magic Items Store, such as "Product," "Order," "Customer," and "Inventory." This involves reviewing user stories, requirements, and existing systems, followed by collaborating with stakeholders to ensure everyone shares a consistent understanding of each term. Establishing a clear, shared vocabulary is essential for accurate modeling and effective communication, helping the API align with both business needs and developer expectations. We'll collect terminology from various sources, review and define each term, and then gain stakeholder agreement on the final definitions. Here's how this process might unfold.

When building a shared vocabulary for the Magic Items Store, key domain terms can be identified from various sources such as user stories, requirements documents, existing system interfaces, wireframes and mockups, and customer support logs. The following are examples of how each source can help define essential terms:

- **User stories**: An example of a user story could be "As a customer, I want to browse available spellbooks and add them to my cart so I can purchase them later." Based on this, we can identify the following key terms:

    - **Customer**: A person browsing or buying magical items from the Magic Items Store
    - **Spellbook**: A type of magical item available for sale in the store
    - **Cart**: A temporary holding area for items the customer intends to buy
    - **Purchase**: The action of completing a transaction for items in the cart

- **Requirements documents**: "The system must support an inventory management feature to allow store admins to add, remove, or update magical items." Based on this, we can identify the following key terms:

    - **Inventory**: The collection of all magical items available for sale
    - **Store admin**: An employee responsible for managing products and fulfilling orders
    - **Add item/Remove item/Update item**: Actions performed by store admins to manage items in the inventory

- **Existing system interfaces**: For instance, this could be "An internal catalog system that classifies magical items," with the following key terms identified:

    - **Product ID**: A unique identifier assigned to each magical item
    - **Stock level**: The quantity of a specific magical item available for purchase
    - **Price**: The cost of each item in the store

- **Wireframes and mockups**: A mockup example could be "A checkout page showing a wishlist, cart, and payment options," where we can identify the following:

  - **Wishlist**: A feature allowing customers to save items for future consideration
  - **Checkout**: The process a customer follows to complete a purchase
  - **Payment options**: Methods available (e.g., credit card, magical token, etc.) to finalize a transaction

- **Customer support logs**: We can consider the inquiry example "How can I check the status of my order or request a return?" where we can identify the following terms:

  - **Order status**: The current state of an order, which may be "Pending," "Shipped," or "Delivered"
  - **Return request**: A customer's action to initiate the return of an item

After collecting and reviewing terms from all artifacts, this will result in a well-defined, unified vocabulary:

- **Customer**: A user who browses or buys items from the Magic Items Store
- **Store admin**: An employee responsible for managing items and orders
- **Product**: Any magical item, such as a spellbook, potion, or talisman, available for sale
- **Inventory**: The entire collection of products in the store
- **Cart**: Temporary storage for items a customer intends to purchase
- **Wishlist**: A list where customers can save items they may purchase later
- **Order status**: The current progress of a customer's order
- **Return request**: A customer's request to return an item
- **Checkout**: The final process to complete a purchase
- **Payment options**: Available methods for payment

With this dictionary, all stakeholders and developers now have a shared understanding of the terms that will shape the Magic Items Store's API, ensuring clarity and consistency across the design and development process.

> Note
>
> For a deeper dive into domain-driven design and the importance of a ubiquitous language, refer to *Chapter 5*. By developing a shared vocabulary, you will not only identify the key entities and concepts within your domain but also lay a solid foundation for the subsequent steps in the API design process.

By defining a ubiquitous language, we have established a shared vocabulary that aligns both technical and business perspectives. This ensures that all stakeholders are on the same page, eliminating ambiguity and forming a strong foundation for API design. With these core terms in place, the next step is to move from terminology to use case definition, where we'll focus on how users interact with the system and translate those interactions into actionable API requirements.

Step 2: Define the use cases

Understanding what your customers aim to achieve is crucial for designing an API that meets their needs. In this step, you will define the use cases that represent the various ways users interact with the Magic Items Store. Common use cases may include browsing products, placing orders, and managing inventory.

Start by documenting all the actions that users will perform within the system, from the perspective of both customers and store administrators. Each use case should be described in terms of business requirements, which define what the system must achieve, and technical specifications, which translate these requirements into concrete API operations. Once you have listed all the use cases, prioritize them based on their importance and frequency of use. Focusing on the most critical use cases first ensures that essential functionality is addressed early in the design process and provides a clear roadmap for implementing the corresponding API endpoints.

Here's how we would approach this for the Magic Items Store. First, let's look at some customer use cases:

- **Browse products**: Customers want to explore the store's magical items, filtering by type, price range, and magical properties:
  - **Business requirement**: Make all products easily searchable and filterable
  - **Technical specification**: Design endpoints such as `GET /products` with optional query parameters for filtering
- **View product details**: Customers may want to see detailed information about a specific item before purchasing:
  - **Business requirement**: Provide in-depth descriptions for each item, including attributes such as price, stock level, and magical effects
  - **Technical specification**: Implement `GET /products/{productId}` to fetch individual product details

- **Add to cart**: Customers should be able to add items to a cart for future purchase:

  - **Business requirement**: Enable users to prepare multiple items for checkout, with the option to adjust quantities

  - **Technical specification**: Use endpoints such as POST /cart/items to add items and PUT /cart/items/{itemId} to update quantities

- **Check out and place order**: When ready, customers proceed to checkout, finalize their purchase, and provide payment details:

  - **Business requirement**: Allow users to complete purchases securely, with payment and shipping options

  - **Technical specification**: Implement POST /orders for order placement, with fields for payment and delivery options

- **Track order status**: Customers should be able to view the status of their order at any time:

  - **Business requirement**: Keep customers informed about order progress

  - **Technical specification**: Use GET /orders/{orderId}/status to retrieve the current status

Second, let's look at some store administrator use cases:

- **Manage inventory**: Admins need to add, update, and remove products from the store's catalog:

  - **Business requirement**: Ensure that inventory can be modified to reflect stock levels, new items, and discontinued products

  - **Technical specification**: Implement POST /inventory, PUT /inventory/{productId}, and DELETE /inventory/{productId}

- **Process orders**: Admins should have the ability to view, confirm, and update order statuses:

  - **Business requirement**: Provide tools for processing orders efficiently to maintain customer satisfaction

  - **Technical specification**: Use PUT /orders/{orderId}/status to update order statuses from pending to confirmed, shipped, or delivered

- **Handle returns and refunds:** In cases where a customer initiates a return, admins need to manage refunds and return processing:

    - **Business requirement:** Allow flexible handling of customer returns while maintaining accurate inventory
    - **Technical specification:** Implement `POST /orders/{orderId}/return` to initiate a return and `POST /orders/{orderId}/refund` for refunds

By analyzing the use cases, we can prioritize them based on user importance and frequency:

1. **High priority** (essential for initial release):

    - Browse products
    - View product details
    - Add to cart
    - Check out and place order
    - Manage inventory (admins)
    - Process orders (admins)

2. **Medium priority:**

    - Track order status (customers)
    - Handle returns and refunds (admins)

3. **Low priority:**

    - Wishlist (future feature allowing customers to save items they're interested in)

By translating business requirements into technical specifications, you gain a clearer understanding of how the system should behave. This step also helps in prioritizing features based on user needs, which is vital for delivering a product that provides real value to its users.

Step 3: Map use cases to REST API verbs

With a clear understanding of the use cases, the next step is to map these actions to RESTful API endpoints using HTTP verbs. RESTful APIs leverage HTTP verbs such as GET, POST, PUT, and DELETE to represent actions on resources.

By defining the endpoints, we also establish a clear framework for how different resources—such as products, orders, and inventory—are accessed and modified. Each endpoint corresponds to a specific action within the system, ensuring that all primary functions are covered.

In terms of the Magic Items Store, let's map some customer endpoints:

- **Browse products**: To retrieve the available magical items, we can create an endpoint that allows users to access the full product catalog:

    - **Endpoint**: `GET /products`
    - **Purpose**: Retrieves a list of products with optional filters (e.g., by category, price)

- **View product details**: To view detailed information about a specific product, customers can use a targeted endpoint:

    - **Endpoint**: `GET /products/{productId}`
    - **Purpose**: Fetches details of a single product, identified by its unique ID

- **Add to cart**: This action allows customers to prepare items for purchase:

    - **Endpoint**: `POST /cart/items`
    - **Purpose**: Adds an item to the customer's cart

- **Update cart item**: Customers may adjust the quantity of items in their cart:

    - **Endpoint**: `PUT /cart/items/{itemId}`
    - **Purpose**: Updates the quantity of an item in the cart

- **Check out and place order**: This endpoint finalizes the cart contents into an order:

    - **Endpoint**: `POST /orders`
    - **Purpose**: Places a new order with payment and shipping details

- **Track order status**: Customers can track the progress of their order:

    - **Endpoint**: `GET /orders/{orderId}/status`
    - **Purpose**: Retrieves the current status of the specified order

And now, let's map some store administrator endpoints:

- **Manage inventory**:

    - **Add product**:

        - **Endpoint**: `POST /inventory`
        - **Purpose**: Adds a new product to the inventory

- **Update product:**

  - **Endpoint:** `PUT /inventory/{productId}`
  - **Purpose:** Updates details of an existing product

- **Remove product:**

  - **Endpoint:** `DELETE /inventory/{productId}`
  - **Purpose:** Removes a product from the inventory

- **Process orders:**

  - **Confirm order:**

    - **Endpoint:** `PUT /orders/{orderId}/status`
    - **Purpose:** Updates the status of an order to "confirmed" after successful payment

  - **Ship order:**

    - **Endpoint:** `PUT /orders/{orderId}/status`
    - **Purpose:** Changes the status of an order to "shipped" once it's dispatched

- **Handle returns:**

  - **Return product:**

    - **Endpoint:** `POST /orders/{orderId}/return`
    - **Purpose:** Initiates the return process for an order

  - **Issue refund:**

    - **Endpoint:** `POST /orders/{orderId}/refund`
    - **Purpose:** Processes a refund for a returned order

By directly mapping use cases to HTTP methods, we align the API's structure with real-world business needs, allowing it to intuitively reflect domain logic. This approach not only ensures coverage of all essential functions but also makes the API easy to navigate and understand for developers. Using state machine diagrams for entities such as orders further supports this structure by providing a visual guide to the transitions and endpoints required, enabling a well-organized and maintainable API.

Step 4: Define the resource model using JSON Schema

Once the API endpoints are defined, it's essential to specify the structure of the data that will be exchanged.

Create JSON Schemas for each resource in your API. For instance, the Product resource might have properties such as productId, name, description, price, and stock. By defining the data types and constraints for each property, you establish clear expectations for both clients and servers interacting with the API.

Here's an example of a JSON Schema for the Product resource:

```
{
  "$schema": "http://json-schema.org/draft-07/schema#",
  "title": "Product",
  "type": "object",
  "properties": {
    "productId": {
      "type": "string",
      "format": "uuid"
    },
    "name": {
      "type": "string"
    },
    "description": {
      "type": "string"
    },
    "price": {
      "type": "number",
      "minimum": 0
    },
    "stock": {
      "type": "integer",
      "minimum": 0
    }
  },
  "required": ["productId", "name", "price"]
}
```

Defining data structures using JSON Schema not only ensures that data is validated but also promotes consistency across different parts of the application. This step is critical for preventing data-related errors and facilitating integration with other systems.

Step 5: Define state transitions and input models

Understanding how entities change state over time is essential for defining endpoints and payloads that accurately reflect business processes. By modeling entity life cycles, you can ensure that your API supports all necessary operations and handles state changes appropriately.

Take, for example, the Order entity. An order might go through several states:

- **Pending**: The order has been created but not yet processed
- **Confirmed**: Payment has been received, and the order is confirmed
- **Shipped**: The order has been dispatched to the customer
- **Delivered**: The customer has received the order

By defining these state transitions, you can identify the actions that cause state changes and the corresponding API operations needed to support them. Input models specify the data required for each operation. For instance, creating an order would require customer details and a list of items, while updating an order's status might be an administrative action that changes the order's state.

By modeling entity life cycles and defining input and output models for API operations, you ensure that your API can handle all necessary scenarios and provide a seamless experience for both users and administrators.

Step 6: Compile everything into the OpenAPI Specification

The final step is documenting your API design with the OpenAPI Specification. While chapters 9 and 10 will explore OpenAPI in detail, it's important to understand now that OpenAPI provides a standardized, machine-readable format for describing your API. This description serves as a foundation for documentation, code generation, and testing.

In your OpenAPI file, you will define the paths (endpoints) and the operations (HTTP methods) that your API supports. You will also specify components such as reusable schemas, parameters, and responses. Additionally, you can define security schemes to outline authentication and authorization requirements.

Here's an example snippet of an OpenAPI file for the Magic Items Store API:

```
openapi: 3.0.0
info:
  title: Magic Items Store API
  version: 1.0.0
paths:
  /products:
    get:
      summary: Retrieve a list of products
      responses:
        '200':
          description: A list of products
          content:
            application/json:
              schema:
                $ref: '#/components/schemas/ProductList'
components:
  schemas:
    ProductList:
      type: array
      items:
        $ref: '#/components/schemas/Product'
    Product:
      # JSON Schema for Product
```

Compiling your API definitions into the OpenAPI format not only standardizes your documentation but also enables the use of various tools that support OpenAPI. These tools can assist with code generation, testing, and creating interactive API documentation, significantly streamlining the development process.

By utilizing the OpenAPI Specification, you ensure that your API is well-documented and accessible to other developers, facilitating integration and collaboration.

Bringing it all together

By following these steps, you have constructed a comprehensive API design domain model for the Magic Items Store. You've established a shared vocabulary, defined use cases, mapped them to RESTful endpoints, specified data models with JSON Schema, and documented everything using OpenAPI. This process not only ensures that your API aligns with business needs but also sets the stage for efficient development and maintenance. In the next section, we'll summarize the key takeaways and explore how these elements contribute to a cohesive API design.

Summary

In this chapter, we explored how to create an API model that serves as a strong foundation for RESTful API design. We emphasized the strategic importance of API modeling in aligning APIs with business goals and providing real value to consumers. Using the MagicStore example, we demonstrated how to transform domain knowledge into a robust API structure by defining key entities, relationships, and real-world use cases.

We also introduced the minimal API surface principle as a technique to streamline design, reduce complexity, and enhance security. JSON Schema was highlighted as a powerful tool for schema-driven validation, ensuring consistency, improving documentation, and providing a reliable contract between API producers and consumers.

By following a structured approach—defining a ubiquitous language, identifying use cases, and integrating these elements into an OpenAPI specification—you can ensure that your API model remains clear, adaptable, and user friendly. In the next chapter, *Chapter 8*, we'll focus on how design documents formalize your API model into a practical contract that ensures consistency, reliability, and transparency for all stakeholders.

Get This Book's PDF Version and Exclusive Extras

UNLOCK NOW

Scan the QR code (or go to `packtpub.com/unlock`). Search for this book by name, confirm the edition, and then follow the steps on the page.

Note: Keep your invoice handy. Purchases made directly from Packt don't require an invoice.

8

Designing and Managing Effective API Contracts

In today's rapidly evolving digital ecosystem, APIs have become the cornerstone of software development and integration. They enable different software systems to communicate seamlessly, fostering innovation and efficiency across industries. However, as the reliance on APIs grows, so does the complexity of managing them effectively. This is where the concept of API contracts comes into play.

An API contract serves as a formal agreement that defines the expectations and responsibilities of both API providers and consumers. It outlines how an API behaves, the data it exposes, the protocols it uses, and the terms under which it operates. Crafting an effective API contract is not just about technical specifications; it's about establishing a mutual understanding that ensures consistency, security, and reliability.

This chapter delves into the significance of well-crafted API contracts, exploring their definition and importance in the API lifecycle. We aim to streamline future API usage and promote open communication among all stakeholders from the outset. By anticipating future applications and incorporating concepts such as consumer-driven design and API maturity models, we can design APIs that are robust, scalable, and adaptable to changing needs. This chapter explores the *why and how* of crafting robust API contracts. You'll learn about the following:

- Why API contracts are essential to scaling API programs and reducing integration friction
- The core building blocks of an API contract, including endpoints, request/response schemas, authentication methods, and error handling

- Best practices for managing API contracts over time, including contract versioning, testing for compatibility, and adopting consumer-driven contract testing

- How to align your contracts with API lifecycle and governance processes, from initial design to deprecation

By the end of this chapter, you'll understand how API contracts shape the developer experience, reduce misunderstandings, and help your APIs evolve safely while keeping your consumers in sync.

Technical requirements

- **Basic API knowledge**: Familiarity with API types (REST, gRPC, and GraphQL) and HTTP methods

- **API specification tools**: Experience with OpenAPI, AsyncAPI, or gRPC, and an understanding of JSON/YAML syntax

- **Understanding of software development concepts**: Knowledge of data modeling, schema validation, and security practices (authentication and rate limiting)

- **Understanding of version control and CI/CD**: Basic Git/GitHub knowledge and awareness of automated testing and validation

- **Business context**: Understanding of **Service-Level Agreements (SLAs)**, usage policies, and how APIs align with business goals

Understanding the concept and importance of API contracts

API contracts are the backbone of effective API communication. They define how APIs behave, the data they expose, and the rules for how consumers should interact with them. These contracts ensure that API providers and consumers have a shared understanding, reducing ambiguity and fostering collaboration.

In this section, we'll break down the key elements of an API contract and explain how each component contributes to consistency, security, and reliability. We'll start by exploring the core building blocks that form a well-defined API contract, such as resource definitions, data models, and security protocols. Next, we'll discuss how adopting standardized specifications such as OpenAPI and AsyncAPI can simplify API management and ensure long-term scalability.

What is an API contract?

An **API contract** is a detailed agreement that defines the expected behavior, capabilities, and usage of an API. It acts as a blueprint and a formal handshake between providers and consumers, outlining what the API offers and the guidelines for its usage. At its core, an API contract represents an approved API design, ensuring consistent and predictable interactions.

API Consumer   API Contract   API Provider

Figure 8.1: API contract

At its core, an API contract includes the following:

- **Invocation details**: Detailed descriptions of the API endpoints, including URLs, HTTP methods, request parameters, and response formats
- **Data models**: Schemas that define the structure of the data being sent and received, including field types, constraints, and validation rules
- **Security protocols and access**: Specifications of authentication and authorization mechanisms, encryption standards, and other security measures
- **Usage policies**: Terms of service, rate limits, quotas, and any legal considerations or compliance requirements
- **Performance expectations**: SLAs that outline uptime guarantees, response times, and support commitments

API contracts frequently adopt widely used specifications, such as the following:

- OpenAPI
- gRPC
- GraphQL
- AsyncAPI

These standards streamline the process for API users by doing the following:

- Offering **clear guidelines** that reduce the effort required to design and maintain API contracts
- Providing **robust toolsets and active community support**, making them a practical choice over custom solutions
- Enhancing **developer onboarding**, allowing new developers to understand the API's structure and functionality more easily through familiar conventions

Typically, these standards define key elements, including the following:

- API functionality
- Data structures and schemas
- Security mechanisms
- Error responses
- Usage limitations

OpenAPI extensibility

Leveraging an API specification is typically sufficient to encapsulate all aspects of an API contract. For instance, the OpenAPI Specification provides powerful extensibility through custom properties known as extensions, which are prefixed with x-, like so:

```
openapi: 3.0.0
info:
  title: Example API
  version: 1.0.0
  x-business-owner: "Product Strategy Team"
  x-support-tier: "Premium"
  x-deprecation-timeline: "Q4 2025"
...
```

These extensions allow you to capture details or functionality not inherently covered by the core standard, ensuring a more comprehensive API contract.

With a solid understanding of what constitutes an API contract, the next step is to explore why these contracts are so vital, examining how they foster alignment between teams, mitigate risks, and ensure seamless integrations. By understanding their value, you'll gain deeper insights into how API contracts contribute to both the technical and strategic success of APIs.

The importance of API contracts

API contracts are foundational to modern software development, serving as the blueprint for how APIs function, communicate, and integrate across systems. Their role in driving consistency, collaboration, security, and efficiency cannot be overstated. Organizations that prioritize well-defined API contracts gain a competitive edge in delivering high-quality software faster, reducing incidents, and fostering better collaboration.

Ensuring consistency and predictability

A well-crafted API contract accelerates application delivery while reducing API-related incidents. According to the Postman State of API Report 2023 (https://www.postman.com/state-of-api/2023/), organizations with formal API contracts report up to 70% faster time to market for new features. This speed is attributed to reduced ambiguity in API behavior, allowing developers to focus on building features rather than troubleshooting integration issues. For example, Netflix uses API contracts extensively to streamline feature rollouts across their global platform, ensuring smooth integration between microservices.

This acceleration stems largely from the standardization that API contracts bring to development workflows. By establishing consistent definitions of request and response structures, API contracts enable developers to predict API behavior with confidence, eliminating the need for time-consuming clarifications between teams. Consider Stripe's API contract, which provides detailed specifications on endpoints and error codes, allowing developers to integrate payment systems seamlessly without constant back and forth with support. This predictability becomes especially valuable when managing complex integrations across multiple services.

The consistency provided by API contracts also translates directly into reduced operational overhead. Teams with standardized API contracts experience a 65% reduction in API-related incidents, and the average resolution time for incidents decreases by 45%. For example, Shopify's use of API contracts ensures early error detection during integration testing, enabling them to prevent downtime for their merchants globally. This proactive approach to incident prevention is made possible through the structured validation that contracts enable.

Building on this foundation of standardization, API contracts facilitate automated validation processes that maintain ecosystem reliability. By defining expected inputs and outputs, contracts enable testing tools to verify compliance before deployment, creating a safety net that catches issues before they reach production environments.

These validation capabilities extend naturally into enhanced monitoring and observability practices. By explicitly defining what constitutes normal behavior versus anomalies, contracts make it easier to set up alerts and dashboards that provide meaningful insights. For example, Amazon API Gateway leverages API contracts to enable real-time monitoring, helping organizations identify and address performance bottlenecks more effectively.

Beyond the technical benefits, API contracts foster stronger relationships between API providers and consumers by establishing clear expectations and mutual trust. When Twilio publishes detailed contracts for its communication APIs, developers worldwide gain confidence in integrating voice, messaging, and video services, knowing the specifications are reliable and accurate. This trust becomes the foundation for broader collaboration across teams and organizations.

Establishing consistency and predictability in APIs does more than streamline development—it fosters an environment where collaboration can thrive. When API behavior is well defined and predictable, teams can align more easily, reducing confusion and building confidence in how different services interact. This clarity serves as a powerful foundation for cross-team collaboration, ensuring that both internal and external stakeholders can contribute effectively to API projects.

Facilitating collaboration

API contracts significantly enhance collaboration by acting as a shared reference point for all stakeholders, including backend and frontend developers, quality assurance teams, and business analysts. By providing clarity on API capabilities, contracts reduce communication overhead by 40% and cut integration-related questions by 50%. For example, Amazon uses API contracts to align teams during feature development, minimizing misunderstandings and delays.

This collaborative foundation becomes even more essential as organizations scale their API ecosystems. In microservices architectures, where dozens or even hundreds of teams manage separate services, API contracts serve as a single source of truth that eliminates ambiguity and ensures everyone works toward the same goals. adidas's adoption of API contracts exemplifies this approach, allowing their engineering teams to scale efficiently while maintaining consistent communication across services.

The benefits of this unified approach extend beyond internal teams to encompass external partnerships as well. Enterprises adopting comprehensive API contracts report a 60% reduction in onboarding time for new API consumers, as clear specifications eliminate guesswork and accelerate integration processes. For instance, HubSpot's detailed API documentation, built on robust contracts, enables partners to integrate CRM capabilities faster and with fewer errors.

Within internal development workflows, different stakeholders leverage API contracts in specialized ways that support their unique responsibilities. Quality assurance teams, for example, use contracts as a foundation for automated testing and validation, enabling them to identify integration issues early in the development cycle. GitHub Actions demonstrates this approach effectively, with workflows that leverage API contracts to validate GitHub API integrations before deployment.

Similarly, business analysts find value in API contracts as they provide clear insights into API functionality and potential business opportunities. Analysts at Spotify, for instance, use API contracts to identify opportunities for new integrations and assess potential business impact, ensuring the API ecosystem aligns with strategic objectives and drives meaningful business outcomes.

This comprehensive approach to stakeholder alignment ultimately creates an environment where external consumers can build with confidence. Companies such as Slack have leveraged robust contracts to create thriving developer ecosystems, where third-party developers can confidently build apps and integrations knowing they have a reliable reference for expected API behavior. This trust forms the backbone of successful API partnerships and platform growth.

While collaboration is key to developing and scaling successful APIs, evolving APIs over time without breaking existing integrations is equally important. Effective version management and change control strategies are essential to balancing innovation with stability. By embedding versioning policies into API contracts, teams can introduce new features while maintaining compatibility, ensuring a smooth transition for all consumers.

Mitigating change and managing versions

Managing changes to APIs is a complex but critical task. API contracts help mitigate the risks associated with change by embedding robust versioning strategies. For example, Stripes's use of versioned API contracts ensures that developers can continue using older versions while adapting to new features over time.

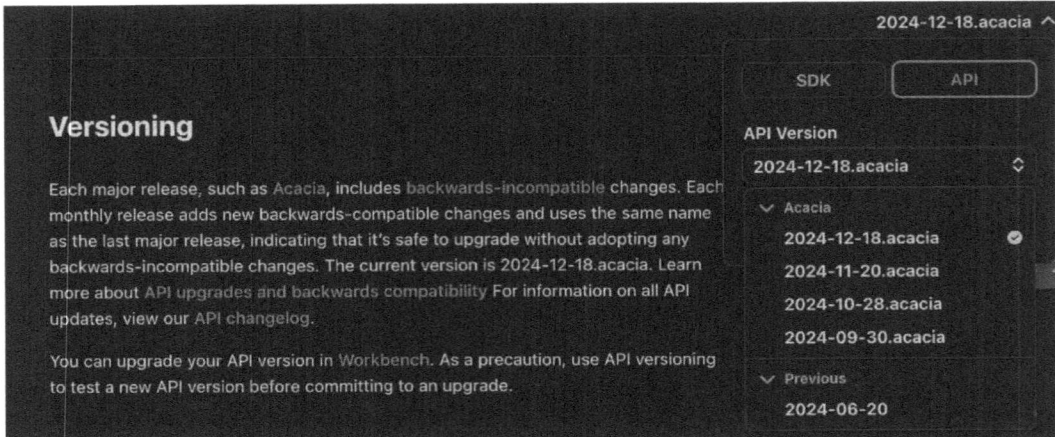

Figure 8.2: Stripe API versioning

🔍 **Quick tip**: Need to see a high-resolution version of this image? Open this book in the next-gen Packt Reader or view it in the PDF/ePub copy.

📖 **The next-gen Packt Reader** is included for free with the purchase of this book. Scan the QR code OR go to `https://packtpub.com/unlock`, then use the search bar to find this book by name. Double-check the edition shown to make sure you get the right one.

Semantic versioning, communicated through API contracts, is another common strategy for managing changes. It signals whether updates are minor, patch-level fixes or major breaking changes. GitHub employs semantic versioning in its API updates, giving developers clear expectations for backward compatibility and adaptation timelines.

Building on this transparent communication approach, many organizations extend their versioning strategy to include early access programs that give consumers advance notice of upcoming changes. Advanced access to new versions of API contracts enables consumers to plan and test integrations proactively, turning potential disruptions into managed transitions. For example, the Google Maps API provides detailed beta contracts for upcoming features, allowing developers to test and adapt their applications ahead of public releases.

API contracts also streamline deprecation policies, ensuring that consumers have ample time to migrate to new versions. AWS offers deprecation notices embedded in API contracts, allowing developers to transition without disruptions.

In microservices architectures, versioning becomes even more critical. Contracts ensure that changes in one service do not inadvertently break dependencies in others. Netflix's implementation of API contracts across its microservices ensures smooth updates without affecting the overall user experience.

Finally, robust change management enabled by API contracts reduces the risk of integration failures. For example, Shopify's versioned API contracts help merchants update their apps seamlessly, maintaining business continuity during platform changes.

Effectively managing API changes ensures stability and adaptability, but it's only part of the equation. Security and reliability are equally critical to maintaining a successful API ecosystem. API contracts play a vital role in safeguarding sensitive data and ensuring compliance with industry regulations. Beyond change management, these contracts provide the foundation for robust security practices, proactive monitoring, and enhanced reliability.

Enhancing security and reliability

APIs are gateways to sensitive data, making security a top priority. API contracts outline authentication methods, authorization scopes, and encryption standards, acting as a safeguard against unauthorized access and data breaches. The previously mentioned Postman report reveals that teams leveraging API contracts report 55% fewer security incidents, underscoring their importance in proactive security management.

API contracts also specify rate limits and performance expectations, reducing the likelihood of abuse or outages. GitHub API contracts include rate-limiting details, protecting the platform from excessive requests while ensuring fair usage for all developers.

For compliance-sensitive industries, such as finance or healthcare, API contracts are indispensable. Contracts explicitly outline data-handling practices and compliance requirements, such as GDPR or HIPAA.

Monitoring and observability improve significantly with API contracts in place. By defining SLAs and metrics within contracts, organizations can ensure reliability and availability.

Finally, API contracts enable consistent security reviews during the development life cycle. By integrating ad hoc API security tools, organizations can automate security testing and identify vulnerabilities early.

While security and reliability are essential for protecting your API ecosystem, an **API-first approach** takes it a step further by making the API contract the foundation of development. This proactive strategy enables teams to collaborate effectively and deliver features faster without compromising stability or quality. API contracts not only streamline development but also foster innovation by aligning technical implementation with business goals from the start.

Supporting API-first design and development

In an API-first approach, the API contract serves as the foundation for development, often created before any code is written. This allows downstream teams to build mocks and prototypes, enabling parallel development and faster time to market. For example, adidas's API-first strategy empowers its teams to release new product features rapidly.

API contracts ensure alignment across teams, reducing rework and delays. By establishing clear expectations up front, developers can build against a consistent specification. Spotify, for instance, uses API contracts to maintain alignment between its backend services and third-party integrations.

API contracts also facilitate stakeholder buy-in early in the process. By providing a tangible artifact for review, teams can gather feedback and iterate before committing to development. For example, adidas's use of API contracts helps its teams refine functionality before implementation.

Finally, an API-first approach supported by contracts accelerates innovation. By decoupling development cycles, teams can experiment with new ideas while maintaining stability.

To harness the full potential of API contracts, it's crucial to understand their foundational elements. API contracts are built using a combination of specifications, tools, and best practices that ensure their reliability and effectiveness across development life cycles. In the next section, we will explore these key components. By breaking down these building blocks, you can gain actionable insights into creating robust API contracts tailored to your needs.

Introducing API contract building blocks

An effective API contract is composed of several key components that collectively define every aspect of the API's functionality, usage, and governance. Understanding these building blocks is essential for creating contracts that are both comprehensive and manageable. In this section, I will focus on REST APIs and OpenAPI as the primary frameworks for defining and standardizing API contracts, offering practical insights into their unique features and best practices for implementation.

Technical specifications

An API contract's technical specification serves as a comprehensive guide for developers, outlining precise instructions on interacting with the API. It provides detailed model schemas, enabling developers to implement robust data handling in their applications while ensuring consistency and accuracy. Additionally, the specification clearly defines security requirements, helping to prevent unauthorized access and safeguard sensitive data effectively.

Endpoints definition

The API description outlines the technical aspects of the API, including the following:

- **Endpoints and methods:** Detailed information on each endpoint, including URLs and supported HTTP methods (GET, POST, PUT, DELETE, etc.)
- **Request parameters:** Definitions of required and optional parameters for each endpoint, including path parameters, query parameters, headers, and body content
- **Response formats:** Descriptions of the expected responses, including status codes, headers, and response bodies

This is an example of the /users endpoint definition, which returns a list of users. The endpoint accepts filter and pagination parameters, enabling developers to refine their queries. It responds with an array of User objects in application/json format:

```
...
paths:
  /users:
    get:
      summary: "Retrieve a list of users"
      description: "Returns an array of users with basic information."
      parameters:
        - name: page
```

```
                in: query
                description: "Page number for pagination"
                required: false
                schema:
                  type: integer
                  example: 1
            - name: limit
              in: query
              description: "Maximum number of items to return per page"
              required: false
              schema:
                type: integer
                example: 10
            - name: filter
              in: query
              description: "Filter criteria for the list of users (e.g., by
role, status)"
              required: false
              schema:
                type: string
                example: "role=admin"
        responses:
          '200':
            description: "A list of users"
            content:
              application/json:
                schema:
                  type: array
                  items:
                    $ref: '#/components/schemas/User'
```

After defining the API contract endpoints, the next critical technical component to describe is the data models and their schemas.

Data models and schemas

Defining data models and schemas is crucial for ensuring that data exchanged via the API is structured and validated consistently. This includes the following:

- **Field definitions**: Names, data types, and constraints for each field in the request and response bodies

- **Validation rules**: Conditions that data must meet, such as minimum and maximum values, string lengths, and pattern matching

- **Example payloads**: Sample requests and responses that illustrate the expected data formats

This is an example of defining a User data model, including its properties:

```
components:
  schemas:
    User:
      type: object
      properties:
        id:
          type: string
          description: "Unique identifier for the user"
        name:
          type: string
          description: "Full name of the user"
        email:
          type: string
          format: email
          description: "Email address of the user"
        createdAt:
          type: string
          format: date-time
          description: "Timestamp when the user was created"
      required:
        - id
        - name
        - email
```

Note

We primarily use JSON Schema to define these models. For a deeper understanding of JSON Schema, refer to *Chapter 11*.

Now that we've covered data models and schemas, let's move on to the final technical aspect of an API contract, security protocols:

Security framework

Security protocols are a critical component of the API contract. They define the following:

- **Authentication methods**: Whether the API uses API keys, OAuth 2.0, JWT tokens, or other authentication mechanisms
- **Authorization scopes**: Permissions and access levels granted to different users or applications
- **Encryption standards**: Requirements for data encryption in transit and at rest

As an example, an API contract might define multiple security methods. Some endpoints may be protected using an API key, and others may be protected using the OAuth2 protocol. Both are shown here:

```
components:
  securitySchemes:
    ApiKeyAuth:
      type: apiKey
      in: header
      name: X-API-Key
    OAuth2:
      type: oauth2
      flows:
        authorizationCode:
          authorizationUrl: https://example.com/oauth/authorize
          tokenUrl: https://example.com/oauth/token
          scopes:
            read: "Read access to protected resources"
            write: "Write access to protected resources"

security:
  - ApiKeyAuth: []
  - OAuth2:
      - read
      - write
```

Having grasped the technical specification building block of an API contract, let's explore the second building block, which focuses on defining the business aspects of an API contract.

Business commitments

Beyond the technical aspects, API contracts must also address their usage from a business perspective—an area that is often underrepresented today. This oversight typically occurs because API contracts are traditionally seen as purely technical artifacts focused on endpoints, data models, and security protocols. However, neglecting business-related elements such as SLAs, **usage policies**, and **monetization models** can create gaps in consumer expectations, leading to misalignment and reduced trust.

Documenting business aspects in API contracts fosters better collaboration between providers and consumers by setting clear expectations around performance, usage limits, and operational policies. This transparency builds trust and helps consumers plan their integration more effectively, ensuring the API meets both technical and business needs. In this section, we'll explore how OpenAPI can be extended to capture these business elements, creating a more comprehensive and consumer-friendly API contract.

Service-Level Agreements (SLAs)

The API contract should outline how the API is intended to be used from a business perspective. This includes the following:

- **Monetization models**: Information on pricing, billing cycles, and payment methods if the API is offered as a paid service
- **Usage limits**: Rate limits, quotas, and throttling policies that govern how frequently the API can be called
- **Onboarding processes**: Steps required to gain access to the API, such as registration, application approval, and API key issuance

Understanding these business aspects helps consumers plan their usage and integrate the API in a way that aligns with their business goals.

That's where SLAs come in. They define the performance and reliability expectations of the API, including the following:

- **Uptime guarantees**: The expected availability of the API, often expressed as a percentage (e.g., 99.9% uptime)
- **Response times**: Maximum acceptable latency for API responses

- **Support and maintenance**: Details on technical support availability, maintenance windows, and incident response times

These metrics ensure that API consumers have a clear understanding of what they can expect in terms of performance, reliability, and support. However, capturing and communicating SLAs effectively can be challenging without a standardized approach. This is where the **SLA4OAI Specification** becomes valuable, offering a draft framework for defining SLAs in conjunction with OpenAPI. By using this framework, providers can detail SLAs in a machine-readable format, enhancing transparency and building trust with consumers.

Although **OpenAPI** does not natively support SLA descriptions, the SLA4OAI Specification offers a draft framework for defining SLAs in conjunction with OpenAPI. This allows providers to detail SLAs in a machine-readable format, enhancing transparency and trust with consumers.

The following example demonstrates how SLA4OAI can define three distinct plans for an API:

```
sla: 1.0.0
context:
  id: magicstore-sample
  type: plans
  api:
    $ref: ./magicstore-service.yml
  provider: ISAGroup
metrics:
  requests:
    type: "int64"
    description: "Number of requests"
plans:
  base:
    availability: R/00:00:00Z/23:00:00Z
  free:
    rates:
      /products/{id}:
        get:
          requests:
            - max: 1
              period: second
    quotas:
      /products:
```

```
            post:
              requests:
                - max: 10
                  period: minute
      pro:
        pricing:
          cost: 5
          currency: EUR
          billing: monthly
        rates:
          /products/{id}:
            get:
              requests:
                - max: 100
                  period: second
```

This structure enables API providers to transparently define SLAs, fostering better alignment with consumer expectations.

- `base`: Ensures daily availability but does not enforce specific usage limits or pricing. Suitable for general or test usage.

- `free`: Offers limited usage with strict rate limits, such as 1 request per second for GET operations and 10 requests per minute for POST operations.

- `pro`: Introduces higher usage limits, such as 100 requests per second for GET operations, and includes a paid monthly subscription priced at 5 EUR.

> **Note**
>
> If you're not ready to adopt SLA4OAI, there are alternative methods to incorporate SLAs into API contracts:
>
> **Custom OpenAPI extensions**: Use x- fields to add SLA-related details such as uptime guarantees and rate limits
>
> **API management platforms**: Platforms such as Apigee, Amazon API Gateway, and Azure API Management support SLA enforcement through built-in tools

In addition to defining your API SLA, an API contract should also outline operational policies. These policies govern how the API is managed, secured, and monitored in real-world scenarios.

Operational policies

Operational policies establish the processes and standards necessary for ensuring that the API runs efficiently, securely, and consistently. These policies help maintain a seamless experience for API consumers while protecting the API from misuse. Key components of operational policies include the following:

- **Rate limiting and throttling**: Mechanisms to control traffic flow, prevent abuse, and ensure fair usage among API consumers
- **Versioning**: Clear guidelines for managing API lifecycle updates, including strategies for introducing new versions, deprecating old ones, and maintaining backward compatibility
- **Error handling**: Standardized approaches for communicating errors, including consistent error codes, meaningful messages, and guidance for resolving issues

The following example demonstrates a *429 Too Many Requests* response for the /users endpoint. This response is returned when an API consumer exceeds the allowed usage limits, providing clear feedback on the restriction:

```
paths:
  /users:
    get:
      responses:
        '429':
          description: "Too Many Requests"
          content:
            application/json:
              schema:
                type: object
                properties:
                  error:
                    type: string
                    example: "Rate limit exceeded"
```

This example illustrates how operational policies can be codified in the API contract to ensure transparency and provide clear communication to consumers. By defining such policies upfront, API providers can foster better reliability, scalability, and consumer trust.

While the business commitments building block ensures clarity around usage limits, monetization models, and SLAs, it's equally important to address the regulatory and compliance framework governing the API. This brings us to the next critical aspect of an API contract: compliance and legal requirements.

Compliance and legal requirements

Depending on the nature of the data and the industry, the API contract may need to address compliance with regulations such as the following:

- **General Data Protection Regulation (GDPR)**: For handling personal data in the European Union
- **Health Insurance Portability and Accountability Act (HIPAA)**: For healthcare information in the United States
- **Payment Card Industry Data Security Standard (PCI DSS)**: For processing credit card information

API contracts can also be utilized by automated tools to verify adherence to compliance requirements, such as GDPR and HIPAA. By embedding metadata or annotations within the API contract, these tools can identify sensitive data, enforce data-handling policies, and validate the API's alignment with regulatory standards.

Including compliance requirements in the API contract ensures that both providers and consumers are aware of their legal obligations. The legal section of the API contract covers the following:

- **Terms of service**: Rules governing how the API can be used, including prohibited activities
- **Intellectual property rights**: Ownership of the API and any derivative works
- **Liability and indemnification**: Limitations of liability and responsibilities in case of data breaches or other issues

The `termsOfService` field in OpenAPI allows you to link to an external *Terms of Service* document that defines the legal terms for using the API. This document typically outlines key legal aspects, such as acceptable use, intellectual property rights, liability limitations, privacy policies, and compliance requirements. Here's an example:

```
openapi: 3.0.3
info:
  title: User management API
  version: 1.0.0
  termsOfService: "https://example.com/terms"
```

```
contact:
  name: API Support
  email: support@example.com
  url: "https://example.com/support"
...
```

In this example, the `termsOfService` field links to `https://example.com/terms`, which contains the full legal agreement. The API contract itself does not include these legal terms directly but refers to the external document, ensuring that consumers have easy access to the completex legal framework. This protects both the API provider and the consumer by clearly defining rights, responsibilities, and usage conditions, reducing the risk of disputes.

Having covered the core elements of API contracts, the next section will dive into managing API contracts, emphasizing the importance of building a single source of API truth for your organization. We will see that as your APIs evolve, managing their contracts becomes increasingly important to maintain quality, compliance, and API consumer trust.

Managing your API contracts

Managing API contracts effectively is vital for building a resilient, scalable, and secure API ecosystem. APIs are the backbone of digital transformation, enabling systems to interact seamlessly and facilitating innovation across industries. However, without proper management, the proliferation of APIs can lead to significant challenges, such as duplication, inconsistency, and security vulnerabilities.

Effective API contract management involves strategic governance, collaboration, and centralization to ensure that APIs remain assets rather than liabilities. It is not merely a technical task but a critical organizational capability that requires attention to detail, robust processes, and the right tools.

The challenge of API sprawl

One of the most significant risks of poor API contract management is API sprawl. This occurs when an organization creates numerous APIs without a centralized strategy or governance. Over time, these APIs grow into a fragmented ecosystem, creating operational inefficiencies and eroding the developer experience. API sprawl introduces multiple layers of challenges that can undermine the effectiveness of an organization's API strategy.

When APIs are created without oversight, teams often reinvent the wheel, developing redundant APIs with overlapping or identical functionality. This duplication not only increases maintenance overhead but also complicates debugging and wastes valuable resources. As the number of redundant APIs grows, organizations face escalating costs and operational inefficiencies that could have been avoided with a more centralized approach.

Building on the issue of duplication, fragmented API ecosystems often lack standardization. Disconnected development efforts result in varied protocols, inconsistent documentation quality, and differing naming conventions or design patterns. This lack of uniformity creates significant hurdles for API users, making it difficult to integrate APIs seamlessly and ultimately leading to a fractured developer experience.

The challenges of inconsistency are compounded by the security risks inherent in a fragmented API landscape. Without a unified strategy, it becomes difficult to enforce consistent security practices across the ecosystem. Vulnerabilities in poorly managed APIs can be exploited by malicious actors, leading to data breaches, compliance violations, and reputational damage. The absence of a centralized governance framework further exacerbates these risks, leaving organizations exposed to potential threats.

In addition to security concerns, unorganized API ecosystems suffer from reduced discoverability. Developers often struggle to find or understand the APIs they need, resulting in the underutilization of available resources. APIs that are difficult to discover or comprehend fail to deliver their intended value, limiting their contribution to organizational goals and frustrating developers who seek streamlined solutions.

By understanding the interconnected nature of these challenges—duplication, inconsistency, security risks, and reduced discoverability—organizations can better appreciate the critical need for centralized governance and strategic management of their APIs. Recognizing and addressing these issues is the first step toward creating a cohesive and effective API ecosystem.

Addressing API sprawl

Tackling API sprawl requires a proactive and structured approach that addresses its root causes. Without deliberate strategies, the challenges of duplication, inconsistency, security vulnerabilities, and poor discoverability can overwhelm even the most well-intentioned API programs. Regaining control and fostering a well-managed API ecosystem begins with establishing a clear and unified strategy.

Single Source of API Truth (SSOT)

At the heart of this strategy is the concept of a **Single Source of API Truth (SSOT)**. An SSOT serves as the authoritative reference point for all API-related information within an organization. It ensures that every team works with consistent, standardized data, providing a shared understanding of the API ecosystem. For API-first organizations, the SSOT is typically the API specification, while for others, the implementation may take precedence as the central reference.

Consolidating APIs into a single reference point eliminates silos and fosters alignment across teams. This centralized approach reduces duplication by ensuring that teams are aware of existing APIs and can build upon them rather than creating redundant ones. It also streamlines collaboration, as developers, business stakeholders, and consumers operate from the same source of truth, enabling more informed and effective decision-making.

A prime example of this approach is adidas, which improved its API delivery by establishing a bold single source of truth for APIs. According to adidas's API guidelines (`https://adidas.gitbook.io/api-guidelines`), the organization follows an API-first principle, which extends the design-first approach. This principle mandates that API development always begins with design, not with coding. For adidas, the API design, including its description and schema, serves as the master of truth—not the implementation. Every API implementation must strictly adhere to the API design, which acts as the binding contract between the API and its consumers. This strategy has empowered adidas to maintain consistency across its APIs, align its teams, and ensure that its API ecosystem delivers value effectively and efficiently.

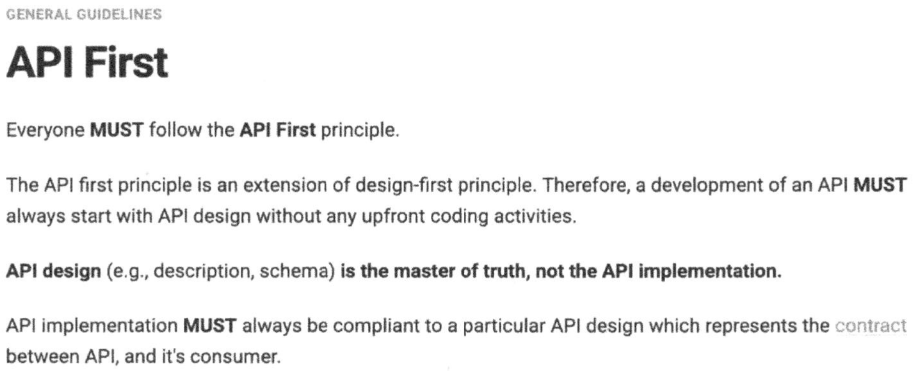

GENERAL GUIDELINES

API First

Everyone **MUST** follow the **API First** principle.

The API first principle is an extension of design-first principle. Therefore, a development of an API **MUST** always start with API design without any upfront coding activities.

API design (e.g., description, schema) **is the master of truth, not the API implementation.**

API implementation **MUST** always be compliant to a particular API design which represents the contract between API, and it's consumer.

Figure 8.3: Extract from adidas's API guidelines

The importance of an SSOT goes beyond technical alignment; it embodies a state of organizational harmony. While tools and systems play a critical role, the true power of an SSOT lies in its human-centric nature. APIs exist to address human needs, whether facilitating collaboration between teams or delivering value to end users. The success of an SSOT hinges on consensus among stakeholders—API producers, consumers, and business leaders—who must agree on what the API should deliver. This shared understanding transforms the SSOT from a technical artifact into a cornerstone of organizational strategy.

Ultimately, an SSOT is as much about fostering collaboration as it is about maintaining technical consistency. By centering the SSOT around the people who build and use APIs, organizations can create a foundation of trust, alignment, and shared purpose that transcends individual tools or processes. This human-centric approach ensures that the API ecosystem remains aligned with organizational goals and capable of delivering sustainable value.

Implementing a central API design repository

A central API design repository serves as a dedicated platform for managing and sharing API contracts, acting as the backbone of API lifecycle management. By providing a centralized location for all API specifications, a design repository supports critical activities such as versioning, feedback collection, and integration with development workflows. It creates a unified environment where developers and stakeholders can collaborate effectively, ensuring that APIs remain consistent, discoverable, and aligned with organizational goals.

One of the key benefits of a central repository is its ability to enhance discoverability. When API contracts are stored in a single, accessible location, developers can quickly locate the APIs they need, reducing the duplication of effort and encouraging the reuse of existing resources. This not only streamlines development but also fosters a more cohesive API ecosystem where redundant APIs are minimized, and innovation is directed toward building new capabilities rather than recreating existing ones.

In addition to discoverability, a central repository provides robust version control capabilities. By tracking changes to API specifications over time, teams can manage multiple versions effectively, ensuring that updates do not disrupt existing consumers. Version control also plays a vital role in maintaining backward compatibility, allowing organizations to evolve their APIs without alienating users who rely on earlier versions.

Collaboration is another significant advantage of a central API design repository. By creating a shared space for API producers and consumers to engage, the repository facilitates meaningful feedback and alignment during the design phase. This collaborative environment ensures that API designs meet user needs before implementation begins, reducing the likelihood of costly revisions later in the development life cycle.

A notable example of this approach is **Back Market**, an online marketplace for refurbished electronics that significantly improved its API delivery and security by implementing an API design repository. Their centralized repository enhanced collaboration, streamlined feedback processes, and strengthened security practices across their API ecosystem, enabling faster and more reliable integrations.

> Note
>
> To learn more about how Back Market achieved these results, visit the case study here: `https://engineering.backmarket.com/leveling-up-apis-at-back-market-659e43d7e063`.

Back Market's success demonstrates how a centralized API design repository can transform API management, improving collaboration and security while accelerating delivery. However, the true power of such a repository lies in how well it integrates with existing development workflows.

For example, *automating the validation of API specifications through CI/CD pipelines* ensures that every API adheres to organizational standards before deployment. Feedback mechanisms embedded within the repository allow developers and stakeholders to propose changes or improvements directly, fostering continuous refinement of API contracts. Moreover, **life cycle support** ensures that APIs are managed from inception to deprecation, providing a structured framework for creating, testing, deploying, and eventually retiring APIs.

By integrating these features into a central repository, organizations can create an environment that supports both the technical and collaborative aspects of API development. This approach not only reduces inefficiencies and redundancies but also lays the groundwork for effective API governance, making it easier to manage APIs at scale.

To illustrate how this can be achieved in practice, let's implement this using our **MagicAPI Store**.

Managing API contracts with GitHub: Magic Items Store use case

Magic Items Store has scaled to hundreds of teams, each generating APIs to power their services. While the pace of innovation is remarkable, the lack of a centralized strategy has resulted in API sprawl—redundant APIs, inconsistent designs, and security blind spots. To regain control and ensure a well-governed API ecosystem, MagicAPI Store adopts GitHub as its central API design repository, leveraging open source tools to streamline its API management practices.

Here's how MagicAPI Store effectively uses GitHub to manage its API contracts:

- **Store API specifications**: MagicAPI Store hosts all its OpenAPI and AsyncAPI specifications in GitHub repositories. Each repository is dedicated to a specific API or a group of related APIs. By storing these specifications in GitHub, the company ensures they are **version-controlled**, easily accessible, and organized for all teams. This structured approach prevents duplication and encourages teams to build on existing APIs rather than creating redundant ones.

- **Collaborate using Pull Requests (PRs)**: To introduce changes to API contracts, MagicAPI Store requires teams to submit PRs. These PRs serve as a collaboration point where API producers and consumers can discuss proposed updates, provide feedback, and ensure alignment. Take the following example:

  - A developer working on the Inventory API submits a PR to add a new endpoint for retrieving product stock levels

  - Reviewers, including API consumers and platform architects, validate the design for consistency with organizational standards before approval

- **Automated validation**: MagicAPI Store integrates open source tools such as Spectral and Prism into its GitHub workflows to automate validation of API specifications. Take the following example:

  - **Spectral** lints the API specifications, ensuring they comply with predefined guidelines such as naming conventions, required fields, and security standards

  - **Prism** simulates the API, allowing teams to test its behavior before implementation

By automating validation during PRs, MagicAPI Store ensures that every change to an API contract meets organizational standards, reducing manual effort and enhancing quality control.

```
name: API Spec Validation
on:
```

```
  pull_request:
    paths:
      - "apis/**.yaml"

jobs:
  validate:
    runs-on: ubuntu-latest
    steps:
      - name: Checkout Code
        uses: actions/checkout@v2

      - name: Install Spectral
        run: npm install -g @stoplight/spectral-cli

      - name: Lint API Specification
        run: spectral lint apis/magic-inventory-api.yaml
```

In this example, the workflow is triggered for every PR involving changes to API specifications in the apis/**.yaml path. The steps include checking out the code, installing Spectral, and running a linting process on the magic-inventory-api.yaml file. This automated validation ensures that the API specification adheres to organizational standards and reduces the risk of errors or inconsistencies being introduced.

This process not only fosters collaboration but also ensures that changes are thoroughly reviewed, reducing the risk of introducing errors or inconsistencies.

At MagicAPI Store, the API contract workflow goes beyond validation to improve reliability and integration. Incorporating **contract testing** ensures API providers meet consumer expectations, minimizing miscommunication and guaranteeing functionality. The workflow also **automates documentation generation and deployment**, giving developers easy access to up-to-date resources. Seamless integration with provisioning systems enables automatic API configuration and deployment, reducing manual overhead and boosting efficiency. Together, these practices foster a scalable, well-governed API ecosystem.

Summary

Crafting and managing effective API contracts is foundational to building a robust, scalable, and efficient API ecosystem. This chapter explored the concept of API contracts, emphasizing their role as formal agreements that define the expectations and responsibilities of API providers and consumers. With clear guidelines for invocation details, data models, security protocols, usage policies, and performance expectations, API contracts ensure consistency, reliability, and alignment between stakeholders.

The importance of API contracts extends beyond technical specifications to include strategic benefits such as fostering collaboration, mitigating risks, managing changes, and enhancing security. By enabling automated validation, streamlining documentation generation, and integrating provisioning systems, API contract workflows reduce manual effort, minimize miscommunication, and accelerate innovation. Furthermore, centralizing API specifications in a design repository helps address API sprawl, ensuring discoverability, reducing duplication, and improving governance.

In conclusion, well-defined and well-managed API contracts are not just technical artifacts but strategic tools that enable organizations to scale efficiently, maintain quality, and support innovation. By adopting best practices such as contract testing, centralized repositories, and automated workflows, organizations can transform their API ecosystems into assets that drive collaboration, reduce time to market, and foster trust among stakeholders.

In the next chapter, we will focus on understanding the OpenAPI Specification. We'll explore its origins and purpose, examine how it supports effective REST API design, and walk through the structure that makes it such a powerful tool. This chapter will provide clear guidance to help you get the most value from OpenAPI in your own API design work. Stay tuned!

Get This Book's PDF Version and Exclusive Extras

UNLOCK NOW

Scan the QR code (or go to `packtpub.com/unlock`). Search for this book by name, confirm the edition, and then follow the steps on the page.

Note: Keep your invoice handy. Purchases made directly from Packt don't require an invoice.

Part 3

The Archmage's Circle — Forging and Evolving API Contracts

In this advanced part, you are welcomed into the archmage's circle, where the most sophisticated arts of API mastery are revealed. Here, you'll learn to forge, enchant, and evolve API contracts that stand as monuments to both technical excellence and enduring power. This is where your apprentice knowledge and wizard-level skills converge into the supreme abilities needed to create APIs that transcend time itself.

You'll master the arcane tools of OpenAPI Specification and JSON Schema, learning not merely their syntax but how to wield them as living contracts that govern entire magical realms of development. We'll unlock the mysteries of hypermedia to create self-describing APIs and confront the greatest challenge faced by all archmages: the art of evolution and change without breaking the ancient bonds of compatibility.

Within this circle, you achieve the ultimate transformation from API designer to API architect—one who not only creates magnificent APIs but guides them through eternal lifecycles of growth and adaptation. You'll learn to perceive future changes before they manifest, craft evolutionary paths that honor the past while embracing innovation, and establish processes that ensure your APIs remain powerful artifacts for generations to come.

This part includes the following chapters:

- Chapter 9, Understanding the OpenAPI Specification
- Chapter 10, OpenAPI as a Contract: Best Practices and Implementation
- Chapter 11, Using JSON Schema to Define Your Object Models
- Chapter 12, Don't hate your Hypermedia : Creating APIs for Humans and AIs
- Chapter 13, API Change Management: Strategies for Versioning and Evolution

9

Understanding the OpenAPI Specification

OpenAPI Specification provides a standardized way to describe REST APIs. This chapter introduces OpenAPI's fundamentals: its history, purpose, and structure. Through our Magic Items store example, you'll learn how to structure an OpenAPI document and define its core components, from basic metadata to endpoints, parameters, responses, and security definitions.

We will cover the following main topics:

- The origins and purpose of OpenAPI
- Designing REST APIs with OpenAPI Specification
- The structure of OpenAPI Specification

By the end of this chapter, you will have a clear understanding of how to effectively describe all key aspects of your API's design and formalize them using the OpenAPI Specification format. You will also gain insight into the structure of your API and learn how to avoid common pitfalls associated with each element.

The origins and purpose of OpenAPI

OpenAPI Specification (OAS) is a standardized, language-agnostic way to describe RESTful APIs. Think of OAS documents as clear contracts that spell out exactly what your API can do, just like we talked about in earlier chapters. OAS is a powerful tool that supports the **API as a product** concept by giving both humans and computers a clear, readable definition of your interface, without needing to dig through source code or separate documentation.

The story of OAS starts back in 2011 with the Swagger project, created by Tony Tam, who was working at the dictionary site Wordnik. Tam and his team were frustrated with documentation headaches and the challenge of generating client SDKs, so they created Swagger as a solution. Developers loved how it made API documentation interactive and easier to work with, and by 2014, Swagger 2.0 took things to the next level.

In 2015, SmartBear Software bought the Swagger project from Reverb Technologies and, later that year, made a game-changing move: they donated the specification to the newly formed OpenAPI Initiative under the Linux Foundation. This is when Swagger Specification officially became OpenAPI Specification, though both names hung around together for a while during the transition.

Since then, the OpenAPI Initiative has kept improving the specification, releasing version 3.0 in 2017 and version 3.1 in 2021, which plays nicer with JSON Schema and handles modern API design patterns better. Today, major tech players such as Google, IBM, Microsoft, and Salesforce back the OpenAPI Initiative, showing just how important this standard has become.

This journey from a team's homegrown solution to an industry standard shows how central APIs have become in modern software development, and how the industry is increasingly recognizing the need for standardized ways to design and document them.

Why use OAS?

In the world of API development, clear communication and standardization aren't just nice to have; they're essential for success. OAS gives you a powerful tool that speaks to both humans and machines, creating a shared language for designing, building, and using APIs. OAS fits perfectly with the **design-first approach** we explored in *Chapter 3*, letting you map out your API's structure before writing a single line of code. This makes planning more effective and helps you avoid painful issues later in development.

OAS brings tons of benefits throughout your API's lifecycle. It lets you generate interactive, user-friendly documentation that helps developers actually understand and use your API. You can automatically create server stubs and client libraries in different programming languages, seriously speeding up development work. It helps teams and organizations stay on the same page with consistent practices that make collaboration smoother. Plus, it gives you solid foundations for API governance to keep quality and compliance in check across your API portfolio. These advantages become especially valuable when you're dealing with complex projects involving multiple teams and stakeholders.

How to use OAS

OAS isn't just for documentation; it's a versatile tool that enhances every aspect of your API lifecycle. To make the most of OAS, start by using it as your API's formal description. Define your endpoints, operations, parameters, and responses in a structured way using JSON or YAML format. This standardized approach keeps everything clear and consistent, making life easier for your team and anyone consuming your API.

Take advantage of the fantastic ecosystem of OAS-compatible tools to boost your productivity. Generate slick, interactive documentation using tools such as Swagger UI or ReDoc that transform your OAS document into user-friendly interfaces. Use code generators such as OpenAPI Generator to create client libraries and server implementations in various languages, keeping everything consistent while saving tons of development time.

OAS works brilliantly as a contract between API providers and consumers. By clearly spelling out expectations and capabilities, it prevents confusion and reduces integration headaches. This contract-first approach aligns perfectly with the *API as a product* concept we talked about in *Chapter 2*, ensuring your API is designed with real users in mind from day one.

Testing and validation are another area where OAS shines. Use your specification document to generate test cases and validate implementations against your defined standard. This helps you catch problems early, following the shift-left approach to development. Tools such as Postman and SoapUI can import your OAS documents to create automated test suites, making your testing more efficient and dependable.

By making OAS your organization's standard for API documentation, you ensure consistency across different teams and projects. This standardization leads to better collaboration, easier knowledge sharing, and smoother onboarding for new team members. Consider applying OAS to your entire API ecosystem, including internal APIs, microservices, and even legacy system integrations, to create a comprehensive API catalog that serves as a single source of truth for your entire API landscape.

Now that we've covered the why and how of OAS, let's roll up our sleeves and get hands-on. Theory is great, but seeing OAS in action with a real-world example will really cement your understanding. In the next section, we'll build a complete API specification for a Magic Items store from scratch, putting into practice all the concepts we've discussed so far. This practical walkthrough will show you exactly how OAS transforms abstract API design principles into concrete, implementable specifications.

Designing REST APIs with OAS

In this section, we'll dive into using OAS by designing an API for a Magic Items store. We want to introduce you to the practical aspect of API design with OAS and see how it works in the real world. You'll learn how to set up API endpoints, structure data for requests and responses, and add cool features such as security and reusable bits. We'll explain why these things matter and how they make your API shine. All of these are based on the knowledge you have already gained previously in this book.

OpenAPI and Swagger

As we already mentioned in the section about the origins and purpose of OAS, it used to be called Swagger Specification. This terminology often persists to this day, interchangeably. In this book, when talking about the specification, we will always refer to it as **OpenAPI Specification (OAS)**. There are noticeable and significant differences between the two specifications. OpenAPI 3.x (the current version) offers more flexibility and features compared to Swagger 2.0, such as centralized reusable components and expanded support for JSON Schema. Whenever we refer to Swagger, we will be talking about a set of tools around OAS built by SmartBear.

Introducing the Magic Items store API

Our goal is to design an API to manage the inventory and basic processes of a magic items store. From the initial lifecycle stage of requirements gathering, we know that our store will show a catalog of items that the store sells, as well as detailed information about each item, manage the inventory of the items in the catalog, and process orders. These actions are our application's affordances. This API will be consumed by our web front and mobile application. On top of that, we want to enable public access to the data about our magic items catalog. With that knowledge, we can start designing our API to be at an appropriate maturity level. At this stage, we decide to aim for level 3 of the **Web API Design Maturity Model (WADMM)**, so an affordance-centric API crafted around the actions it exposes. We will also aim for level 2 of the **Richardson Maturity Model (RMM)**, so an API designed in accordance with the HTTP protocol semantics. In *Chapter 12*, we will introduce hypermedia controls to our API and bump it up to RMM level 3 maturity. Both of these maturity models were previously introduced in *Chapter 6*.

> JSON-Schema in this chapter
>
> We cover JSON Schema and object modeling in detail in *Chapter 11*, so we won't be focusing on schema specifics in this chapter. It's worth noting that OAS leverages JSON Schema to define its data models, making them a crucial part of your API contract. The schema examples in this chapter demonstrate basic usage, but *Chapter 11* will provide comprehensive guidance on creating robust, reusable schema definitions for your APIs.

Now that we've established the requirements and goals for our Magic Items store API, let's dive into how we'll represent this design using OAS. Understanding the basic structure of OpenAPI will help us translate our API concepts into a standardized format that tools and developers can easily understand.

The structure of OAS

Now that we're ready to design our Magic Items store API, let's look at what actually goes into an OAS file. Whether you choose YAML or JSON format (most developers prefer YAML for its readability), every OAS document follows a consistent structure. Let's start with the basic skeleton and build it up as we go:

```
openapi: 3.1.0
info:
servers:
paths:
components:
security:
```

💡 **Quick tip**: Enhance your coding experience with the **AI Code Explainer** and **Quick Copy** features. Open this book in the next-gen Packt Reader. Click the **Copy** button

(1) to quickly copy code into your coding environment, or click the **Explain** button

(2) to get the AI assistant to explain a block of code to you.

```
                                                              Copy       Explain
function calculate(a, b) {                                     ①          ②
    return {sum: a + b};
};
```

📖 **The next-gen Packt Reader** is included for free with the purchase of this book. Scan the QR code OR go to `https://packtpub.com/unlock`, then use the search bar to find this book by name. Double-check the edition shown to make sure you get the right one.

This simple outline shows the six main building blocks of an OpenAPI document. Each plays an important role in defining different aspects of your API:

- openapi: This specifies which version of OAS you're using. It's like declaring which rule-book you're following. This isn't just a technicality; it signals which features and syntax rules apply to your document. Tools such as code generators and validators need this to process your document correctly, avoiding those frustrating compatibility errors. We're using version 3.1.0, the latest and greatest.

- info: This is basically your API's ID card. It contains all the metadata, such as the title, version, description, and contact details. This is required and gives developers the essential background about your API before they dive into technical details.

- servers: This lists the URLs where your API can actually be accessed. While it's technically optional, it's super helpful for anyone trying to use your API. Since we're still in the design phase for our Magic Items store, we won't focus much on this section in this chapter.

- paths: This is the star of the show! Here's where you define all your API endpoints and the HTTP methods they support. Technically, you could have an OAS document without paths, but it would be like a restaurant without food – not very useful! Most of our work in this chapter will be around building out this section for our Magic Items store.

- components: Think of this as your toolbox of pre-defined parts that you can reference throughout your API. It's where you store reusable pieces of your API definition, such as data schemas, response templates, parameters, and security schemes. It's optional but incredibly useful for keeping your specification DRY (Don't Repeat Yourself).

- security: This defines how your API is protected, whether that's with API keys, OAuth2, or other mechanisms. While optional, it's crucial for any production API to keep the bad guys out.

These six elements work together to create a complete picture of your API, covering both how it's designed and how it runs in the real world. There are a few other top-level elements (such as webhooks, which we'll touch on later), but these core six will handle most of what you need.

> **The entire specification**
>
> Throughout this chapter, we'll explore the most important aspects of OpenAPI as we build our Magic Items store API. We won't cover every last detail of the specification – that would take an entire book on its own! If you want the complete reference, head over to the official specification website: `https://spec.openapis.org/oas/latest`.

The info object: your API's first impression

The `info` object acts as your API's business card, offering essential metadata that introduces everyone to what your API does, who owns it, and where it's at in its lifecycle. Beyond just basic identification, it ensures good governance by establishing clear versioning and ownership details that are crucial when multiple teams are collaborating.

```
openapi: 3.1.0
info:
  title: Magic Items Store API
  version: 1.2.0
  description: |
    # Welcome to the Magic Items E-store API
    Manage magical inventory and orders.
```

```
    Supports filtering by item type, rarity, and enchantment level.
  termsOfService: https://magic-store.com/terms
  contact:
    name: Arcane Support Team
    email: support@magic-store.com
    url: https://magic-store.com/contact
  license:
    name: Magical Commons License v2.0
    url: https://magic-store.com/license
```

Let's break down each part of this `info` object:

- `title` (Required): This is your API's unique name. Keep it concise but descriptive, and avoid vague terms such as "API Service" that don't tell you anything. This is especially important if you're working in an ecosystem with lots of APIs. A good title should give users a decent idea of what your API actually does.

- `version` (Required): This shows the current semantic version of your API (such as 1.2.0). It's super critical for tracking compatibility. If this number changes unexpectedly, it can break integrations for your users. We'll dive deeper into versioning strategies in *Chapter 13*.

- `description` (Optional but recommended): This is your chance to provide a Markdown-enabled overview of what your API can do. Use this space to highlight key features, mention authentication requirements, or explain domain-specific rules (such as "Only Level 5+ wizards can purchase Legendary items").

- `termsOfService` (Optional): This is a URL that links to your legal terms. It's often overlooked, but it's vital for public APIs to limit liability and clearly define usage rights. Since we're planning for our Magic Items API to be public, we definitely need to include this.

- `contact` (Optional): This provides support details for when your users inevitably run into issues. Make sure any emails or URLs you list here are actively monitored. Nothing frustrates API consumers more than sending support requests into a black hole. This is important for both internal and external APIs.

- `license` (Optional): This clarifies how others can use your API. For internal APIs, you might consider adding your company's compliance guidelines here instead of an open source license.

A well-crafted `info` object makes sure everyone involved: developers, legal teams, and API consumers, can understand your API's scope and rules at a glance. It also helps enforce good governance by requiring version discipline and making ownership transparent.

Next, we'll explore the `paths` element, where your API's endpoints and operations really come to life.

The `paths` object: mapping your API's capabilities

The `paths` object is where your API's functionality takes shape. It defines not just endpoints and HTTP methods, but also the precise interaction model between clients and your service. Think of it as a blueprint that specifies *what* actions users can perform and *how* they execute them.

```
paths:
  /items:
    summary: Manage items collection
    description: Operations for managing the collection of magical items.
    get:
      tags: [Inventory]
      summary: List all magic items
      description: |
        Retrieve a paginated list of magical items.
        Supports filtering by rarity, spell type, and price range.
        Maximum of 100 items per response.
      operationId: listItems
      parameters:
        - $ref: '#/components/parameters/RarityFilter'
        - $ref: '#/components/parameters/Page'
        - $ref: '#/components/parameters/PageSize'
      responses:
        '200':
          $ref: '#/components/schemas/Items'
        '400':
          $ref: '#/components/responses/BadRequest'
        '500':
          $ref: '#/components/responses/InternalError'
```

- This code defines the `/items` endpoint in our Magic Items Store API, showing a GET operation that retrieves a paginated list of magical items with filtering options, along with possible success and error responses. Let's break down each part:

- `/items` (Required): This is a path item object. Basically, it's a relative path to an individual API endpoint. It always needs to start with a forward slash `/` since it gets added to the server URL we defined earlier. Avoid trailing slashes such as in `/items/`. For our

Magic Items store, we're using noun-based paths referring to resources (such as items). Stay away from action-based paths such as /getItems; they break REST principles and would make our API less intuitive. Use path parameters for resource identifiers, such as /items/{itemId} (we'll see these in action soon).

- get (Required): This is an operation object that defines what happens when someone makes a GET request to our /items endpoint. This keyword can be any HTTP method: GET, POST, PUT, DELETE, PATCH, and so on. The method you choose affects what other keywords you can use. For example, GET methods can't have a requestBody, while POST methods typically need one.

- summary (Optional): This gives users a quick idea of what this resource is for in plain language. Start with verbs for clarity. We used "Manage items collection" to clearly communicate the purpose.

- description (Optional): This provides more detailed documentation with Markdown support. It's a great place to include any context users need to use the endpoint effectively, such as business rules or usage tips.

- tags (Optional): This groups related operations in documentation. Our Magic Items API has endpoints for both inventory management and order processing, so we're using tags to keep things organized. Just make sure you use consistent casing throughout (Inventory versus inventory). If you're managing multiple APIs, try to keep the same casing standards across all of them.

- operationId (Optional but recommended): This is a unique identifier that's super helpful for code generation. Many tools use it to create clean SDK method names or define workflows. Each operationId must be unique across your entire specification.

- parameters (Conditional): This defines the inputs for your endpoint – things such as path, query, or header parameters. It's required for POST/PUT/PATCH requests but optional for others. We're using $ref to point to our components section for consistency (we'll cover the $ref keyword in more detail later).

- responses (Required): This declares all the possible outcomes when someone calls this operation. For good documentation and tool support, make sure you document all potential 4xx/5xx error scenarios. It's also good practice to standardize error formats using components/responses.

Arazzo Specification

The Arazzo specification is a great new standard that complements OpenAPI by defining API workflows, basically sequences of related API calls that work together to accomplish specific business objectives. Released in 2024 by the OpenAPI Initiative, Arazzo lets developers document complex, multi-step API interactions in a machine-readable format (YAML or JSON). This makes it especially valuable for generating interactive documentation, enabling code generation, supporting automated testing, and providing clear guidance for AI-based API consumption. You can learn more at https://www.openapis.org/arazzo.

As you can see from our example, we've declared only the top-level elements of our operation, while keeping most of the details as references. This approach helps with the readability of our OAS document and keeps it clean. It also helps us define potentially reusable components in one place. Let's focus now on the details of the more complex elements of the *operation object*, starting with defining its request parameters.

The parameters object: configuring your API's inputs

In our previous discussion of the Magic Items store API, we introduced path and operation objects using the /items endpoint. Now, let's dig into the Parameter Object, which lets you define all the different ways users can customize their API requests beyond just the request body.

Parameter types and locations

OpenAPI gives you four different places to put parameters, which you specify using the in field:

- Path parameters (in: path): These are like the variable parts of your URL route, such as /items/{itemId}, where you identify a specific magical item:

```
parameters:
  - name: itemId
    in: path
    required: true  # Always required for path parameters
    description: Unique identifier of the magical item
    schema:
      type: string
```

Path parameters are always required, and they must appear in the path surrounded by curly braces. Use these sparingly; they should only be for truly essential resource identifiers. Also, remember not to put two consecutive path parameters one after another to maintain the readability and simplicity of your API.

- Query parameters (in: query): These are the extra bits you add to the URL after a question mark. They're perfect for filtering, sorting, and pagination:

```
parameters:
  - name: rarity
    in: query
    description: Filter items by rarity level
    required: false
    schema:
      type: string
      enum: [common, uncommon, rare, legendary]
```

Query parameters are your best friends for filtering – for example, when a customer only wants to see rare or legendary items that match their budget. When possible, avoid making them required. This makes your API more future-proof and backward compatible. If you later need to change how filtering works, you won't break existing clients.

- Header parameters (in: header): These are HTTP headers that come with the request. They're great for API keys, caching directives, or telling your API where the consumer is shopping from:

```
parameters:
  - name: X-Magical-Realm
    in: header
    description: Restrict search to a specific magical realm
    required: false
    schema:
      type: string
```

Try sticking with established HTTP headers when you can and avoid making up custom ones unless you really need to. This helps your API play nicely with existing tools and languages right out of the box. Custom headers really shine when you need to track events across a complex ecosystem.

- Cookie parameters (`in: cookie`): These are values passed in the `cookie` header, often used for keeping track of sessions:

```
parameters:
  - name: session-id
    in: cookie
    description: Session identifier
    schema:
      type: string
```

Parameter object fields

Each parameter object requires these mandatory fields:

- `name`: Case-sensitive identifier for the parameter
- `in`: Where it lives (path, query, header, or cookie)

Here are some optional fields that you'll definitely want to use:

- `description`: A human-readable explanation that can include Markdown. It is great for explaining to developers things such as what `potency_level` actually means for magical items.
- `required`: Whether the parameter is mandatory (defaults to `false`).
- `deprecated`: Flags parameters you're phasing out (defaults to `false`). For example, such as when you're transitioning from `spell_power` to the more precise `arcane_potency`.
- `schema`: Defines the parameter's data type and constraints using JSON Schema (we'll dive deep into this in *Chapter 11*).

Handling objects and arrays in parameters

Simple parameters are straightforward, but what if you need something more complex? For example, what if customers want to filter magical items by multiple properties at once?

```
parameters:
  - name: filter
    in: query
    description: Complex filter criteria
    schema:
      type: object
      properties:
```

```
    minPower:
      type: integer
    elementType:
      type: string
  style: deepObject  # Serializes as
filter[minPower]=5&filter[elementType]=fire
  explode: true
```

When designing APIs that need structured data in query parameters, OpenAPI gives you style and explode properties to control how things get formatted in the URL. The style property determines the format (such as form for simple key-value pairs, deepObject for nested properties with bracket notation, or pipeDelimited for pipe-separated values). The explode property controls whether arrays and objects generate separate parameter instances. With explode: true, something such as colors: ['red', 'blue'] becomes colors=red&colors=blue in the URL.

For our Magic Items store, these properties let us create sophisticated filtering options that balance power with URL readability. This means customers can easily search for, say, wands with fire elemental affinity and a minimum power level of 7, without requiring a complex request body.

While parameters manage all the URL and header-based data, many operations (especially POST, PUT, and PATCH) need more complex structures sent in the request payload. That's where the requestBody object comes in, which we'll explore next for our Magic Items store API.

The requestBody object: structuring your API's payloads

The requestBody object is where you define what data clients send to your API in operations such as POST, PUT, and PATCH. While parameters handle the simple stuff in URLs and headers, requestBody is designed for the complex, structured data that comes in the request payload. It's perfect for when your customers want to add that new enchanted battle axe to your inventory.

Basic structure and key fields

Here's what a typical requestBody definition looks like for our Magic Items store:

```
requestBody:
  description: Magical item to add to the inventory
  required: true
  content:
    application/json:
      schema:
        $ref: '#/components/schemas/MagicItemCreate'
```

Let's break down the key parts:

- `description`: This explains what the request body is for, helping developers understand they're adding a magical item to your inventory

- `required`: A simple boolean that tells you whether the request body is mandatory (it defaults to **false**, but really, you can't add an item without describing it!)

- `content`: This maps media types to their schema definitions, saying "here's what your data should look like in JSON format"

Multiple content types

Your API can be flexible and accept different content types for the same operation:

```
requestBody:
  content:
    application/json:
      schema:
        $ref: '#/components/schemas/MagicItemCreate'
    application/xml:
      schema:
        $ref: '#/components/schemas/MagicItemCreate'
    multipart/form-data:
      schema:
        $ref: '#/components/schemas/MagicItemUpload'
```

This flexibility is like having multilingual staff in your Magic Items store. Clients can speak their preferred language (format) while interacting with your API. Some clients may prefer the elegance of JSON, while other might still use XML. Each content type can optionally use different schema definitions, letting you optimize for each format's strengths, such as using `multipart/form-data` when a customer wants to upload an image of their new custom item.

This versatility is especially important for customer-centric APIs. When combined with proper content negotiation, your affordance-centric API (WADMM level 3, as we discussed earlier) can serve the same magical catalog in different formats for diverse needs: JSON for your web interface and CSV for data scientists analyzing your data in languages such as R.

The critical importance of examples

Examples are like the difference between reading a spell description and seeing it performed. They transform abstract schema definitions into concrete illustrations that show developers exactly what your API expects. Instead of just describing the properties of a potion, you show exactly how to structure one:

```
requestBody:
  content:
    application/json:
      schema:
        $ref: '#/components/schemas/PotionCreate'
      examples:
        healingPotion:
          summary: Basic healing potion
          value:
            name: "Minor Healing Potion"
            effect: "Restores 25 health points"
            duration: 30
            ingredients: ["Herbs", "Fairy Dust"]
        strengthPotion:
          summary: Strength enhancement potion
          value:
            name: "Giant's Strength"
            effect: "Increases strength by 50%"
            duration: 120
            ingredients: ["Troll Blood", "Mountain Herbs"]
```

Examples work like magic throughout your API lifecycle. They transform your technical specifications into practical guides, showing exactly what potion data should look like. Tools can use them to generate realistic mock responses, so your frontend developers can start building the shopping interface before the backend is even finished. Your test suites can leverage examples as baseline test cases, ensuring your implementation accepts valid data formats right from the start.

They also serve as known-good templates for request validation. Client libraries can use examples to generate model constructors with sensible defaults, and new developers joining your team can understand expected formats immediately without having to decipher complex schemas.

For our Magic Items store, well-crafted examples illustrate the precise structure of potions, wands, and scrolls, making it immediately clear how magical properties should be formatted. A good example is worth a thousand words of schema documentation, especially when explaining a difference such as the one between a "Wand of Fireballs" and a "Staff of Fireballs."

By designing your requestBody objects with comprehensive examples, you create a clear guide that helps clients understand exactly what data your Magic Items API expects. This improves the developer experience and reduces those frustrating integration errors that can turn a smooth shopping experience into a nightmare.

Just as requestBody defines what clients send to your API, the response object, which we'll explore next, defines what your API sends back, completing the request-response cycle that forms the foundation of your REST API communications.

The responses object: defining your API's output contracts

The responses object is where the real magic happens in OAS. It's the other half of the promise you make to your API consumers – if they send you a well-formed request, here's exactly what they'll get back. For our Magic Items store, properly defined responses ensure customers know exactly what to expect when they're browsing the catalog, adding a new item to their cart, or dealing with errors when a product is out of stock.

Key fields of the responses object

Each response in your responses map is defined using a responses object with these key ingredients:

- description (required): This is the only field you absolutely must include. It's a human-readable explanation of what the response means:

```
responses:
  '200':
    description: The magical item was successfully retrieved
  '404':
    description: The requested magical item could not be found
```

You can use Markdown formatting here, so feel free to add rich text, bullet points, or even tables to explain complex responses. It's perfect for describing the difference between a 404 "item not found" and a 403 "you're not powerful enough to view this artifact."

- `headers`: Here, you can define any special headers that might come back with the response. This is super useful for pagination (so shoppers can browse through pages of magical items), caching directives, or rate-limiting information:

```
headers:
  Cache-Control:
    description: Directives for caching mechanisms
    schema:
      type: string
      example: "max-age=3600, must-revalidate"
  ETag:
    description: Version identifier for the resource
    schema:
      type: string
      example: "W/\"12345\""
```

Just remember that if you define a `Content-Type` header here, it'll be ignored; this is determined by the content field instead.

- `content`: This maps media types to their response payload definitions. Just like with request bodies, you can specify different formats for your responses:

```
content:
  application/json:
    # Schema definition goes here
  application/xml:
    # Alternative schema for XML format
```

You can even use wildcards for media types, with specific definitions taking priority over general ones. So, if you define both `text/plain` and `text/*`, the `text/plain` definition wins when that specific format is requested.

- `links`: This defines potential links to other operations, enabling hypermedia capabilities. We'll dive deep into this in *Chapter 12*, when we talk about hypermedia APIs and how they can make navigating your Magic Items catalog feel intuitive and interconnected.

HTTP status codes in the responses map

In your responses map, you can use any valid HTTP status code, status code ranges (such as 4xx), or the default keyword as keys:

```
responses:
  '200':
    description: Successful retrieval of magical items
  '4XX':
    description: Client error
  '500':
    description: Server error
```

The importance of defining all possible responses

You should always document all possible responses for your API endpoints, not just the happy path. This is like a good guidebook that tells you not only how a spell works when cast perfectly, but also what might happen if something goes wrong.

Complete response definitions serve multiple purposes in your API design. They create a comprehensive contract that specifies all expected behaviors, giving consumers confidence in how your API will behave. Well-defined error responses help developers implement proper error handling, so they know exactly what to do when a customer tries to purchase an item without sufficient permissions.

Your documentation tools and SDK generators also work better with complete response definitions, enabling more accurate mock servers and client libraries. From a practical standpoint, clear response documentation saves developers hours of frustrating trial-and-error during integration. They'll know exactly what to expect when calling your Magic Items API.

For our store, this means documenting not just successful responses but also what happens when an item is out of stock, when a user lacks permission to view rare artifacts, or when someone tries to combine incompatible enchantments on a single item.

Why to avoid the default response

While OpenAPI includes the default response as a catch-all mechanism, we recommend staying away from it in most cases. Using default is like labelling a potion bottle with "miscellaneous effects" – it's not very helpful for the person drinking it!

There's often confusion about what default actually means. Some people think it covers only status codes you haven't explicitly defined, while others see it as covering entire ranges you haven't mentioned. This ambiguity makes your API contract less precise and can lead to misunderstandings.

APIs that rely heavily on default responses tend to be under-documented, leaving consumers guessing about possible outcomes. It also makes testing more difficult. It's much easier to create comprehensive test cases when you know exactly which status codes to expect.

Instead of using default, it's better to explicitly document each status code your API might return or use range definitions, such as 4XX and 5XX, for groups of similar responses. Your Magic Items store customers will appreciate knowing exactly what to expect!

Closing the communication loop

By thoroughly defining your API's responses, you complete the request-response communication contract. While requestBody objects define what your API expects to receive, response objects define what consumers can expect in return. Together, they form a comprehensive contract that reduces ambiguity and improves integration success rates.

Properly documented responses are particularly crucial for error conditions. Clear guidance helps developers build robust applications that gracefully handle exceptions.

Next, we'll explore how to document security requirements in OAS. The security object defines the authentication and authorization mechanisms that protect your API, ensuring that only authorized clients can access sensitive operations such as deleting items from your catalog.

The security object: protecting your API resources

The security object in OpenAPI defines how you protect your API's valuable resources from unauthorized access. Just as you wouldn't leave valuable items unsecured in your store, you shouldn't leave your API endpoints unprotected. You can set up security in two ways:

- **Global security**: This is the default protection applied across your entire API, defined at the root level of your OpenAPI document and applied to all operations by default.
- **Operation security**: These are special protections for specific endpoints. Defined at the operation level, they override global settings when you need different security for particular operations.

Here's how it looks in your OpenAPI document:

```
# Global security definition (applied to all endpoints)
security:
  - OAuth2: [read:items]
paths:
  /items:
    get:
      # Inherits global security
    post:
      # Override for this specific operation
      security:
        - OAuth2: [write:items]
```

In this example, we are defining global security for all the operations to be OAuth2 with a scope of read:items. Then, we are overriding the required scope for the POST operation on the /items resource collection to be write:items.

Understanding security requirements and scopes

The arrays in your security requirement object (such as [read:items] in the preceding example) define the permissions needed to access an endpoint. These scopes are permission identifiers specifying exactly what actions a client is allowed to perform.

For our Magic Items store, we might use scopes such as the following:

- read:items: Permission to view items in the catalog
- write:items: Permission to create or modify items
- admin:inventory: Permission to manage the entire inventory

An empty array ([]) means "no specific permissions needed for this scheme," while an empty security requirement object (security: []) makes an endpoint publicly accessible, like the public-facing parts of your store that anyone can access without authentication.

Multiple entries in the security array represent alternative security schemes (logical OR): "you can use either this credential OR that one," while multiple scopes within a scheme represent combined requirements (logical AND): "you need BOTH this permission AND that permission to access this resource."

Security schemes

Security schemes define the authentication mechanisms your API supports. These are declared in the `components/securitySchemes` section (which we'll cover in more detail later). OpenAPI supports several standard authentication methods:

API keys

These are simple tokens that identify the client, passed in headers, query parameters, or cookies:

```
components:
  securitySchemes:
    ApiKeyAuth:
      type: apiKey
      in: header
      name: X-API-Key
```

API keys are easy to implement but have limitations: they don't expire automatically, they grant all-or-nothing access, and if one gets stolen, it's hard to revoke without affecting all your legitimate users.

HTTP authentication

These are standard HTTP-based authentication methods, including `Basic` (encoded username/password) and `Bearer` (token-based) schemes:

```
components:
  securitySchemes:
    BasicAuth:
      type: http
      scheme: basic
    BearerAuth:
      type: http
      scheme: bearer
      bearerFormat: JWT
```

Basic authentication is straightforward but should only be used with HTTPS to prevent credentials from being intercepted. *Bearer* is commonly used with JWT tokens, which provide structure and validation capabilities for more secure access control.

OAuth 2.0

OAuth 2.0 offers a more sophisticated approach to API security:

```
components:
  securitySchemes:
    OAuth2:
      type: oauth2
      flows:
        authorizationCode:
          authorizationUrl: https://auth.magicitems.com/oauth/authorize
          tokenUrl: https://auth.magicitems.com/oauth/token
          refreshUrl: https://auth.magicitems.com/oauth/refresh
          scopes:
            read:items: Read magical items
            write:items: Create or modify items
            delete:items: Remove items from inventory
```

OAuth 2.0 provides multiple "flows" for different client types, token expiration, fine-grained scopes for permissions, and standardized token handling. It separates authentication (proving who you are) from authorization (what you're allowed to do) and supports refreshing access without requiring re-authentication.

OpenID Connect

Built as an identity layer on top of OAuth 2.0, OpenID Connect adds standardized authentication:

```
components:
  securitySchemes:
    OpenIDConnect:
      type: openIdConnect
      openIdConnectUrl: https://auth.magicitems.com/.well-known/openid-
configuration
```

OpenID Connect provides verified identity information about users through a well-defined token format (JWT) containing claims about the authenticated user. It's ideal when you need to know not just what permissions a user has, but who they actually are.

Why OAuth 2.0 is preferred for most APIs

For our Magic Items store (and as best practice in modern API design), we recommend OAuth 2.0 over simpler schemes. OAuth 2.0 gives you fine-grained permissions control. Store owners need full inventory management, while customers only need read access to available items. It also includes token expiration, so access isn't permanent. Tokens should expire to limit potential damage if they're stolen.

If a user's credentials are compromised, you can revoke their access without affecting other users. OAuth 2.0 also allows delegation without sharing credentials. Third-party applications can access a user's data without needing their password. It also supports standardized flows for various client types (web apps, mobile apps, server-to-server) with appropriate authentication mechanisms for each.

Securing your magical realm

Security isn't just a technical checkbox; it's a fundamental aspect of your API's design. By properly documenting security requirements in your OpenAPI specification, you create a clear contract that helps developers understand how to authenticate and what permissions they need for different operations in your Magic Items store.

Now that we've covered how to secure our Magic Items API, let's turn our attention to the components object – the central repository for reusable elements in your OpenAPI specification. This powerful feature allows you to define schemas, parameters, responses, and security schemes once and reference them throughout your API, promoting consistency and reducing duplication, just like having a standard reference that all your API elements can draw from.

The components object: your API's reusable building blocks

The components object is like your API's parts inventory – a central repository for storing reusable elements that you can reference throughout your OpenAPI specification. Instead of defining the same schema or parameter over and over, you define it once in components and reference it wherever you need it. This makes your API specification cleaner, more consistent, and easier to maintain.

```
components:
  schemas:
    MagicItem: { }
  parameters:
    RarityParameter: { }
  responses:
```

```
    NotFoundError: { }
  examples:
    SamplePotion: { }
  requestBodies:
    CreateItemRequest: { }
  headers:
    RateLimit: { }
  securitySchemes:
    OAuth2: { }
  links:
    GetRelatedItems: { }
  callbacks:
    ItemCreated: { }
```

The value of centralized definitions

Moving reusable elements to the components object gives you several major advantages in your API design. You get a single source of truth – when you need to update a component (such as adding a new property to your MagicItem schema), you only need to change it in one place, and the update applies everywhere it's referenced.

Your API specification becomes more concise since referencing a component takes much less space than duplicating its definition throughout your document. This makes your specification easier to understand and maintain.

For teams working on larger APIs (like our growing Magic Items store), centralized definitions make governance easier. You can ensure all endpoints consistently use the same error format or pagination parameters. The modular approach also improves readability by separating reusable components from their usage, making the specification easier to navigate.

Most OpenAPI tools provide specific features for managing and visualizing components, which can help you keep track of dependencies and ensure consistency across your API design.

Components and their references

While we've covered most component types in previous sections, let us clarify how they fit into the components object:

Headers defined in components are specifically for reuse in response definitions. Unlike parameter-defined headers, components/headers are referenced when you need the same header definition across multiple responses, such as rate limiting headers that appear in many endpoints.

Examples provide concrete illustrations of data structures. When defined in components, you can reuse them across multiple request bodies and responses, so your example potion doesn't need to be redefined for each endpoint that returns potions.

Callbacks define webhook-like patterns for asynchronous communication. In our Magic Items store, we might use callbacks when a rare item becomes available or when a custom enchantment is completed.

Links enable hypermedia capabilities in your API and will be explored in detail in *Chapter 12* on Hypermedia APIs. They'll help customers navigate between related magical items or follow a purchasing workflow.

Understanding $ref: the glue that binds components

The $ref keyword is what ties everything together – it's a JSON reference that points to component definitions, allowing you to use them throughout your API specification. For local references within the same document, it typically starts with #/, followed by the path to the referenced element:

```
/items:
  get:
    parameters:
      - $ref: '#/components/parameters/RarityFilter'
    responses:
      '200':
        description: A list of magical items
        content:
          application/json:
            schema:
              type: array
              items:
                $ref: '#/components/schemas/MagicItem'
      '404':
        $ref: '#/components/responses/NotFound'
```

You can also use external references by including the file path or URL before the fragment identifier:

```
$ref: './common.yaml#/components/parameters/userId'
```

This allows you to break larger specifications into multiple files or reference shared components across multiple APIs. This is perfect when you're expanding your Magic Items store with a separate API that shares some common data types.

Bringing it all together: the OAS structure

Through our exploration of the Magic Items store API, we've now covered all the major structural elements of an OpenAPI document: the `info` obje, which provides essential metadata; the `paths` object, which defines endpoints and operations; the `parameters` and `requestBody` objects, which specify inputs; the `responses` object, which defines outputs; the `security` object, which documents authentication requirements; and the `components` object, which houses reusable definitions.

Understanding this structure is crucial for creating effective API specifications. Each element plays a specific role in describing your API's capabilities and requirements, forming a complete description that both humans and machines can interpret. The structure isn't just about organization. It directly impacts how tools interact with your specification and how developers understand your API.

Now that we've examined the building blocks of OpenAPI, we're ready to explore a deeper concept: how OpenAPI functions not just as documentation but as a binding contract between API providers and consumers. In the next chapter, *Chapter 10*, we'll look at how the specification creates clear expectations, enables tooling that enforces those expectations, and ultimately builds trust in your API ecosystem.

Summary

In this chapter, we explored the foundations of **OpenAPI Specification (OAS)** and its fundamental components. We traced the evolution from Swagger to the standardized OpenAPI under the Linux Foundation, understanding why it has become essential in modern API development. Using our Magic Items store as a practical example, we examined the core structure of OAS documents: from the `info` object, which provides essential metadata, to the `paths` object, which defines endpoints and operations.

We dove into the key building blocks of an OpenAPI document, including parameters for configuring inputs, `requestBody` for structured payloads, `responses` for defining output contracts, security mechanisms for protecting resources, and `components` for creating reusable elements. Each section provided practical examples showing how these elements apply to real-world API design scenarios.

With this foundation in OpenAPI's structure and syntax, you're now prepared to explore how it functions as a living contract between API providers and consumers, which we'll cover in the next chapter.

Get This Book's PDF Version and Exclusive Extras

Scan the QR code (or go to packtpub.com/unlock). Search for this book by name, confirm the edition, and then follow the steps on the page.

Note: Keep your invoice handy. Purchases made directly from Packt don't require an invoice.

10

OpenAPI as a Contract: Best Practices and Implementation

Beyond documentation, OpenAPI serves as an executable contract for API development. This chapter explores practical implementation patterns, from contract validation to tool integration. You'll learn how to design intuitive APIs with consistent resources, error handling, and asynchronous operations while discovering how contract-first approaches transform team collaboration. In this chapter, we will talk about the following:

- OpenAPI as a contract for your API
- Best practices for using OpenAPI Specification

By the end of this chapter, you will be able to implement OpenAPI as a binding contract for your APIs and apply industry best practices for API design, including resource structuring, error handling, and asynchronous operations. You will also know how to leverage the OpenAPI ecosystem to transform your development workflow through contract-first approaches and automated tooling.

OpenAPI as a contract for your API

Remember when we talked about APIs as products in earlier chapters, and how important it is to treat API design as a contract between you and your users? Well, OpenAPI Specification is where that idea comes to life. It's not just documentation; it's your API contract in a format that both computers and humans can understand.

Think of your OpenAPI document as the official rulebook for your API. It clearly states what items customers can buy, how they can search the inventory, what information they need to provide when placing an order, and what responses they'll get back. Both your developers and your API users can rely on this contract to know exactly what to expect.

The beauty of OpenAPI is that once you've created this contract, it powers a whole toolkit of helpful solutions. Your single OAS document can generate interactive documentation that lets developers try out API calls right in their browser—imagine letting potential customers browse your Magic Items catalog before they even write a line of code. You can spin up mock servers that return example responses, so frontend developers can start building the shopping interface before the backend team has finished implementing inventory management.

When it's time to write code, the same OAS contract can generate client libraries in different programming languages, so users don't have to write boilerplate code to call your API. And for your own development team, it can generate server stubs that match the API design exactly, ensuring your implementation stays true to the contract.

Testing becomes much easier too. Your QA team can use the OAS contract to automatically generate test cases and validate that your API responses match what you promised. If someone accidentally changes an endpoint to return different data, automated tests will catch the contract violation before it affects your users.

This means everyone stays on the same page. The enchantment specialists who design new magical items, the inventory managers who track stock levels, and the customer-facing portal developers all work from the same contract. When a change is needed, such as adding a new "rarity score" field to each magical item, you update the OpenAPI contract first, and everyone can immediately see how it affects their part of the system.

By putting OpenAPI at the center of your API development process, you build trust with your users. They know exactly what to expect from your API and can rely on its consistency. This reliability is essential whether you're selling magical artifacts or any other type of API product. Users need to know they can depend on your contract before they build their systems around it.

In the following sections, we'll look at some practical tools and workflows that help you make the most of your OpenAPI-defined API contract throughout the development lifecycle.

OAS as your single source of truth

When we talk about a "single source of truth" in API development, we're tackling one of the biggest headaches teams face: keeping documentation, code, and expectations all lined up. OpenAPI Specification solves this problem by giving you one definitive, executable definition of your API contract.

Unlike traditional documentation that can drift away from what your code actually does (we've all been there!), an OAS document serves as the reference point that everyone can rely on: your developers, testers, product managers, and the people using your API. For our Magic Items store, this means when we define the /items endpoint in our specification, it's not just a suggestion or some documentation that might be outdated; it's a binding agreement that clearly states what parameters customers can use, what responses they'll get back, and what errors might pop up.

This precision eliminates those frustrating "but I thought it worked like this" conversations and creates a foundation where tools can automatically check that your API does exactly what you promised it would. The specification becomes the referee, ensuring your API delivers exactly what it promises throughout its lifecycle.

How OpenAPI implements the contract concept in practice

OpenAPI transforms abstract contract concepts into something you can actually enforce through precisely defined schemas, operations, and response patterns. Let's see how this works with our Magic Items store:

Let's say we define an endpoint such as /items/{itemId} in our OAS document with its operations, parameters, and responses:

```
/items/{itemId}:
  get:
    parameters:
      - name: itemId
        in: path
        required: true
        schema:
          type: string
          pattern: "^[a-zA-Z0-9-]+$"
    responses:
      '200':
        content:
```

```
        application/json:
          schema:
            $ref: '#/components/schemas/MagicItem'
    '404':
      $ref: '#/components/responses/NotFound'
```

When we do this, we don't only create documentation; we create a binding contract that clearly states the following:

- First, there are input requirements. The itemId parameter must be present (since we marked it as required: true) and must match the specified pattern. Any customer who sends invalid identifiers, such as item@123, is breaking the rules of the contract.

- Second, it provides output guarantees. Your API promises to return a MagicItem object for valid requests. If a developer builds a client expecting a price field because it's defined in the MagicItem schema, that field better be there!

- Third, it specifies error handling. The contract explicitly states which errors can occur (in this case, 404 if the item doesn't exist).

This contractual precision matters throughout the system. When adding a new item to the inventory, the POST operation contract defines exactly what properties are required. The shopping cart system relies on the contract to know how to request item details. And the ordering system can count on a consistent item structure across all endpoints.

This contract gets enforced through validation tools that can verify both requests and responses match the specification. If an API update accidentally changes the structure of MagicItem, contract validation tools immediately flag this as a breaking change, preventing the kind of silent failures that can cause major headaches with loosely defined APIs.

The great thing about OAS as a contract is that it's both human-readable and machine-enforceable, ensuring everyone, from your developers to business stakeholders, has a shared understanding of exactly what your API delivers.

Translating abstract API contracts into executable OAS documents

So, how do you actually move from abstract API requirements to a concrete OpenAPI contract? It's all about translating your business concepts and rules into structured OAS elements. Let's see how this works for our Magic Items store.

Imagine you have a business requirement that "Customers must be able to browse items by rarity (common, uncommon, rare, legendary)." In your OpenAPI document, this translates to the following:

```
paths:
  /items:
    get:
      parameters:
        - name: rarity
          in: query
          schema:
            type: string
            enum: [common, uncommon, rare, legendary]
            description: Filter items by their magical rarity
```

Now your API contract clearly states that customers can filter the items catalog by these specific rarity levels.

What about domain constraints? Say you have a rule that "Magic item prices must be positive numbers with up to 2 decimal places" (because who wants to deal with fractions of a gold coin?). This becomes a schema validation rule:

```
components:
  schemas:
    MagicItem:
      properties:
        price:
          type: number
          minimum: 0.01
          multipleOf: 0.01
          description: Item price in gold coins
```

Now your contract enforces that no one can set negative prices or use weird fractional values that your checkout system can't handle.

Security requirements get the same treatment. If "Only authenticated shop owners can discount items," you can translate this to OAS security definitions:

```
paths:
  /items/{itemId}/discount:
    post:
```

```
security:
  - OAuth2: [items:write]
requestBody:
  content:
    application/json:
      schema:
        properties:
          discountPercentage:
            type: number
            minimum: 1
            maximum: 75
```

Even complex business rules can be represented. If "When an item is purchased, the inventory count must be updated," this becomes a documented API behavior with appropriate status codes:

```
paths:
  /orders:
    post:
      responses:
        '201':
          description: Purchase successful
        '409':
          description: Item no longer in stock
          content:
            application/json:
              schema:
                $ref: '#/components/schemas/OutOfStockError'
```

What makes these OAS translations so powerful is that they're "executable"—tools can actually enforce these rules. Validators can check that request payloads match your specified schemas, so no one tries to discount an item by 200%. API gateways can enforce the security policies you've defined, keeping unauthorized users from messing with your prices.

Your test frameworks can verify that your implementation behaves exactly as promised in the responses section. And you can spin up mock servers that simulate your entire API based solely on the contract, without writing a line of backend code.

For our Magic Items store, this means a developer building a shopping cart feature doesn't need to guess how to filter items or what errors might occur during checkout. They can just look at your OAS document for clear, definitive answers, and even better, they can use tools that directly act on this information to generate client code, validate requests, or simulate responses.

By translating your abstract requirements into concrete OAS elements, you create a contract that's not just documentation; it's an actionable blueprint that drives your entire API lifecycle.

Key elements that make OAS effective as a binding agreement

What exactly transforms OpenAPI from just another documentation format into a real, binding contract? There are several critical elements that give it this power. Let's see how they work in our Magic Items store API.

Schema definitions with validation rules are perhaps the most important part. In the components/ schemas section, you precisely define data structures in a way that tools can enforce:

```
components:
  schemas:
    MagicWand:
      type: object
      required: [name, wandType, powerLevel]
      properties:
        name:
          type: string
          minLength: 3
          maxLength: 50
        wandType:
          type: string
          enum: [oak, elder, phoenix, dragon]
        powerLevel:
          type: integer
          minimum: 1
          maximum: 10
```

This schema doesn't just describe what MagicWand looks like. It also creates rules that must be followed. Every MagicWand in your store must have a name (between 3 and 50 characters), a type that's one of your approved materials, and a power level from 1-10. Your API has to reject any MagicWand submission that breaks these rules, which means both you and your API users are bound by these constraints. We'll dive deeper into schema definitions in *Chapter 11*.

Throughout your OpenAPI document, you can clearly mark what's required versus what's optional. This distinction is crucial for a binding contract. Everyone needs to know exactly what's mandatory:

```
/orders:
  post:
    requestBody:
      required: true
      content:
        application/json:
          schema:
            type: object
            required: [itemId, quantity]
            properties:
              itemId:
                type: string
              quantity:
                type: integer
                minimum: 1
              giftWrap:
                type: boolean
                default: false
```

Here, your contract says that customers must provide an order request body, and within it, they absolutely need to include which item they want and how many. The giftWrap option is nice to have, but it is not required. It defaults to false if not specified. This clarity eliminates those annoying "but I didn't know I needed to provide that" conversations.

Response status codes and structures are another key part of the binding agreement. OpenAPI encourages you to spell out all possible responses:

```
/items/{itemId}:
  get:
    responses:
      '200':
        description: Successful retrieval of magic item
        content:
          application/json:
            schema:
              $ref: '#/components/schemas/MagicItem'
```

```
          '404':
            description: Item not found
            content:
              application/json:
                schema:
                  $ref: '#/components/schemas/Error'
```

This part of your contract commits you to return either a valid `MagicItem` or a standardized `Error` structure—nothing else is allowed. Customers can confidently build their shopping interfaces knowing exactly what to expect from your API.

Parameter constraints let you set precise boundaries on what inputs your API will accept:

```
/spells:
  get:
    parameters:
      - name: elemType
        in: query
        schema:
          type: string
          enum: [fire, water, earth, air]
      - name: minPower
        in: query
        schema:
          type: integer
          minimum: 1
          maximum: 10
```

This guarantees that when customers are filtering spells, they can only use valid elemental types (fire, water, earth, air) and power levels between 1 and 10. Your implementation must enforce these constraints. You can't suddenly decide to accept "lightning" as an element if it's not in the contract!

Examples and default values provide concrete illustrations that make expected behavior crystal clear:

```
/potions:
  get:
    responses:
      '200':
        content:
```

```
application/json:
  example:
    - id: "health-potion"
      name: "Minor Healing Potion"
      effect: "Restores 25 health points"
      price: 50
```

These examples give everyone a shared understanding of what your API responses should look like. They serve as reference points that your implementation should match, making your contract much clearer than abstract descriptions alone.

What makes OpenAPI truly powerful as a binding agreement is that all these elements are machine-readable. Validation tools can automatically check that both customer requests and your server responses follow the rules. For our Magic Items store, this means we can automatically ensure that every spell, potion, wand, and magical artifact follows the promised structure, creating confidence throughout your magical marketplace.

With OpenAPI established as your API's binding contract, the question becomes: how do you leverage this machine-readable agreement throughout your development process? The true power of OAS emerges when you connect it to the ecosystem of tools designed to understand and act on your design documents. Let's explore how different types of OAS-powered tools can transform each stage of your workflow, from designing your Magic Items catalog to testing and deploying your final API.

OAS-powered tools across your workflow

One of the best reasons to use OpenAPI Specification is all the cool tools you get access to. When your API is defined in OAS format, it becomes way more than just documentation. It powers automation throughout your entire development process.

From showing your Magic Items API to stakeholders in an interactive format to generating server code that matches your design exactly, these tools can save you tons of time while making sure your implementation stays true to what you promised. Let's look at how different types of tools can help you at each stage of building your API.

Documentation generators: bringing your API to life

Documentation generators take your dry OpenAPI specification and transform it into interactive, user-friendly documentation that people will actually want to use. Instead of handing your API users a technical spec, you're giving them an interactive playground where they can explore how everything works.

For our Magic Items store, a documentation generator would take our /items endpoint definition and turn it into an attractive web page where developers can see all the available query parameters (such as filtering by rarity or magical properties), check out the expected response format, and even try out example responses showing what items look like. This lets a developer understand not just what endpoints are available, but exactly how to use them without having to dig through code or bother other team members with questions.

These documentation tools do all kinds of helpful things. They'll show syntax-highlighted request and response examples, so patterns are easy to spot. Many include "Try it" consoles where developers can test endpoints right from the documentation page—perfect for when a customer wants to see if they can filter items by both rarity and magical element before writing any code.

They'll organize your API with collapsible sections, so users aren't overwhelmed by all your endpoints at once. Most support Markdown, so you can add rich explanations and guidance, such as special notes about how potion effects stack or wand compatibility. You can usually customize the theme to match your brand's style, so your magical marketplace documentation feels like part of your overall experience.

The real magic of documentation generators is that they keep your docs and implementation perfectly in sync. When someone on your team adds a new field to the MagicItem schema or updates the authentication requirements, the documentation automatically shows these changes the next time it's generated. This solves that annoying problem of outdated documentation that frustrates so many API users.

Documentation generation tools

Among the many solutions available for generating documentation from OpenAPI specifications, a few notable examples include **SwaggerUI**, which embeds a "Try it out" console for live API testing; **Redoc**, which delivers a responsive, three-column layout ideal for complex APIs; and **GitBook**, which produces rich, wiki-style guides with built-in team collaboration. While these are just a few examples from a broad market, the ideal choice will depend on your specific project needs, whether for interactivity, design, or collaboration. Ultimately, these tools automate the creation of high-quality, developer-friendly documentation directly from your spec.

Mock servers: development without waiting

Mock servers are like conjuring an illusion of your API before you've written any real backend code. These tools read all the paths, operations, parameters, and response schemas in your OAS document and create a functioning fake API that returns realistic-looking data matching your schemas.

For our Magic Items store, a mock server would let your frontend team start building the shopping interface without waiting for the backend team to finish implementing inventory management. When a developer sends a GET request to /items?rarity=legendary, the mock server returns a collection of legendary items with all the properties defined in your MagicItem schema: names, descriptions, magical properties, all filled with realistic sample data.

This approach delivers several big benefits. Your teams can work in parallel: frontend developers don't have to wait for the backend to be finished before they start building. You can prototype and validate your API design early, finding out if it actually meets everyone's needs before investing a lot of development time.

Mock servers also give you realistic testing environments for development and QA work. You can set up demonstration environments to show stakeholders how the API will work, helping them visualize the final product. You can even configure them to simulate specific edge cases or error scenarios that might be hard to trigger in a real environment, such as what happens when a legendary item is out of stock.

By using a mock server based on your OAS document, your team can spot issues with the API design early. Frontend developers might realize they need additional item properties or different filtering options, letting you refine your API design before you've invested heavily in implementation.

Mock server generation tools

For solutions that create mock servers from OpenAPI specifications, **Stoplight Prism** offers real-time request validation and dynamic response generation; **Microcks** provides a comprehensive platform for running and managing mocks and virtual services; and **WireMock** delivers powerful request matching, response templating, and extension capabilities. These examples illustrate a few options to consider—each of these tools is open source, and the best fit will depend on your setup, customization needs, and workflow integration.

Validators: ensuring contract compliance

Validators are like quality control inspectors for your API. They check that both your OAS document itself and your actual API implementation comply with the OpenAPI specification and any custom rules you've set up. They help maintain quality by catching issues before they affect your users.

For our Magic Items store, validators would verify that our OAS document is structurally correct and that our implemented API actually matches what we've defined. If a developer accidentally returns a non-standard HTTP status code or forgets to include the "rarity" field in item responses, validators will flag these inconsistencies early in the development process.

Validators do much more than basic checking. They'll make sure your OAS document syntax is correct and follows the OpenAPI structure. You can set up custom rulesets to enforce your organization's API standards, such as requiring all endpoints to have examples or making sure error responses follow a consistent format.

They can check your actual running API by comparing real responses against the schemas you defined. Many validators integrate with CI/CD pipelines to catch issues automatically whenever code is committed or deployed. They also provide detailed error reports that help developers understand and fix issues quickly.

By building validators into your workflow, you enforce your API contract throughout development. This shifts quality control earlier in the process, finding issues during development rather than after deployment, when they're much more expensive to fix and might have already frustrated your customers.

OpenAPI validation tools

To maintain high quality and consistency in your API definitions, consider the following open source validators. **Spectral** is a flexible, rule-based linter that comes with built-in rulesets and allows you to define custom checks to enforce style and consistency across your API definitions. **Open Policy Agent** enables policy-as-code by letting you write sophisticated validation and security rules in Rego, so you can enforce organizational governance within your CI/CD pipelines. These tools can be combined or extended to enforce quality, security, and governance for your API specifications.

Code generators: from definition to implementation

Code generators are like magical crafting tools that transform your OpenAPI specification into real, working code for both servers and clients. Instead of writing everything by hand, these tools can instantly create baseline implementations that match your API design exactly.

For our Magic Items store, a code generator could take our OAS document and produce a complete server implementation with all the endpoints we've defined. It would automatically set up request validation (so nobody can submit invalid magic items), proper response formatting, and consistent error handling. On the client side, it could create ready-to-use libraries in JavaScript, Python, or other languages that your API users can simply import into their projects. No more figuring out how to format requests or parse responses!

Code generators deliver some seriously impressive benefits:

- They dramatically speed up development by handling all the repetitive coding tasks, letting your developers focus on the unique business logic instead of writing boilerplate code.
- They ensure consistent implementation patterns across all your APIs. If you're building both a Magic Items API and a Spell Books API, the generated code keeps them consistent.
- They create type-safe client libraries that perfectly match your API contract, so developers get autocomplete and compile-time error checking.
- They build request validation directly into the server code, automatically rejecting invalid requests before they even reach your business logic.
- They significantly reduce the risk of implementation errors or contract violations, since the generated code is directly based on your specification.

By generating code straight from your OAS document, you're ensuring that what gets built actually matches what you designed. This tackles one of the most common API headaches—the frustrating mismatch between documentation and actual behavior.

Gateway configurations: managing API traffic

API gateways act as the front door to your API, handling important cross-cutting concerns such as authentication, rate limiting, and request routing. Many modern gateways can read your OpenAPI specification and automatically configure themselves based on your defined API contract.

For our Magic Items store, a gateway configuration tool might use our OAS security definitions to implement API key validation for the /orders endpoint, while keeping the /items catalog endpoint publicly accessible. It could enforce rate limits (so nobody can overwhelm your inventory system with too many requests) and route different types of requests to the appropriate backend services.

Gateway configuration tools handle several critical functions:

- They automatically set up authentication and authorization based on your OAS security schemes, so access control works exactly as designed

- They validate incoming requests according to your parameter definitions and schemas, rejecting invalid requests before they hit your servers

- They transform and format responses to match your defined schemas, ensuring consistent output even if backend systems change

- They manage traffic with rate limiting and quota enforcement, protecting your API from abuse or overload

- They provide analytics and monitoring for API usage, giving you visibility into how customers are using your API

By configuring your gateway directly from your OAS document, you ensure the operational aspects of your API align perfectly with your design, reducing the risk of security gaps or configuration errors.

Testing frameworks: verifying contract compliance

Testing frameworks use your OpenAPI specification as a blueprint for automated tests that verify your API behaves exactly as defined. Instead of writing test cases manually, these tools generate them directly from your OAS document and run them against your API.

For our Magic Items store, a testing framework might create tests to verify that each endpoint returns the expected status codes and response formats. It would check that our /items/{itemId} endpoint correctly returns 404 when a customer requests a non-existent magical artifact, or that our pagination parameters for browsing the catalog work exactly as documented.

These testing frameworks provide several key advantages:

- They automatically generate comprehensive tests based on your API contract, saving enormous amounts of time and ensuring complete coverage

- They verify all your defined operations and responses, not just the happy paths that developers typically focus on when writing manual tests

- They catch regressions or breaking changes early, before they affect your customers or integration partners

- They validate both normal scenarios and error conditions, ensuring your API handles problems gracefully

- They integrate with CI/CD pipelines for continuous verification, so every code change is automatically tested against your API contract

By incorporating contract-based testing into your development workflow, you continuously verify that your implementation honors the promises made in your API contract. This builds confidence in your API and helps maintain the trust of your customers over time.

This rich ecosystem of OAS-powered tools transforms your API specification from a static document into a dynamic asset that drives quality and efficiency throughout your API lifecycle. From interactive documentation and mock servers to code generation and automated testing, these tools ensure consistency between design and implementation while accelerating development and reducing errors.

However, to fully capitalize on these capabilities, we need to move validation earlier in the development process. Let's explore how OpenAPI enables a shift-left approach to API quality, catching potential issues before they impact your users or integration partners.

API testing tools

To validate your implementation against your OpenAPI specifications, you can use multiple tools. For example, **Prism** can mock and validate HTTP requests and responses in real time according to your spec, while **Schemathesis** performs property-based and fuzz testing by generating smart test cases from OpenAPI files. These open source tools help ensure your API consistently matches its specification.

Shifting left: catching API issues before they happen

In traditional API development, validation often happens way too late—after code is written, during QA testing, or worse, when your customers report issues in production. "Shifting left" means moving these validation activities earlier in the development lifecycle, catching problems when they're cheapest and easiest to fix.

OpenAPI Specification is the perfect foundation for this approach because it gives you a machine-readable contract that can be automatically validated at multiple stages. With your Magic Items store API defined in OAS format, you can check that both your design decisions and implementation choices honor your API contract long before any customer tries to order a magical artifact that doesn't match your schema.

Detecting contract violations before deployment

Contract validation should start during the design phase before you write a single line of code. You can verify that your OAS document itself is structurally sound and follows best practices:

```
# Conceptual: Validating the contract itself using spectral
spectral lint magic-items-api.yaml
```

Think of this as checking your magical blueprint before construction begins. If your OAS document has issues, such as circular references or missing required fields, it's much better to catch them now than after you've built your entire API.

During development, you can incorporate runtime validation to catch implementation discrepancies:

- **Request validation** ensures all incoming data meets your defined constraints. This prevents invalid submissions, such as a customer trying to add a "Legendary" potion with no effect description or a wand with an invalid material type.

- **Response validation** verifies that your implementation returns data matching your schema definitions. It catches issues such as returning a 204 status when your contract specifies 200 or forgetting to include the "rarity" field in item responses.

These validation layers form a protective spell around your API, catching structural issues before they reach your customers.

Test everything against your contract

Your test suite should use your OAS document as an executable test specification rather than creating tests from scratch:

- Generate comprehensive test cases directly from your endpoints and schemas
- Verify the correct handling of edge cases defined in your contract
- Ensure security requirements are properly enforced
- Test that error responses match your defined schemas

This means automatically testing that item categories follow the defined enumeration values (no made-up categories such as "ultra-legendary"), price ranges respect minimum and maximum constraints, and appropriate errors are returned when business rules are violated, such as when someone tries to order more invisibility cloaks than you have in stock.

Building validation gates in your pipeline

Embed contract validation as automated quality gates in your deployment pipeline:

1. **Specification validation**: First, verify that your OAS document is correct and complete
2. **Static analysis**: Check for breaking changes against previous API versions
3. **Contract testing**: Deploy to a test environment and verify all endpoints behave as specified
4. **Schema validation**: Ensure all responses match your defined schemas

These gates act like barriers that prevent contract violations from reaching production, where they could break client applications or disrupt customers trying to browse and purchase items from your store.

This GitHub Actions workflow enforces API contract quality by linting your OpenAPI document, detecting breaking changes, validating live endpoints against the spec, and checking response schemas before merging to the main branch:

```
name: API Contract Validation
on:
  push:
    branches: [ main ]
jobs:
  validate-contract:
    runs-on: ubuntu-latest
    steps:
      - name: Checkout code
        uses: actions/checkout@v3
      - name: Set up Node.js
        uses: actions/setup-node@v3
        with:
          node-version: '16'
      - name: Install dependencies
        run: npm ci
      # 1. Specification validation with Spectral
      - name: Lint OpenAPI spec
        run: npx @stoplight/spectral lint api/magic-items-api.yaml
      # 2. Static analysis (breaking-change detection) with openapi-
changes
      - name: Check for breaking changes
```

```
            run: npx openapi-changes api/openapi-prev.yaml api/openapi.yaml
    --fail-on breaking
        # 3. Contract testing with Prism
        - name: Start test environment
            run: docker-compose -f docker-compose.test.yml up -d
        - name: Validate contract with Prism
            run: npx @stoplight/prism validate api/magic-items-api.yaml
    http://localhost:3000
        # 4. Schema validation in responses with Schemathesis
        - name: Validate response schemas
            run: npx schemathesis run api/magic-items-api.yaml --checks all
        - name: Tear down test environment
            if: always()
            run: docker-compose -f docker-compose.test.yml down
```

In the preceding example, we do the following:

- **Lint OpenAPI spec**: Spectral checks `api/magic-items-api.yaml` for style, formatting, and completeness issues

- **Check for breaking changes: openapi-changes** compares `api/openapi-prev.yaml` with the current spec and fails the job on any breaking changes

- **Validate contract with Prism**: Prism spins up the test environment via Docker Compose and sends real requests to `http://localhost:3000`, ensuring responses match the spec.

- **Validate response schemas**: Schemathesis runs property-based tests against live endpoints to confirm all API responses conform to defined schemas

Embedding these validation gates in your CI pipeline blocks merges on any contract violation limiting errors, breaking changes, or schema mismatches, preventing faulty API updates from reaching production.

By implementing these validation layers, your API remains reliable and consistent. Each validation step builds confidence, reducing bugs and ensuring that customers can depend on your contract's promises without any unexpectation.

By implementing OAS validation throughout the development lifecycle, you transform your API contract from mere documentation into an executable quality standard. This shift-left approach catches issues early: during design, development, testing, and deployment, ensuring your Magic Items API consistently meets its promises.

But beyond these technical improvements, OAS adoption has profound effects on how teams collaborate and deliver APIs. Let's explore how embracing OpenAPI Specification transforms team dynamics, standardizes design decisions, and accelerates the entire development process.

Transforming teams with OAS adoption

Now that we've covered the technical benefits of OpenAPI Specification and its powerful validation tools, let's talk about something even more important: how OAS transforms the way your teams work together.

Beyond all the technical advantages, OAS acts as a catalyst for organizational change, breaking down those traditional walls between your business folks, developers, and operations teams. It gives everyone a common language to discuss API design and development, creating measurable standards that align your teams around shared goals.

Making API design decisions clear and consistent

Have you ever been in a situation where people argued about naming conventions or parameter patterns? OpenAPI helps solve that problem by providing objective standards for judging API quality.

For our Magic Items store, this means every part of your API follows consistent patterns:

- **Consistent resource naming**: All your inventory items follow the same logical pattern (/items, /orders) rather than a confusing mix of approaches such as some endpoints using /get-artifacts while others use /magicItemSearch
- **Predictable parameter patterns**: Filtering works the same way across all endpoints, so the rarity and minPower query parameters behave identically whether your customers are browsing for wands or potions
- **Uniform error handling**: When someone submits an invalid order or requests a magical artifact you don't have in stock, the error format stays consistent, making it easier for developers to handle errors properly

The beauty of these standards is that they're enforceable through automated validation. This removes those subjective debates about API design. Instead of arguing about whether a parameter should be called itemType or just type, your teams can simply reference the established patterns in your OAS document.

Getting everyone speaking the same language

OAS creates a universal translation layer between your different team members. Your product managers write user stories about magical inventory features. Your designers create frontend mockups for browsing magical items. Backend developers implement inventory databases and business logic. Frontend developers build the customer-facing catalog interface. And QA engineers verify that the entire purchasing flow works correctly.

Without OpenAPI, each group might interpret requirements differently. But with a shared OAS contract, your product manager's "filterable inventory" becomes concrete query parameters, your designer's "item details" screen maps to specific response fields, and your developers implement exactly what QA will test.

This shared understanding reduces the "telephone game" effect, where requirements gradually change as they pass between teams. When everyone can refer to the same contract, they're all working from the same playbook.

Speeding up development with contract-first practices

With contract-first development, your teams define the OAS document before writing any implementation code:

Business Requirements → OAS Contract → Implementation

Taking a contract-first approach really boosts how efficiently your team can work. By separating the frontend and backend tasks, your frontend developers can build the shopping interface using the API contract, while backend developers focus on the item catalog. No one has to wait around for someone else to finish first. The OpenAPI document sets the ground rules for what "done" means: if the API passes validation against the contract, it's ready. This takes the guesswork and debate out of whether a feature is complete, and it means both sides are much more likely to integrate smoothly the first time, since they're building to the same spec.

There are bigger picture benefits too. Having a shared contract helps all the stakeholders. Everyone, from product managers to QA and DevOps, speaks the same language and follows the same patterns. As your API ecosystem grows and more teams get involved, this consistency is a lifesaver, especially when you're handling things such as partner integrations or third-party extensions. OpenAPI stops being just a technical document and becomes a collaboration tool that keeps everyone aligned as your digital marketplace gets more complex.

Best practices for using OpenAPI

Now that we understand how OpenAPI serves as a contract for your API, the question becomes: how do we create OAS documents that really shine? While any syntactically valid OpenAPI document can describe an API, not all specs are equally effective as contracts. Creating a truly valuable API specification requires thoughtful design choices, careful organization, and attention to detail.

In this section, we'll explore practical best practices for creating OpenAPI documents that serve as clear, consistent, and effective contracts. We'll continue using our Magic Items store example to illustrate these practices, showing how proper API design can make the difference between a frustrating integration experience and a delightful one.

From designing intuitive resource structures and leveraging reusable components to implementing common patterns such as pagination and filtering, we'll address the real-world challenges you'll likely face when designing APIs. We'll also cover documentation techniques, error handling strategies, versioning approaches, and security best practices that will help you create APIs that aren't just functional, but truly developer-friendly.

By applying these best practices to your own OpenAPI documents, you'll create specifications that serve as reliable contracts, enabling all the benefits we discussed in previous sections while avoiding common pitfalls that can undermine your API's usability and maintainability. Whether you're defining endpoints for browsing magical artifacts or processing enchanted orders, these practices will help ensure your API is both powerful and pleasant to use.

Designing clear and consistent API structures

In the world of API design, clarity and consistency aren't just nice-to-have features; they're absolutely essential for creating APIs that developers can quickly understand and effectively use. A well-structured API reduces the learning curve, minimizes integration errors, and creates a more intuitive experience for everyone. Let's explore how to design APIs that follow consistent patterns and conventions, all documented clearly in your OpenAPI Specification.

Organizing resources logically

The foundation of any well-designed API is the logical organization of resources. Your resources should represent the key business entities in your domain and be structured in a way that reflects their natural relationships.

For our Magic Items store, we need to identify our primary resources: items, categories, orders, and users. Each of these represents something important in our magical marketplace. Within items, we have different types: potions, wands, scrolls, and other magical artifacts, that share common properties but also have their own unique characteristics.

Here's how we might structure these resources in our OpenAPI definition:

```
paths:
  /items:
    description: Collection of all magical items in the store
    # Operations on the collection
  /items/{itemId}:
    description: Individual magical item identified by its unique ID
    # Operations on a specific item
  /categories:
    description: Types of magical items (potions, wands, scrolls, etc.)
    # Operations on the collection of categories
  /categories/{categoryId}:
    description: A specific category of magical items
    # Operations on a specific category
  /items/{itemId}/effects:
    description: Magical effects associated with a specific item
    # Operations related to a specific item's effects
```

This structure follows the principle of resource hierarchies, where related resources are nested logically. The /items endpoint represents the collection of all magical items, while /items/{itemId} represents a specific item, such as that legendary staff of fireballs. The relationship between items and their effects is expressed through the /items/{itemId}/effects nested path.

Establishing consistent URL patterns

Consistency in URL patterns is crucial for making your API predictable and easy to use. Developers should be able to guess endpoint URLs based on patterns they've already learned.

For our Magic Items store, we'll follow these URL pattern conventions:

- Use plural nouns for collection resources (e.g., /items, not /item)
- Use concrete, specific names rather than ambiguous terms (e.g., /potions is clearer than /products)
- Use hyphens for multi-word resource names (e.g., /brewing-ingredients)

- Use lowercase for all URL segments
- Use resource identifiers in path parameters (e.g., /items/{itemId})

This approach maintains consistency while allowing for resource-specific endpoints when needed. We could alternatively structure this using a category parameter (/items?category=potion), but dedicated endpoints can be more intuitive and way easier to use for primary resource types. Remember, we're aiming for level 3 of WADMM, creating an API based on the actions your customers need to perform.

Defining meaningful operations

Each endpoint should support a clear set of operations using appropriate HTTP methods. The operations should align with the resource's nature and follow REST principles.

Here's how we define operations for our Magic Items store:

```
paths:
  /items:
    get:
      summary: List all magical items
      description: Returns a paginated list of magical items with optional
filtering
      operationId: listItems
      # Parameters, responses, etc.
    post:
      summary: Create a new magical item
      description: Adds a new item to the magical inventory
      operationId: createItem
      # Request body, responses, etc.
  /items/{itemId}:
    get:
      summary: Get a specific magical item
      description: Returns detailed information about a magical item
      operationId: getItem
      # Parameters, responses, etc.
    put:
      summary: Update a magical item
      description: Replaces all properties of an existing magical item
      operationId: updateItem
      # Parameters, request body, responses, etc.
```

```
patch:
  summary: Partially update a magical item
  description: Updates specific properties of an existing magical item
  operationId: patchItem
  # Parameters, request body, responses, etc.
delete:
  summary: Remove a magical item
  description: Deletes a magical item from the inventory
  operationId: deleteItem
  # Parameters, responses, etc.
```

For each operation, we've included a clear summary and description and assigned a unique operation ID that follows consistent naming conventions. These operation IDs are crucial for code generation and maintaining consistency in your API.

By organizing your resources logically, establishing consistent URL patterns, and defining meaningful operations, you create an API that feels intuitive and predictable. Developers working with your Magic Items API will appreciate how quickly they can understand and integrate with your endpoints, whether they're listing available potions or placing an order for that perfect enchanted wand.

Establishing naming conventions

Consistent naming conventions make your API feel intuitive and reduce the mental effort developers need to use it. This becomes especially important when you're managing multiple APIs across your organization. Let's apply consistent naming to all elements of our API: paths, operations, parameters, and schemas.

For our Magic Items store, we'll follow these naming conventions:

- Use **camelCase** for operationIds (e.g., `listItems`, `createPotion`)
- Use **snake_case** for parameter names and schema properties
- Use **PascalCase** for schema names (e.g., `MagicItem`)
- Use **Hyphenated-Pascal-Case** for header names (e.g. `Content-Type`)
- Prefix query parameters with their purpose (e.g., `filter_rarity`)
- Use consistent verbs in operation IDs (`list`, `get`, `create`, etc.)

Here's how these conventions look in a schema definition:

```
components:
  schemas:
    MagicItem:
      type: object
      properties:
        id:
          type: string
          readOnly: true
          description: Unique identifier for the item
        name:
          type: string
          description: The name of the magical item
        rarity:
          type: string
          enum: [common, uncommon, rare, very_rare, legendary, artifact]
          description: The rarity classification of the item
        magic_type:
          type: string
          description: The type of magic imbued in the item
```

Notice how all property names use **snake case** and have clear, descriptive names. The schema itself uses **PascalCase** (`MagicItem`). These conventions make your API more predictable and easier to remember.

Creating consistent resource patterns

To make your API feel cohesive, establish patterns for common operations that you'll use across different resource types. For example, all collection endpoints should support similar filtering, sorting, and pagination mechanics.

For our Magic Items store, here's how we maintain consistency across different types of magical inventory:

```
paths:
  /potions:
    get:
      summary: List all potions
      parameters:
```

```
          - $ref: '#/components/parameters/Page'
          - $ref: '#/components/parameters/PageSize'
          - name: filter_effect
            in: query
            schema:
              type: string
          - name: sort_price
            in: query
            schema:
              type: string
              enum: [asc, desc]
              default: asc
      # Responses, etc.
  /wands:
    get:
      summary: List all wands
      parameters:
        - $ref: '#/components/parameters/Page'
        - $ref: '#/components/parameters/PageSize'
        - name: filter_wood_type
          in: query
          schema:
            type: string
        - name: sort_price
          in: query
          schema:
            type: string
            enum: [asc, desc]
            default: asc
      # Responses, etc.
```

Notice how we reuse common pagination parameters via $ref and maintain consistent naming for filter and sort parameters. Even though potions and wands have different properties (effects versus wood types), the patterns for interacting with them remain consistent.

Pagination, filtering, and sorting

Consistent handling of pagination, filtering, and sorting is essential for collection resources. Define these parameters as reusable components to ensure consistency across your API.

For our Magic Items store, we could define common parameters like this:

```
components:
  parameters:
    Page:
      name: page
      in: query
      description: Page number for pagination
      schema:
        type: integer
        default: 1
        minimum: 1
    PageSize:
      name: page_size
      in: query
      description: Number of items per page
      schema:
        type: integer
        default: 20
        minimum: 1
        maximum: 100
    SortDirection:
      name: sort_direction
      in: query
      description: Direction to sort results
      schema:
        type: string
        enum: [asc, desc]
        default: asc
```

These parameters can be referenced in any collection endpoint, ensuring that paging through potions works exactly the same way as paging through wands or scrolls. Your developers will appreciate this consistency when building features such as browsing and searching your magical inventory.

Designing clear and consistent API structures is fundamental to creating a positive developer experience. By organizing resources logically, establishing consistent URL patterns, defining meaningful operations, and applying consistent naming conventions, you create an API that's intuitive and easy to use.

For our Magic Items store, we've seen how to structure different types of magical items while maintaining consistency in how they're accessed and manipulated. This approach makes our API more predictable and reduces the learning curve for developers integrating with our service.

In the next section, we'll explore how to leverage reusable components in OpenAPI to further enhance consistency and reduce duplication in your API specification.

Leveraging reusable components

One of OpenAPI's most powerful features is its component reuse system. Instead of defining the same structures repeatedly throughout your specification, you can define them once and reference them wherever needed. This approach is like creating a library of magical ingredients that you can mix and match to create different items. It improves maintainability, ensures consistency, and significantly reduces the size of your OpenAPI document.

Creating component schemas for common data structures

For our Magic Items store, several data structures appear across multiple endpoints. By defining these once in the `components/schemas` section, we ensure consistency while making our specifications easier to maintain.

```
components:
  schemas:
    Rarity:
      type: string
      enum: [common, uncommon, rare, very_rare, legendary]
    MagicalEffect:
      type: object
      properties:
        name:
          type: string
        duration:
          type: string
```

Now we can reference these components in our item schemas:

```
Potion:
  properties:
    name:
      type: string
    rarity:
      $ref: '#/components/schemas/Rarity'
    effects:
      type: array
      items:
        $ref: '#/components/schemas/MagicalEffect'
```

This approach ensures that all potions, wands, and scrolls use the same structure for magical effects and rarity values. When a customer browses your magical inventory, they'll see consistent information regardless of which type of item they're viewing.

You should apply this same reuse pattern to your parameters, responses, and request bodies as well. For example, define standard error responses once and reference them throughout your API, so customers always get consistent error information.

Organizing components for maintainability

As your OpenAPI specification grows in complexity, organizing your components becomes crucial for long-term maintainability. The components section serves as a centralized repository for reusable elements, but without proper organization, it can quickly become unwieldy—like a wizard's workshop with ingredients scattered everywhere!

Group related schemas logically

One effective approach is to organize components by domain or functional area. For our Magic Items store, we might organize schemas into categories:

```
components:
  schemas:
    # Base structures
    MagicItemBase:
      type: object
      properties:
        id:
          type: string
```

```
      name:
        type: string
# Item type definitions
Potion:
  allOf:
    - $ref: '#/components/schemas/MagicItemBase'
    - type: object
      # Potion-specific properties
# Common structures
PaginationInfo:
  type: object
  properties:
    total:
      type: integer
```

This logical grouping makes it easier for developers to locate related components and understand their relationships. When you need to add a new property to all magical items, you know exactly where to make the change—in the MagicItemBase schema.

Consider modularization for large specifications

For extensive APIs such as our complete Magic Items store, consider splitting your specification into multiple files:

- Core components in a central definitions file
- Resource-specific components grouped by domain
- Shared response patterns and error definitions

This modular approach improves maintainability by reducing file sizes and allowing focused updates. Teams can work on different modules simultaneously without conflicts: your potions team can update their schemas while the wands team works on theirs. Just remember to carefully manage references between files to maintain consistency across your entire API.

By leveraging reusable components effectively, you'll create an OpenAPI specification that's not only more maintainable but also ensures a consistent experience for developers integrating with your Magic Items store API. This reuse pattern is especially valuable as your API grows over time, helping you maintain quality and consistency even as you add new features and capabilities.

Implementing common API patterns

RESTful APIs commonly face recurring design challenges that you'll need to solve in consistent ways. Let's look at some of the most important patterns you'll want to implement in your Magic Items store.

Implementing robust error handling with problem details

OpenAPI Specification gives you excellent tools for documenting standardized error responses using the Problem Details standard (RFC 9457, formerly RFC 7807). This standard defines a consistent format for error responses, making life easier for your API users and simplifying error handling in client applications.

For our Magic Items store, implementing the Problem Details standard looks like this:

```
components:
  schemas:
    Problem:
      type: object
      properties:
        type:
          type: string
          format: uri
          description: URI reference identifying the problem type
        title:
          type: string
          description: Short, human-readable summary of the problem
        status:
          type: integer
          description: HTTP status code
        detail:
          type: string
          description: Human-readable explanation specific to this
occurrence
        instance:
          type: string
          format: uri
          description: URI reference identifying the specific occurrence
```

This standardized approach allows you to provide consistent error responses across your entire API. When a customer tries to enchant an item but doesn't have enough magical energy, they'll receive a structured response they can easily understand and process:

```
responses:
  '400':
    description: Bad Request
    content:
      application/problem+json:
        schema:
          $ref: '#/components/schemas/Problem'
        example:
          type: "https://api.magicitems.com/problems/insufficient-magic"
          title: "Insufficient magical energy"
          status: 400
          detail: "This enchantment requires 50 mana, but only 30 is
available"
          instance: "/enchantments/failed/12345"
```

The Problem Details standard has become widely adopted because it offers so many benefits. You'll find built-in support in many Java libraries, Spring frameworks, and easy implementation patterns for TypeScript/JavaScript. Your developers will appreciate the clear, structured error messages, and your tooling will work better with standardized errors. You can also extend the format with custom fields for specific errors while maintaining the common structure that makes errors predictable.

Handling pagination

Remember when we talked about pagination parameters earlier? There are different approaches to pagination, and it's worth understanding when each works best:

- **Offset-based pagination** works well for stable data such as your catalog of magical artifacts, but can become problematic if your inventory changes frequently during browsing
- **Cursor-based pagination** shines for real-time data such as auction listings or magical effects that are constantly changing, especially in large collections where performance matters

Choose the pagination style that best fits each endpoint in your API. Your catalog items might work fine with offset pagination, while your "real-time enchantment monitoring" might need cursor-based approaches.

Avoiding bulk operations

While your API could support bulk operations (such as adding multiple items to inventory at once), it's generally better to avoid them, especially when they would result in distributed transactions. These introduce several problems:

- Increased complexity in error handling (what if adding 3 out of 5 potions succeeds?)
- Potential performance issues affecting all your customers
- Consistency challenges across system boundaries
- Recovery complications if failures occur mid-transaction

Instead, design your Magic Items API to encourage clients to make individual requests or provide asynchronous processing for necessary bulk operations (such as importing a collection of items).

The importance of examples

Throughout your OpenAPI document, examples play a crucial role in helping developers understand your API:

```
MagicPotion:
  type: object
  properties:
    # Properties definition
  example:
    id: "healing-potion-001"
    name: "Minor Healing Potion"
    effect: "Restores 25 health points"
    duration: "30 seconds"
```

These examples aren't just documentation; they're powerful tools that serve multiple purposes. They enable automated mock server generation for testing, so frontend developers can work without waiting for your backend. They provide clear guidance for developers implementing clients, showing exactly what a potion looks like in your system.

Examples also support documentation tools in creating interactive demos and help validation tools verify that your implementation matches your design. Testing frameworks can generate realistic test cases based on your examples, making quality assurance more effective.

Documenting error codes

When documenting error responses, you need to decide whether to list all possible error codes or just the most important ones. The best practice is to document all error codes your API might return, as this creates a complete contract with your users.

OpenAPI also provides a default response for documenting unexpected errors:

```
responses:
  '400':
    # Specific 400 error documentation
  '404':
    # Specific 404 error documentation
  default:
    description: Unexpected error
    content:
      application/problem+json:
        schema:
          $ref: '#/components/schemas/Problem'
```

Use the default response to handle unexpected errors or those not explicitly documented, but don't let it replace proper documentation of known error conditions. Your users will appreciate knowing exactly what can go wrong and how to handle each case.

By implementing these common API patterns consistently, you'll create an API that feels polished and professional. Your Magic Items store API will be more predictable, easier to use, and ultimately more successful with developers.

While these patterns work great for typical request-response interactions, some operations take longer to complete. What happens when an operation takes minutes to apply, or when importing a merchant's entire inventory can't be completed within a typical request timeout? Next, we'll explore how to handle these long-running operations effectively in your RESTful API design, ensuring your Magic Items store can handle both quick queries and complex, time-consuming processes with equal grace.

Implementing long-running operations in REST APIs

In the real world, not all API operations can be completed immediately. Processing a large batch of resources, performing complex tasks, or integrating with external systems often takes more time than is reasonable for a synchronous HTTP request. Let's explore how to effectively handle these situations in your Magic Items store API.

Using 202 accepted for asynchronous processing

The HTTP 202 Accepted status code is perfect for long-running operations. It tells your API users, "We've received your request and we're working on it, but it's going to take a while." This allows your server to acknowledge receipt without keeping the connection open for extended periods.

Here's how to implement this pattern in your OpenAPI specification:

```
/orders/bulk-import:
  post:
    summary: Import multiple orders in a single operation
    description: |
      Starts an asynchronous bulk import process.
      Returns 202 Accepted with a Location header pointing to status
resource.
    requestBody:
      content:
        application/json:
          schema:
            $ref: '#/components/schemas/BulkOrderImport'
    responses:
      '202':
        description: Import job accepted for processing
        headers:
          Location:
            schema:
              type: string
              format: uri
            description: URI to check the status of the import job
        content:
          application/json:
            schema:
              $ref: '#/components/schemas/JobStatus'
```

The client can then poll the provided location to check the status:

```
/tasks/{taskId}:
  get:
    summary: Check the status of a long-running task
    parameters:
      # properties definition
    responses:
      '200':
        description: Current status of the task
        content:
          application/json:
            schema:
              $ref: '#/components/schemas/TaskStatus'
      '303':
        description: Task completed, redirect to result
        headers:
          Location:
            schema:
              type: string
              format: uri
            description: URI of the completed resource
```

This could be used for complex processes that require time to complete. Imagine a customer submitting a request to process a very complex operation on their request, something that takes several minutes to process. They'll receive a 202 Accepted response with a link to monitor progress, and can check periodically until the process is completed.

Using 303 See Other for completion redirection

When a long-running task is completed, you can use HTTP 303 See Other to redirect the customer to the result resource. This creates a clean transition from "in progress" to "completed" states:

1. The customer polls the task status endpoint.
2. When the task is completed, your server responds with 303 See Other.
3. The Location header points to the final result resource.
4. The customer follows the redirect using GET to retrieve the result.

Long Running Task

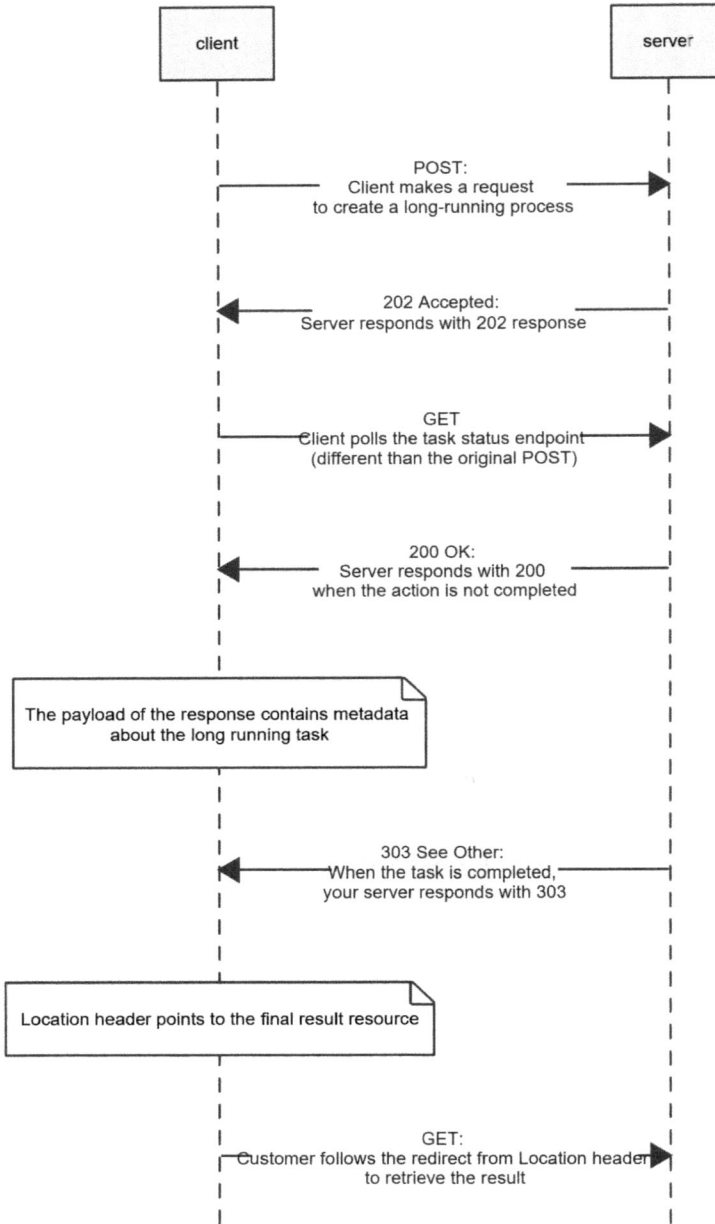

Figure 10.1 – Long Running task

Quick tip: Need to see a high-resolution version of this image? Open this book in the next-gen Packt Reader or view it in the PDF/ePub copy.

The next-gen Packt Reader and a free PDF/ePub copy of this book are included with your purchase. Scan the QR code OR visit `https://packtpub.com/unlock`, then use the search bar to find this book by name. Double-check the edition shown to make sure you get the right one.

This pattern works great for situations such as bulk imports or complex enchantments where you want to guide the customer smoothly from the processing phase to viewing the completed result.

Callbacks and webhooks for notifications

While polling is straightforward, it's not always efficient. Two alternative patterns can improve the experience.

With callbacks, the customer provides a URL in the initial request that your server will call when processing completes. This eliminates the need for continuous polling:

```
/enchantments:
  post:
    summary: Start an enchantment process
    requestBody:
      content:
        application/json:
          schema:
            type: object
            properties:
              # properties definition
              callback_url:
                type: string
                format: uri
                description: URL to be called when enchantment completes
```

```
responses:
  '202':
    description: Enchantment process initiated
callbacks:
  enchantmentComplete:
    '{$request.body#/callback_url}':
      post:
        requestBody:
          content:
            application/json:
              schema:
                $ref: '#/components/schemas/EnchantmentResult'
        responses:
          '200':
            description: Callback received successfully
```

The callback definition includes the following:

- A callback name (enchantmentComplete)

- An expression that resolves to the URL where the callback should be sent ({$request.
  body#/callback_url})

- A Path Item Object that defines the operation, including the HTTP method, request body
  structure, and expected responses

Callbacks are ideal for notifications about completed events that might take time to process but
require customer notification.

Webhooks, the second approach, extend the callback concept but are typically pre-registered
rather than provided with each request. They're ideal for ongoing event notifications rather than
one-time operations:

```
/webhook-registrations:
  post:
    summary: Register a webhook for magical item events
    requestBody:
      content:
        application/json:
          schema:
            type: object
```

```
properties:
  url:
    type: string
    format: uri
  events:
    type: array
    items:
      type: string
      enum: [item.created, item.sold, enchantment.completed]
```

The key difference between regular callbacks and webhook-style callbacks is that webhooks typically involve subscribing to event streams with persistent callback URLs rather than providing a one-time callback for a specific operation. Using these patterns, your Magic Items store can provide rich notification capabilities for inventory changes, price updates, or special events.

Best practices for long-running operations

When implementing long-running operations in your Magic Items API, keep these best practices in mind:

- Always use 202 Accepted for requests that will be processed asynchronously
- Provide a status resource via the Location header or in the response body
- Include estimated completion time when possible, using the Retry-After header
- Design for idempotency so customers can safely retry requests
- Offer cancellation mechanisms for long-running operations
- Consider implementing both polling and callbacks to accommodate different customer needs

Implementing these patterns ensures that even complex operations can be handled efficiently without timeouts or connection issues affecting the user experience.

By properly implementing these asynchronous patterns in your OpenAPI specification, you create a contract that clearly communicates how clients should interact with long-running operations, improving the overall developer experience and making your API more robust for real-world usage.

API versioning approaches

While we'll cover API evolution and versioning strategies in detail in *Chapter 13*, it's worth mentioning how OpenAPI helps you maintain the golden rule of versioning: **any change to your API must not break existing clients.**

OpenAPI gives you powerful tools to plan and document your versioning strategy. When you're designing changes to your Magic Items store API, you can use your OpenAPI document to clearly indicate which elements are stable and which might change in the future.

Remember that modifications to resource identifiers, required fields, response structures, or representation formats can easily break client applications. Your OpenAPI document serves as both documentation of your current API contract and a planning tool for future changes, helping you ensure that your Magic Items store API can evolve without disrupting your existing users.

As you build and maintain your API over time, OpenAPI helps you track these changes and communicate them clearly to your users, ensuring a smooth evolution of your API.

Summary

In this chapter, we explored how OpenAPI Specification transforms from documentation into a binding contract for API development. We examined how OAS serves as a single source of truth that translates abstract business requirements into executable specifications. Through our Magic Items store example, we discovered how this contract-driven approach enables a powerful ecosystem of tools for documentation, mocking, validation, code generation, and testing.

We investigated best practices for designing clear, consistent APIs: establishing logical resource structures, consistent naming conventions, and leveraging reusable components. We explored implementation patterns for common challenges, including error handling, pagination, and long-running operations, all while maintaining OpenAPI as the central contract.

Beyond technical benefits, we saw how OAS adoption transforms team dynamics by providing objective standards, creating shared understanding across roles, and enabling contract-first development that accelerates delivery. While we introduced how OAS uses schemas to define data structures, the next chapter will dive deeper into JSON Schema, exploring advanced modeling techniques and validation strategies for your APIs.

Get This Book's PDF Version and Exclusive Extras

UNLOCK NOW

Scan the QR code (or go to packtpub.com/unlock). Search for this book by name, confirm the edition, and then follow the steps on the page.

Note: Keep your invoice handy. Purchases made directly from Packt don't require an invoice.

11

Using JSON Schema to Define Your Object Models

This chapter explores the use of JSON Schema in designing REST APIs, building on the domain model established in earlier chapters. We focus on defining the data models used in the OpenAPI Specification discussed in the two previous chapters. The chapter covers creating, validating, and documenting complex JSON structures to ensure consistency and reliability in your API design.

In this chapter, we're going to cover the following main topics:

- Understanding JSON Schema
- JSON Schema at work
- Best practices for using JSON Schema

By the end of this chapter, you will know the ins and outs of JSON Schema to create advanced model definitions for your API resources. You will also have explored how to approach the evolution of a schema and how to integrate it into your development workflow, as well as the best practices to consider when creating schemas.

Technical requirements

To effectively work through this JSON Schema chapter, you will need several key technologies and installations to practice the concepts and examples presented. A modern text editor or IDE with JSON and YAML support is essential, such as Visual Studio Code with the JSON Schema Store extension. The environment should also support Git for version control for working with examples. All of the code included in this chapter is available on GitHub at https://github.com/API-Peak/RESTful-Design-Patterns/blob/main/Chapter10-JSON-Schema.

Understanding JSON Schema

Nowadays, almost all REST APIs expose data in JSON format. It is crucial to define this data strictly to ensure that our contract, documented as an OpenAPI Specification file, remains unambiguous. Understanding how to use JSON Schema is essential for creating well-defined APIs. In this section, we will explore its purpose and how to create schema files effectively.

Open nature

Unlike XML schemas, which are closed by nature, JSON Schema is considered *open*. This means JSON Schema inherently allows for flexible definitions that can accommodate additional properties not explicitly defined in the schema. This openness promotes extensibility and interoperability, but it may also introduce ambiguity, requiring you to carefully define all necessary constraints. In contrast, closed schemas ensure that only the elements explicitly defined in your code are permitted.

Introduction to JSON Schema

JSON Schema is a descriptive language used to define the structure and content of JSON data. It offers a clear and concise method for specifying the expected format, types, and constraints of JSON objects, ensuring that data adheres to a predefined schema. JSON Schema is written in JSON itself, making it easy to read and understand for anyone who is already familiar with JSON notation. JSON Schema plays a key role in describing REST APIs, because it is leveraged by OpenAPI Specification to describe all the data models.

OpenAPI and JSON Schema

It is important to note that full support for JSON Schema was introduced in OpenAPI version 3.1.0. Prior to this, especially in version 2.0, OpenAPI used a subset of JSON Schema with certain quirks that did not exist in the standard JSON Schema. This could lead to edge cases that were not entirely compatible. We will explore this topic later in this chapter.

The purpose of JSON Schema is to provide a standardized way to describe the structure, constraints, and relationships of data described in JSON format. Specifically, it allows us to ensure a number of important qualities of JSON data:

- Validate JSON data against a predefined schema. This way, we can ensure that the data is well formed and within all the required constraints. This quality is especially important for REST APIs as consistent data formats are crucial for interoperability.

- JSON Schema serves as a form of documentation for JSON data structures. It provides a clear and unambiguous description of the expected data format, making it easier for developers to understand and work with the data. Because JSON Schema is machine-readable, documentation can be generated from it in a form that is readable not only by developers but also by any other stakeholder involved in the process of building an API.

- By using JSON Schema, different systems and applications can agree on a common data format. This promotes interoperability and reduces the risk of data inconsistencies when exchanging information between systems.

- JSON Schema can be used to automate various aspects of the development process, such as generating code, creating test cases, and validating data. This helps to improve efficiency and reduce the likelihood of errors.

As we can see, there are many benefits of using JSON Schema. Let's learn about the structure of JSON Schema and explore its concepts.

Basic concepts

In this section, we will explore the foundational concepts of JSON Schema. Understanding these core principles is crucial for anyone working with APIs that rely on JSON data, as it ensures data consistency, quality, and reliability.

This section will introduce you to the following key concepts:

- Data types
- Basic structure of a JSON Schema document
- Validation keywords

By the end of this section, you will have a solid understanding of how to create basic schemas, define data types, and apply validation rules to ensure your JSON data is well structured and valid. This knowledge will serve as a foundation for more complex schema designs in later chapters.

Data types

In this section, we will dive into the **data types** supported by JSON Schema, which form the foundation for defining and validating JSON data structures. Specifying data types in JSON Schema is essential for ensuring data consistency and reliability. Defining expected types for each field establishes clear rules that prevent processing invalid or unexpected data. This not only helps avoid errors but also improves the predictability of data interactions, especially in APIs. Additionally, type validation enables early detection of issues, making it easier to catch bugs during development and ensuring that your system handles data as intended.

JSON Schema defines several core data types, each with specific validation rules and use cases. Here's a brief overview of each:

- string: This represents a sequence of Unicode characters. JSON Schema allows for additional validations, such as length constraints and format checks, such as date-time, email, and uri. JSON Schema also allows restricting a string field to follow a specific regular expression pattern.

- number: This represents any numeric value, including integers and floating-point numbers. JSON Schema allows specifying constraints such as minimum/maximum values and whether boundaries are inclusive or exclusive.

- integer: This is a subtype of number that only accepts whole numbers. It can also have constraints such as multipleOf to ensure divisibility by a specific value.

- boolean: This represents a value that is either true or false. It is often used for flags or toggles in data structures.

- array: This represents an ordered list of items. JSON Schema allows specifying the type of items, the minimum/maximum number of items, and whether items must be unique.

- object: This represents a collection of key-value pairs, where keys are strings and values can be any type. JSON Schema enables defining required properties, property dependencies, and restrictions on additional properties.

- null: This represents the absence of a value. It is often used in combination with other types to indicate that a field can either be a specific type or null.

Each of these types has specific keywords for validation, allowing fine-tuned control over the structure and content of JSON data.

Further reading

To learn more about JSON Schema data types, refer to the official website of the JSON Schema organization at `https://json-schema.org/understanding-json-schema/reference/type`.

Basic structure of a JSON schema

A JSON schema is itself a JSON object that contains a set of keywords used to define the structure and validation rules for JSON data.

The basic structure of a JSON schema includes the following elements:

- The `$schema` keyword defines the version of the JSON Schema specification being used. It is optional but recommended for clarity. The schema value is a URI of the schema that is used:

```
{
    "$schema": "http://json-schema.org/2020-12/schema#"
}
```

This example illustrates a properly defined $schema parameter with a value that references the 2020-12 version of JSON Schema.

Because there are some differences between versions of JSON Schema, this keyword ensures clarity regarding the interpretation of keywords in the document.

- The `title` and `description` keywords provide a human-readable title and description for the schema, making it easier to understand its purpose:

```
{
    "title": "Magic Item Schema",
    "description": "A schema definition for a Magic Item data object."
}
```

In this example, we can see properly defined `title` and `description` fields.

- The type keyword specifies the type of data being described by the schema, as we have introduced earlier in this chapter.

- The `properties` keyword is used to define the properties of an object. Each property is described by a nested schema that specifies its type and validation rules:

```
{
  "type": "object",
  "properties": {
    "name": {
      "type": "string"
    },
    "weight": {
      "type": "number"
    }
  }
}
```

  In the preceding example, we can see an object with a `string` type with the properties `name` and `weight`, which can be any number.

- The `items` keyword is used to define the schema for the elements within an array. It can specify a single schema that applies to all elements or an array of schemas for tuple validation. The following example defines an array of strings:

```
{
  "type": "array",
  "items": { "type": "string" }
}
```

  In this example, we see a definition of an array consisting of `string` type items.

- The `required` keyword specifies an array of property names that are required in the JSON data:

```
{
  "required": ["name", "age"]
}
```

  In the following example, we require the `name` and `age` fields for an object.

- The `additionalProperties` keyword specifies whether additional properties are allowed in the JSON data. It can be set to `true`, `false`, or a schema that defines the structure of additional properties. In the following example, we specify that the schema cannot have any other properties besides those specified:

```
{
    "additionalProperties": false
}
```

Example of a complete JSON schema

Here's an implementation of a complete JSON Schema file containing the examples discussed in this section:

`https://github.com/PacktPublishing/RESTful-Design-Patterns-and-Best-Practices/blob/main/Chapter-11/basic-structure.json`

So far, we have covered the fundamental building blocks of JSON Schema, including data types and basic validation keywords that help define and enforce the structure of your JSON data. Now, we will move on to more advanced concepts.

Advanced concepts

In this section, we will delve into modeling more complex data structures. We will explore topics such as schema composition, conditional validation, and reusable components, which will allow for greater flexibility and control in designing complex data models.

Combining schemas (allOf, anyOf, oneOf, and not)

JSON Schema provides powerful keywords for combining multiple schemas to create more complex and flexible data validation rules. These keywords—allOf, anyOf, oneOf, and not—allow developers to define schemas that can accommodate various data structures and constraints. Here's a detailed explanation of each keyword:

- The allOf keyword is used to ensure that the data must validate against all the specified schemas. It is essentially an "and" operation, where all conditions must be met:

```
{
  "allOf": [
    {
      "properties": {
        "name": { "type": "string" }
      },
      "required": ["name"]
    },
    {
```

```
      "properties": {
        "weight": {
          "type": "number",
          "minimum": 0.1
        }
      }
    }
  ]
}
```

This example schema uses allOf to combine two subschemas:

- The first subschema *requires* that the object has name, which must be a string
- The second subschema *doesn't require* that the object has a weight property, but if it does, it must be a number and be at least 0.1

For the data to be valid, it must satisfy *both* subschemas.

The allOf keyword is used to combine multiple schemas. It functions similarly to inheritance in object-oriented programming by allowing one schema to inherit properties from others.

> Best practice
>
> Use allOf to create base schemas for common properties and extend them for specific use cases. This reduces duplication and ensures consistency across API resources.

Inheritance allows schemas to extend other schemas, promoting reuse and reducing redundancy.

> Disclaimer
>
> Only allOf is supported for combining schemas in OpenAPI 2.0 (formerly known as Swagger 2.0).

- The anyOf keyword is used to ensure that the data must validate against at least one of the specified schemas. It is essentially an "or" operation, where at least one condition must be met:

```
{
  "anyOf": [
    { "type": "string" },
    { "type": "number" }
  ]
}
```

In this example, the data can be either a string or a number.

• The oneOf keyword is used to ensure that the data must validate against exactly one of the
  specified schemas. It is a stricter version of anyOf, where only one condition must be met:

```
{
  "oneOf": [
    { "type": "string" },
    { "type": "number" }
  ]
}
```

In this example, the data must be either a string or a number, but not both.

• The not keyword is used to ensure that the data must not validate against the specified
  schema. It is essentially a "not" operation, where the condition must not be met:

```
{
  "not": { "type": "null" }
}
```

In this example, the data must not be null.

OpenAPI compatibility

OpenAPI Specification does not fully support the not keyword in versions
below 3.1.0. Specifically, the subschema used with not must be an OpenAPI
schema, not a standard JSON Schema. This means that while you can use
the not keyword in OpenAPI 3.0.0, it may not behave exactly as it would in
full JSON Schema implementations, and it must follow OpenAPI-specific
rules for schemas.

oneOf, anyOf, and not help to introduce composition to your JSON schemas. Composition involves assembling schemas from smaller, reusable components. Use composition to handle polymorphic data types and optional fields. Doing so ensures that schemas combined with allOf, anyOf, or oneOf do not have conflicting properties (e.g., properties with the same name but different types), as this can lead to validation errors. This approach enhances flexibility while maintaining clear validation rules. Remember to clearly document the use of composition in your API documentation. This helps consumers understand how to interact with your API effectively.

> Practical examples
>
> Here's an implementation of a complete JSON Schema file containing the examples discussed in this section:
>
> `https://github.com/PacktPublishing/RESTful-Design-Patterns-and-Best-Practices/blob/main/Chapter-11/combining-schemas.json`

Exploring conditional subschemas

JSON Schema provides powerful keywords for defining conditional validation rules using if, then, and else. These keywords allow developers to create schemas that apply different validation rules based on the presence or value of certain properties. This feature is particularly useful for handling complex data structures that require conditional logic. Let's walk through each of them:

- if keyword

  The if keyword is used to specify a schema that acts as a condition. If the data matches this schema, the then schema is applied; otherwise, the else schema is applied.

- then keyword

  The then keyword is used to specify the schema that should be applied if the if condition is met.

- else keyword

  The else keyword is used to specify the schema that should be applied if the if condition is not met.

The if, then, and else keywords can be combined to create complex conditional validation rules:

```
{
  "type": "object",
  "properties": {
    "type": { "type": "string" },
    "grade": { "type": "string" },
    "position": { "type": "string" }
  },
  "if": {
    "properties": {
      "type": {
        "const": "student"
      }
    }
  },
  "then": {
    "required": ["grade"]
  },
  "else": {
    "required": ["position"]
  }
}
```

In this example, if the type property is "student", the grade property is required. If the type property is not "student", the position property is required.

Practical examples

Here's an implementation of a complete JSON Schema file containing the examples discussed in this section:

https://github.com/PacktPublishing/RESTful-Design-Patterns-and-Best-Practices/blob/main/Chapter-11/conditional.json

References and reusability ($ref)

One of the powerful features of JSON Schema is its ability to reference other schemas using the $ref keyword. This capability promotes reusability and modularity, allowing developers to define common schemas once and reuse them across multiple parts of their application. By leveraging references, you can create more maintainable and scalable schemas, reducing redundancy and ensuring consistency.

The $ref keyword is used to create a reference to another schema. This can be a schema defined within the same document, or an external schema located at a different URI. When the JSON Schema validator encounters a $ref keyword, it replaces the reference with the actual schema it points to, effectively including the referenced schema in the validation process.

The syntax for using the $ref keyword is straightforward. Here is an example of a schema that references another schema:

```
{
  "definitions": {
    "address": {
      "type": "object",
      "properties": {
        "street": { "type": "string" },
        "city": { "type": "string" },
        "zipcode": { "type": "string" }
      },
      "required": ["street", "city", "zipcode"]
    }
  },
  "type": "object",
  "properties": {
    "name": { "type": "string" },
    "address": { "$ref": "#/definitions/address" }
  },
  "required": ["name", "address"]
}
```

In this example, the address schema is defined in the definitions section and is referenced in the properties section using the $ref keyword. The address property in the main schema will be validated against the address schema defined in the definitions section.

JSON Schema also supports referencing external schemas located at different URIs:

```
{
  "type": "object",
  "properties": {
    "address": { "$ref": "http://api.magicstore.com/schemas/address.json"
}
  },
  "required": ["address"]
}
```

In this example, the user property is validated against the schema located at http://api.magicstore.com/schemas/address.json. As a best practice, define common elements, such as error responses or pagination details, once and reuse them across different endpoints. This ensures consistency and simplifies updates.

Complete example

You can find an example of a whole JSON Schema document leveraging the advanced concepts introduced in this section in our GitHub repository: https://github.com/PacktPublishing/RESTful-Design-Patterns-and-Best-Practices/blob/main/Chapter-11/advanced-concepts.json.

JSON Hyper-Schema

JSON Hyper-Schema is a JSON Schema vocabulary that allows you to annotate JSON documents with hyperlinks. These hyperlinks include attributes describing how to manipulate and interact with remote resources. The main goal of JSON Hyper-Schema is to enable hypermedia-driven APIs, where clients can discover and navigate resources dynamically based on the links provided in the responses. JSON Hyper-Schema adds several elements to the schema. Most importantly, the **hypermedia links** allow you to embed hypermedia information into JSON documents using the links keyword. Hypermedia links leverage a **link description object** to describe the details of a hyperlink, using attributes such as rel (relation type), href, method, and optional schemas for inputs and outputs:

```
{
  "type": "object",
  "properties": {
    "id": { "type": "number" }
  },
  "links": [
    {
      "rel": "self",
      "href": "/resource/{id}",
      "method": "GET",
    }
  ]
}
```

With the help of **dynamic URI templates**, the href field can support templates. This way, we can allow links to be dynamically constructed based on the contextual data:

```
{
  "links": [
    {
      "rel": "next",
      "href": "/resources?cursor={nextCursor}"
    }
  ]
}
```

If we take a look at the rel link attribute, we can see that it defines the relationship between the current document and the target resource. For example, self indicates that the target URI identifies a resource equivalent to the link context. It is used to interact with the resource that the instance document represents. There are two other types of relationships. item represents individual items within a collection, providing semantics for accessing singular resources within a broader collection context. Collection, on the other hand, identifies a resource that represents a collection of items, often used when the target is a collection endpoint.

JSON Hyper-Schema separates the schema from the instance, enabling clients to interact with plain JSON documents while providing hypermedia features for Hyper-Schema-aware applications. These elements make JSON Hyper-Schema a powerful tool for building hypermedia-driven systems, where clients can dynamically discover and interact with related resources based on schema-defined links.

JSON Hyper-Schema example

Refer to a more thorough example of JSON Hyper-Schema in use in our GitHub repository: https://github.com/PacktPublishing/RESTful-Design-Patterns-and-Best-Practices/blob/main/Chapter-11/json-hyper-schema.json.

JSON Schema at work

In this section, we will address the challenges related to versioning and evolving schemas over time. Additionally, we will discuss how JSON Schema integrates seamlessly into modern development workflows, enhancing productivity and reducing errors.

Evolution

As REST APIs evolve, so too must their underlying data schemas. Properly managing the versioning and evolution of JSON Schema documents is crucial to maintaining compatibility and ensuring a smooth transition for API consumers. This section explores strategies for handling schema changes and best practices for versioning.

Handling schema changes

Schema evolution refers to the process of modifying a schema over time to accommodate new requirements or improvements. Changes can include adding new fields, deprecating old ones, or altering validation rules. Effective schema evolution ensures that these changes do not disrupt existing API clients.

In general, we differentiate between two types of schema changes: those that are backward-compatible and those that are not. Backward-compatible changes do not require existing consumers of the data to alter their code in order for their code to function well. Any change, where we add a new optional field, expand allowed values for a field, or increase constraints (such as maxLength, etc.), will be considered backward-compatible. Sometimes, though, there is a need to change the current data model in a way that will potentially break the integration of the consumers of our data. Whenever we remove or rename a field, change the field's data type, or tighten a constraint (e.g., reduce maxLength from 50 to 20), we face a potentially backward-incompatible change. Since JSON Schema does not provide explicit metadata for indicating the version of the schema, we need to adopt alternative approaches. A common method is to version the files containing the JSON Schema models and reference these versions in the OpenAPI documents. Because versioning strategies are more relevant to the entire API context than to an individual data model, we will explore these strategies and more in-depth concepts of versioning in *Chapter 11*.

Integration with development workflows

Integrating JSON Schema into development workflows enhances the robustness and reliability of APIs by ensuring data consistency and facilitating automated validation processes. This section explores how JSON Schema can be effectively utilized in API development and integrated into CI/CD pipelines for automatic validation.

Using JSON Schema in API development

JSON Schema plays a crucial role in defining the structure and constraints of data exchanged via APIs. Its integration into the development workflow can streamline the design, implementation, and testing phases.

By defining clear data models, JSON Schema ensures consistency across different API endpoints, reducing errors caused by mismatched data formats. During development and testing phases, schemas can be used to validate incoming and outgoing data, ensuring it adheres to defined standards before processing. Schemas also serve as a form of documentation that provides developers with a clear understanding of expected data structures, enhancing collaboration and reducing onboarding time for new team members.

Best practices

Adopt a schema-first approach where JSON schemas are developed before implementing API logic. This ensures that all team members have a shared understanding of data requirements from the very beginning, boosting productivity and communication. On top of that, define common schema components that can be reused across multiple endpoints to improve consistency and reusability.

Automating schema validation in CI/CD pipelines

In a project with a well-defined and managed API lifecycle, automating processes is crucial for enhancing quality and minimizing the potential for human error. Automation not only streamlines workflows but also allows development teams to focus on more strategic and innovative tasks, ultimately driving greater efficiency and productivity. One key area where automation can have a significant impact is in schema validation within CI/CD pipelines. By integrating JSON Schema validation into these pipelines, teams can ensure that API changes adhere to predefined data structures and constraints before they are deployed. This proactive approach helps maintain high-quality APIs and prevents regressions or inconsistencies from reaching production environments, where they could cause disruptions or require costly fixes.

When automating JSON Schema validation in CI/CD pipelines, following best practices and employing effective strategies can significantly enhance the reliability and quality of your APIs. When automating your workflows with JSON Schema, think about the following:

- Choosing the right tool to validate your schemas. Focus on options, such as the JSON Schema validator, that are well documented and regularly updated.

- Integrating the validation tool with your testing framework to ensure the data structure.

- Integrating your tests into the CI/CD pipeline to ensure that data validation is automatically performed each time in your development process. This way, you can catch errors early and reliably.

- Updating schemas as your API and application evolve to ensure the tests remain relevant.

Here is a practical example of how such an automated CI pipeline could look in GitHub Actions:

```
name: JSON Schema Validation
on:
  push:
    branches: [ main, develop ]
  pull_request:
    branches: [ main ]

jobs:
  validate-schemas:
    runs-on: ubuntu-latest
    steps:
      - name: Checkout code
        uses: actions/checkout@v4

      - name: Set up Node.js
        uses: actions/setup-node@v4
        with:
          node-version: '18'

      # 1. Install JSON Schema validation tool
      - name: Install AJV CLI
        run: npm install -g ajv-cli
```

```
# 2. Validate schema files are correct
- name: Validate schema syntax
  run: |
    for schema in schemas/*.json; do
      echo "Validating schema: $schema"
      ajv compile -s "$schema"
    done

# 3. Validate test data against schemas
- name: Validate sample data
  run: |
    ajv validate -s schemas/user-schema.json -d test-data/valid-
user.json
    ajv validate -s schemas/product-schema.json -d test-data/valid-
product.json
```

In the preceding code snippet, these three validation steps implement the core automation principles outlined in this section. First, the pipeline installs ajv-cli as the chosen validation tool. It is a well-documented and regularly updated option for reliable schema validation. Next, it validates the syntax and structure of all schema files to ensure they are correctly formatted. This way, it catches schema definition errors before they can impact the API. Finally, the pipeline validates sample test data against the schemas to verify that the data structures work as intended, integrating the validation tool with the testing framework to ensure data integrity. By automating these steps in the CI/CD pipeline, the workflow catches schema-related errors early in the development process, prevents regressions from reaching production, and maintains high-quality APIs without requiring manual intervention from development teams.

We have learned the theory and some best practices around approaching changes in JSON Schema and how to create automated validation processes in your development environment. Now, let's move on to more practical aspects and talk about best practices when working with JSON Schema.

Best practices for using JSON Schema

In this section, we will look at how to maximize the effectiveness of JSON Schema in our products. We will explore how to improve our schema designs, documentation, performance, and security.

Schema design principles

Good design helps with data validation and makes life easier for developers. By following some core principles, you can create schemas that are simple, flexible, and efficient. This section covers essential tips for designing JSON Schemas that balance simplicity with functionality, ensuring your data stays consistent and compatible.

Let's look at the tips:

- **Keep it simple and readable**

  Design schemas that are easy to understand and maintain. Avoid unnecessary complexity by using clear naming conventions and straightforward structures. For example, instead of nesting multiple layers of objects, intend to flatten the structures where possible. This will greatly improve readability and make the client code simpler to write and reason about.

  Example

  Check a detailed example on GitHub: `https://github.com/PacktPublishing/RESTful-Design-Patterns-and-Best-Practices/blob/main/Chapter-11/keep-it-simple-and-readable.json`.

- **Avoid over-validation**

  While it's important to enforce data integrity, over-validation can lead to rigidity. Allow for some flexibility to accommodate future changes. Use the `additionalProperties` parameter if you anticipate the need for extra fields in the future:

  ```
  {
    "type": "object",
    "properties": {
      "id": { "type": "string" }
    },
    "additionalProperties": true
  }
  ```

In the preceding example, by setting the additionalProperties parameter to true, we allow the object model to be open, and thus allow it to contain properties beyond only id. This means that while the object must have an id property of type string, it can also include any number of other properties with any valid JSON values, such as the following:

```
{
"id": "456",
"name": "John",
 "age": 30
}
```

While sacrificing strictness, this will give you the benefit of easier achieved potential future compatibility. This approach depends on how rigid your structure should be, so weigh up all the pros and cons.

- **Use clear descriptions**

  Provide meaningful descriptions for each field using the description keyword to enhance understanding among developers and users:

  ```
  {
      "type": "object",
      "properties": {
        "itemName": {
          "type": "string",
          "description": "The unique identifier for a magic item"
        }
      }
  }
  ```

  In this example, providing a description for the itemName property serves multiple purposes:

  - It explains the property's purpose and intended use
  - It offers meaningful documentation for developers and users
  - It enhances the long-term maintainability of the entire JSON Schema file

By including clear descriptions, we ensure that the schema is not only functional but also self-explanatory and easier to understand and maintain over time.

- **Leverage reusability with $ref**

  Use the $ref keyword to reference common schema components, reducing redundancy and improving maintainability:

  ```
  {
    "$ref": "#/definitions/commonProperties"
  }
  ```

  This practice minimizes the size of your JSON documents and makes it easier to update shared components across multiple schemas.

- **Ensure backward compatibility**

  When updating schemas, maintain backward compatibility to ensure that existing clients are not broken by changes. Avoid removing fields or changing field types in a way that could disrupt current users. Instead, consider adding new optional fields to accommodate new requirements.

Having discussed best practices for working with JSON Schema, let's now explore the importance of providing clear documentation and effective communication about JSON schemas.

Documentation and communication

Clear documentation and effective communication are essential for making JSON schemas understandable and usable by developers. We want to document schemas effectively and use them to enhance team collaboration.

Documenting schemas for developers

To ensure the clear understanding and proper implementation of your JSON schemas, provide detailed documentation for each schema. This documentation should do the following:

- Explain the purpose of each field
- Clarify any constraints applied
- Include comments within the schema files
- Offer links to external documentation when necessary

By providing comprehensive documentation, you enable developers to do the following:

- Quickly grasp the structure and intent of the schema
- Implement the schema correctly in their applications
- Troubleshoot issues more efficiently
- Maintain and update the schema with confidence over time

Remember, well-documented schemas lead to fewer misunderstandings, reduced development time, and improved overall quality of data handling in your projects.

Example

Take a look at the example on GitHub: `https://github.com/PacktPublishing/`
`RESTful-Design-Patterns-and-Best-Practices/blob/main/Chapter-11/`
`documentation-and-communication.json`.

Using JSON Schema for API documentation

Use JSON Schema within OpenAPI specifications to automatically generate API documentation that includes data models. Define schemas in OpenAPI to provide a single source of truth for API documentation. We cover this aspect in depth in *Chapter 9*.

Performance considerations

When using JSON Schema for validation, it's important to balance strictness with performance to ensure efficient processing. Let's explore strategies for optimizing schema validation, helping you maintain high performance without compromising data integrity.

Optimizing schema validation

Optimize your validation logic to minimize overhead, particularly in high-throughput environments. Load and compile a JSON schema once, then reuse it for multiple validations to avoid the repeated overhead of parsing and compiling the schema. Leverage the caching capabilities of your tools to enhance efficiency and performance.

Validate large JSON documents incrementally rather than loading the entire document into memory. This reduces memory usage and speeds up processing, especially for large datasets.

Be careful when working with regular expressions. Simplify and optimize them when used in schemas to improve validation speed. Complex regex patterns can slow down validation significantly.

Balancing validation strictness and performance

To effectively balance validation strictness and performance in JSON Schema, it's important to apply strict validation rules only where necessary, ensuring critical fields are thoroughly validated while allowing optional fields more flexibility. This approach helps maintain data integrity without compromising performance. We talked about this very briefly in the *Schema design principles* subsection. Let's expand on that here.

Firstly, aim to apply strict validation only to fields that are crucial for the application's functionality or security. For example, ensure that fields such as email and password meet specific format and length requirements.

The following example demonstrates how to define and constrain properties within a JSON schema:

```
{
  "type": "object",
  "properties": {
    "email": {
      "type": "string",
      "format": "email",
      "maxLength": 255
    },
    "password": {
      "type": "string",
      "minLength": 8
    }
  },
  "required": ["email", "password"]
}
```

This schema defines an object with two properties:

- `email`:
    - Must be a string
    - Must conform to the predefined email format
    - Cannot exceed 255 characters in length

- password:

    - Must be a string

    - Must be at least eight characters long

Both the email and password properties are set as required fields for this object, meaning they must be present for the object to be considered valid according to this schema. By structuring the schema this way, we ensure that any data validated against it will have properly formatted email addresses and sufficiently secure passwords.

At the same time, for non-critical or optional fields, use more relaxed validation rules to accommodate future changes without requiring schema updates. This can reduce processing overhead and improve performance.

Let's examine a JSON schema that demonstrates a flexible approach to data validation:

```
{
  "type": "object",
  "properties": {
    "nickname": {
      "type": "string"
    },
    "profilePictureUrl": {
      "type": ["string", "null"],
      "format": "uri"
    }
  }
}
```

This schema defines an object with two properties—nickname and profilePictureUrl:

- The nickname property is simply defined as a string, allowing for maximum flexibility in user input.
- The profilePictureUrl property demonstrates even more flexibility:

    - It accepts either a string or null value, using array for the type field
    - When it's string, it should conform to the URI format
    - By allowing null, the schema remains valid even if a user hasn't set a profile picture

Neither property is marked as required, meaning the object can be valid even if one or both properties are missing.

This approach to schema design allows for graceful handling of evolving data structures and user behaviors, reducing the need for frequent schema updates as the application grows and changes.

When using more advanced structures of JSON Schema, be cautious about complexity. anyOf and oneOf can introduce flexibility, but they may also impact performance. Use them when necessary to validate data against multiple potential schemas without being overly permissive:

```
{
  "anyOf": [
    { "$ref": "#/definitions/basicUser" },
    { "$ref": "#/definitions/adminUser" }
  ]
}
```

This schema allows data to be valid if it matches either the basicUser or adminUser schema. While providing flexibility, anyOf can impact performance and complexity, so use it carefully when you need to validate against multiple potential schemas.

By strategically applying strict validation only where necessary and allowing flexibility elsewhere, you can achieve a balance that maintains data integrity while optimizing performance. This approach ensures that your API remains robust and efficient, even as it scales.

Security implications

When using JSON Schema, it's crucial to consider security implications to prevent vulnerabilities and ensure data integrity. This section explores how JSON Schema can help mitigate security risks and highlights common pitfalls to avoid, ensuring that your API remains secure and reliable.

Preventing security vulnerabilities with JSON Schema

Firstly, ensure that the data is validated against a well-defined schema to prevent injection attacks and malformed data from entering the system. This schema ensures that usernames are alphanumeric with optional underscores, and emails conform to a valid format.

To prevent security vulnerabilities using JSON Schema, it's essential to define strict validation rules for incoming data. The following schema demonstrates how to implement these security measures for user registration data:

```json
{
  "type": "object",
  "properties": {
    "username": {
      "type": "string",
      "minLength": 3,
      "maxLength": 20,
      "pattern": "^[a-zA-Z0-9_]+$"
    },
    "email": {
      "type": "string",
      "format": "email"
    }
  },
  "required": ["username", "email"]
}
```

This schema enforces several security-enhancing constraints. It defines an object with two required properties—username and email:

- The username field:
    - Must be a string between 3 and 20 characters long, preventing excessively short or long usernames
    - Is restricted to alphanumeric characters and underscores, mitigating the risk of injection attacks
- The email field:
    - Must be a string conforming to the email format, ensuring valid email addresses

By implementing these constraints, the schema helps prevent common security issues such as SQL injection, **cross-site scripting (XSS)**, and data validation bypasses. It ensures that only properly formatted data enters your system, reducing the attack surface and enhancing overall API security.

Secondly, avoid recursive schemas. They can lead to many unwanted issues, such as **denial-of-service (DoS)** attacks by causing excessive resource consumption. To address this, instead of allowing recursive structures, define a maximum depth of nested objects and follow it rigorously. This not only improves security but also performance and clarity, especially for AI agents.

Also, use the `additionalProperties` parameter wisely. By default, JSON Schema allows additional properties unless explicitly restricted. Use `additionalProperties: false` to prevent unexpected fields. This way, you ensure that only the specified properties are allowed, reducing the risk of processing unexpected or malicious data. As we mentioned previously in the chapter, `additionalProperties` can be a powerful tool for making your schema more flexible and making it easier to introduce changes in the future, but at the same time, this has its implications.

Lastly, define appropriate limits for numeric fields to prevent overflow attacks or excessive resource use:

```
{
  "type": "object",
  "properties": {
    "age": {
      "type": "integer",
      "minimum": 0,
      "maximum": 150
    }
  }
}
```

By restricting age to an integer between 0 and 150, the schema prevents invalid inputs, mitigates potential overflow attacks, and ensures realistic data validation.

Setting realistic bounds on numeric values helps prevent misuse.

This wraps up our section on best practices when working with JSON Schema. Remember that most situations are contextual and you should carefully consider the implications of every decision. In particular, the act of balancing security with performance and extensibility is a tricky one and needs careful consideration.

Summary

In this chapter, we explored the use of JSON Schema in REST API design, building upon the foundation set by the OpenAPI Specification discussed in the previous chapter. We delved into how JSON Schema provides a structured way to define, validate, and document JSON data models, ensuring consistency and reliability in your APIs. Key lessons included understanding JSON Schema's open nature, its integration with OpenAPI, and best practices for schema design, such as keeping schemas simple and readable while avoiding over-validation. These skills are crucial for creating APIs that are both robust and easy to maintain. Using JSON Schema enhances interoperability between systems, reduces data inconsistencies, and supports automation in development processes such as code generation and testing. These capabilities improve efficiency and minimize errors, making JSON Schema an indispensable tool for API developers.

In the next chapter, we will explore leveraging hypermedia in API design. This progression is a natural step from understanding JSON Schema, as hypermedia can further enhance API interactions by enabling clients to dynamically discover and navigate resources through embedded links and address common design pattern issues.

Get This Book's PDF Version and Exclusive Extras

UNLOCK NOW

Scan the QR code (or go to `packtpub.com/unlock`). Search for this book by name, confirm the edition, and then follow the steps on the page.

Note: Keep your invoice handy. Purchases made directly from Packt don't require an invoice.

12

Don't Hate Your Hypermedia: Creating APIs for Humans and AIs

In earlier chapters, we introduced REST's constraints, including the often-overlooked hypermedia. This chapter explores how hypermedia transforms static APIs into dynamic, self-describing systems where clients discover available actions from the API responses rather than relying on hardcoded knowledge of the API structure.

As generative AI and large language models reshape how systems interact, hypermedia's importance grows exponentially. These AI systems thrive when they can discover and navigate API capabilities dynamically, making hypermedia the perfect companion for AI-driven interactions. We'll explore practical implementations, common patterns, and best practices for creating truly RESTful APIs that are not just human-friendly, but AI-ready for today's needs and tomorrow's innovations.

In this chapter, we're going to cover the following main topics:

- The power of hypermedia as a REST constraint
- Navigating hypermedia implementation: patterns, formats, and challenges
- Designing hypermedia APIs for AI consumption

By the end of this chapter, you will have a better understanding of hypermedia's theoretical foundations, be able to implement practical hypermedia patterns in your APIs, overcome common implementation challenges, and design APIs that both human developers and AI systems can effectively discover and navigate.

The power of hypermedia as a REST constraint

In previous chapters, we established that hypermedia is a critical constraint for truly RESTful APIs, but knowing the theory and implementing it effectively are two very different challenges. Even though your Magic Items store API might offer basic CRUD operations without hypermedia, it still lacks the contextual information needed for effective use. It is like giving someone a treasure map without any legends – they have the data, but lack the context to navigate effectively. Hypermedia controls make your API a dynamic, self-describing system where clients can discover capabilities through navigation. Clients can simply follow the links and controls provided by your API instead of hardcoding knowledge about order cancellation or item availability. This is like an interactive map with a legend and all the necessary information. This section explores the practical implementation of adding meaningful hypermedia controls to your Magic Items API, moving beyond theoretical compliance to measure your progress toward true hypermedia maturity.

Beyond basic REST: implementing true hypermedia

You might think your Magic Items store API is RESTful because it uses proper HTTP methods and status codes, such as GET for potion details, POST for adding wands to carts, and 404s for non-existent artifacts. While a great start, this only represents Level 2 of the Richardson Maturity Model discussed in *Chapter 6*. True REST requires hypermedia, enabling clients to navigate your API solely through the controls provided in each response. Many APIs claiming to be RESTful lack this critical ingredient, resulting in what some call "REST-ish" APIs. Let's look at how your current Magic Items API might fall short of true hypermedia implementation, and what practical steps you can take to bridge that gap.

Hypermedia's critical role in REST

Remember the Richardson Maturity Model we explored earlier? Level 1 gave us proper resources and URLs, Level 2 added appropriate HTTP methods and status codes, but it's Level 3 – Hypermedia Controls – that completes the REST puzzle. Without hypermedia, you're building APIs that miss REST's revolutionary core principle: the ability for clients to dynamically discover and navigate API capabilities.

Here's what this looks like in practice with our Magic Items store:

```
// Level 2 API response
{
  "id": "wand-1",
  "name": "Oak Wand with Dragon Heartstring",
  "price": 75.0,
  "inStock": true,
  "powerLevel": 8
}
```

♀ **Quick tip:** Enhance your coding experience with the **AI Code Explainer** and **Quick Copy** features. Open this book in the next-gen Packt Reader. Click the **Copy** button (**1**) to quickly copy code into your coding environment, or click the **Explain** button (**2**) to get the AI assistant to explain a block of code to you.

```
                                              Copy    Explain
function calculate(a, b) {
    return {sum: a + b};                       1        2
};
```

⊟ **The next-gen Packt Reader** is included for free with the purchase of this book. Scan the QR code OR go to https://packtpub.com/unlock, then use the search bar to find this book by name. Double-check the edition shown to make sure you get the right one.

This response gives us data but no indication of what we can do next. Should customers just know they can add this to their cart at /cart/items? What if we later change that endpoint? In contrast, true hypermedia includes controls that guide the client:

```
// Level 3 API response with hypermedia controls
{
  "id": "wand-1",
  "name": "Oak Wand with Dragon Heartstring",
  "price": 75.0,
  "inStock": true,
  "powerLevel": 8,
  "_links": {
    "self": { "href": "/items/wand-1" },
    "add-to-cart": { "href": "/cart/items", "method": "POST" },
    "similar-items": { "href": "/items?type=wand&powerLevel=8" },
    "compatible-potions": { "href": "/items/wand-1/compatible-potions" }
  }
}
```

Another common misconception is that simply including URLs in your response counts as hypermedia. True hypermedia provides not just links but context about what those links represent and how to use them. Notice how our improved response includes both the links and information about how to interact with them, such as the HTTP method to use.

Many APIs fall short by implementing hypermedia inconsistently, adding links to some resources but not others, or failing to include crucial state transitions. For a truly RESTful Magic Items API, every response should contain the controls necessary for clients to take any valid next step, from browsing similar wands to checking compatibility with magical potions.

Assessing your API's hypermedia maturity

How mature is your API's hypermedia implementation? Ask yourself these practical questions:

- Can a client navigate your entire API starting from a single entry point? Try accessing just your root endpoint (/) and see if you can discover how to perform key actions or access different resources without prior knowledge.

- Do state transitions include all necessary information? When a resource is created or updated, does the response include links to view its status, modify it, or access related resources?

- Are link relation types consistent and meaningful? The same relation, such as *edit* or *details* should mean the same thing throughout your API.

Let's look at what an immature implementation might return when a customer places an order:

```
{
  "orderId": "order-1234",
  "status": "confirmed",
  "total": 125.0,
  "link": "/orders/order-1234"
}
```

The client has to guess what to do next. Can they cancel? View items? Check shipping? They don't know!

From theory to practice: implementing hypermedia

Moving from theoretical compliance to practical implementation involves implementing some concrete steps. First, start with an API index. Create a discoverable entry point that lists available resources and actions. In the following example, we see a response from calling the GET method on the root / endpoint of our Magic Items store.

```
GET https://magic-items.com/
{
  "_links": {
    "items": { "href": "/items" },
    "potions": { "href": "/items?type=potion" },
    "wands": { "href": "/items?type=wand" },
    "cart": { "href": "/cart" },
    "orders": { "href": "/orders" }
  }
}
```

As the next step, add contextual links to every response. Don't just return data. Include relevant actions and related resources. In the following example, we are getting an order response with contextual actions to other sensible actions.

```
{
  "orderId": "order-1234",
  "status": "confirmed",
  "total": 125.0,
```

```
    "_links": {
      "self": { "href": "/orders/order-1234" },
      "cancel": {
        "href": "/orders/order-1234/cancel",
        "method": "POST"
      },
      "items": { "href": "/orders/order-1234/items" },
      "payment": { "href": "/orders/order-1234/payment" }
    }
  }
```

Additionally, you should represent state transitions explicitly. If an order's status changes to *shipped*, the available actions should change too. The *cancel* link might disappear while a *track* link appears.

Lastly, remember to use standardized link relations when possible. Use established relations such as *next*, *prev*, *self*, and *collection* for predictability. For domain-specific relations such as *brew-potion* or *enchant-item* ensure consistency throughout your API.

Remember, practical hypermedia isn't about checking a box on the REST compliance list – it's about creating an API that's truly self-describing and adaptable. Your API's consumers shouldn't need to read extensive documentation just to figure out how to list their inventory or process returns – they should be able to follow your API's built-in navigational cues.

> **Link relation types**
>
> You can find the whole list of IANA-registered link relations here: https://www.
> iana.org/assignments/link-relations/link-relations.xhtml

Hypermedia controls in practice

To implement effective hypermedia controls in your API, focus on a structured design rather than superficial additions. Like a well-built engine requiring precise components, hypermedia demands consistent link relations, clear state transitions, and contextual actions. This section will explore how to represent available actions and reflect state changes in a way that guides API users effectively, while balancing comprehensive controls with performance optimization. Avoid complexity that hinders usability. Overengineered solutions are difficult to work with.

Implementing link relations effectively

Link relations are crucial identifiers that inform clients about the purpose of each hypermedia control. In our Magic Items store API, they function like clear labels on products, helping users to understand available actions and resources. It's a good practice to combine standardized link relations, such as those mentioned earlier from IANA, with domain-specific ones that express your API's unique capabilities. This approach ensures your API is both understandable and specific at the same time.

```
{
  "id": "crystal-wand-7",
  "name": "Crystal Wand of Illumination",
  "_links": {
    "self": { "href": "/items/crystal-wand-7" },
    "next": { "href": "/items/phoenix-feather-8" },
    "collection": { "href": "/items?type=wand" },
    "enchant": { "href": "/items/crystal-wand-7/enchantments" }
  }
}
```

In this example, self, next, and collection are standard IANA-registered relations that most clients will immediately understand, while enchant is a domain-specific relation unique to our magical context.

For domain-specific relations, establish clear naming conventions and stick to them consistently. If you use enchant in one place, don't use add-enchantment or enchantment elsewhere for the same concept.

Remember to make your link relations descriptive of the relationship, not the destination. The potions relation name is poor compared to compatible-potions or recommended-potions, which express why these potions are linked to this wand.

State transitions as hypermedia controls

State transitions are where hypermedia truly shines – showing clients exactly what actions are possible given the current state of a resource. Consider a magical potion in your store that exists in multiple states: *brewing, ready, testing,* and *for sale.*

Rather than clients hardcoding the possible transitions, your API can dynamically present the appropriate actions:

```
{
  "id": "healing-potion-42",
  "name": "Greater Healing Potion",
  "state": "brewing",
  "completionTime": "2023-09-15T14:30:00Z",
  "_links": {
    "self": { "href": "/potions/healing-potion-42" },
    "cancel-brewing": {
      "href": "/potions/healing-potion-42/cancel",
      "method": "POST"
    },
    "check-status": { "href": "/brewing-status/healing-potion-42" }
  }
}
```

Then, when this potion changes state from brewing, to ready, its links and properties would change as well:

```
{
  "id": "healing-potion-42",
  "name": "Greater Healing Potion",
  "state": "ready",
  "_links": {
    "self": { "href": "/potions/healing-potion-42" },
    "test-quality": {
      "href": "/potions/healing-potion-42/test",
      "method": "POST"
    },
    "put-for-sale": {
      "href": "/potions/healing-potion-42/sell",
      "method": "POST"
    }
  }
}
```

The available actions change completely based on the potion's state. When brewing, you can cancel or check the status. When the potion is ready, you can test it or put it up for sale. The client doesn't need to know these business rules. They're embedded in the hypermedia controls themselves.

This state-driven approach creates a self-documenting API. Your clients don't need to memorize what actions are possible on potions in various states. They just look at the available controls and understand their options immediately.

Context-sensitive actions

Another powerful feature of hypermedia is when controls adapt not just to resource state, but to the broader context. Things such as who is making the request, what time it is, or what other conditions exist. Consider this response returned for a Magic Items store's client:

```
{
  "name": "Crystal Wand of the Ancients",
  "price": 500.0,
  "_links": {
    "self": { "href": "/items/rare-crystal-wand" },
    "add-to-cart": { "href": "/cart/items", "method": "POST" }
  }
}
```

And the response for the same item, when the request is made by the shop's administrator:

```
{
  "name": "Crystal Wand of the Ancients",
  "price": 500.0,
  "cost": 250.0,
  "_links": {
    "self": { "href": "/items/rare-crystal-wand" },
    "update": { "href": "/admin/items/rare-crystal-wand", "method": "PUT"
},
    "adjust-inventory": { "href": "/admin/inventory/rare-crystal-wand" }
  }
}
```

Notice how the administrative response includes the additional cost data field and management-focused links – update and adjust-inventory – while the customer view only shows purchasing options. This demonstrates hypermedia's ability to adapt both data and actions based on user roles.

Context sensitivity can also reflect temporary conditions. A *buy-now* link might disappear when inventory reaches zero, or special *sale-price* links might appear during promotional periods. This approach means clients don't need to know your business rules; they simply follow the available paths presented to them, just as customers in your magical shop would only see doors they're permitted to enter.

Balancing hypermedia richness with simplicity

While hypermedia controls make your API more discoverable, there's a fine line between helpful guidance and overwhelming complexity. An API that includes every possible link on every response can become cluttered and inefficient. Instead, focus on the most relevant links for each context. Ask yourself: "What would my client typically want to do next with this resource?" Include those links, but save rarely used options for more specific views:

```
{
  "id": "healing-potion-42",
  "name": "Greater Healing Potion",
  "_links": {
    "self": { "href": "/potions/healing-potion-42" },
    "collection": { "href": "/potions" },
    "similar-potions": { "href": "/potions?similar-to=healing-potion-42"
},
    "details": { "href": "/potions/healing-potion-42/details" }
  }
}
```

Another important aspect to consider is offering a specific media type for the right situations, such as bandwidth-sensitive scenarios. In those, think about clients getting responses with minimal hypermedia through content negotiation to serve the appropriate level of detail.

Throughout this section, we've seen how hypermedia transforms your Magic Items API from a collection of disconnected endpoints into a dynamic, self-describing system. We've explored how to implement effective link relations, guide clients through state transitions, create context-sensitive actions, and balance comprehensiveness with simplicity. By embracing true hypermedia controls, your API becomes not just technically RESTful but genuinely adaptable and discoverable. Now that you understand the power of hypermedia, let's dive into the practical details of implementing it in your API through specific patterns and formats.

Navigating hypermedia implementation: patterns, formats, and challenges

Understanding hypermedia's importance is just the first step; now you need to implement it in your API. In this section, we'll explore practical hypermedia patterns, compare formats based on real-world considerations, and address implementation challenges you'll face.

Essential hypermedia design patterns

Successful hypermedia implementation depends on consistent design patterns that guide clients through your API. Think of these patterns as the standard navigation elements in an online store: search bars, category filters, *related items* sections, and checkout buttons. No matter how your store looks, customers expect these elements to behave in predictable ways. We'll explore proven hypermedia patterns for navigating collections, transitioning between states, discovering related resources, and handling conditional actions. These patterns work across different formats, forming the building blocks of a truly navigable API for your Magic Items store.

Navigating collections: pagination, filtering, and sorting

Collection resources, such as your product catalogue, order history, or customer reviews, need consistent navigation patterns. Similar to physical stores, APIs require predictable navigation for large datasets.

Pagination links

The core of collection navigation is pagination, which requires clear signposts:

```
{
  "items": [
    { "id": "product-123", "name": "Healing Potion" }
    // More items...
  ],
  "_links": {
    "self": { "href": "/products?page=2" },
    "next": { "href": "/products?page=3" },
    "prev": { "href": "/products?page=1" }
  }
}
```

This example provides three essential navigation links:

- `self`: The current page, useful for refreshing or sharing
- `next`: The next page of results, absent on the final page
- `prev`: The previous page, absent on the first page

Clients don't need to know your pagination implementation. They simply follow the links provided.

Collection metadata

Always include information about the collection itself:

```
{
  "page": {
    "size": 10,
    "totalElements": 118,
    "totalPages": 12,
    "number": 2
  }
}
```

This metadata enables the following:

- Allows clients to show **Page 2 of 12** in interfaces
- Progress indicators (e.g., **Showing 11-20 of 118 products**)
- Clients to know whether to expect more pages

By providing this context, you help API consumers build more informative and user-friendly interfaces, handle edge cases, such as empty results or last pages, gracefully, and optimize their data-fetching strategies.

Filtering and sorting

For filtering and sorting, templated links show available options:

```
{
  "_links": {
    "filter": {
      "href": "/products{?category,min_price}",
      "templated": true
    }
  }
}
```

This templated link shows that clients can filter by `category` and `min_price` parameters. The templated format indicates that these are optional query parameters, allowing clients to discover filtering capabilities without hardcoding knowledge.

For sorting, indicate available sort fields and directions:

```
{
  "_links": {
    "sort": {
      "href": "/products{?sort}",
      "templated": true,
      "options": ["price_asc", "price_desc", "name"]
    }
  }
}
```

The `options` property lists valid sorting values, preventing clients from having to guess which fields support sorting.

When implementing these patterns, remember that good collection navigation does the following:

- Is consistent across all collection resources in your API
- Preserves context when navigating (filters stay applied when paging)
- Dynamically excludes impossible actions (no `prev` on first page)
- Provides enough metadata for clients to build intuitive interfaces

These patterns create discoverable, predictable navigation that helps clients move through your data collections efficiently.

Related resource discovery patterns

When implementing hypermedia, you need consistent patterns for discovering connected resources. Just like product pages showing **You might also like** sections, your API needs clear ways to expose relationships.

```
{
  "id": "product-123",
  "name": "Healing Potion",
  "_links": {
    "self": { "href": "/products/123" },
    "similar": { "href": "/products/123/similar" },
```

```
        "ingredients": { "href": "/products/123/ingredients" }
    }
}
```

This example shows three essential link types:

- Direct self-reference
- Collection of related resources
- Component resources

For complex relationships, consider embedding previews rather than just links:

```
{
  "id": "cart-456",
  "_embedded": {
    "items": [
      {
        "name": "Healing Potion",
        "quantity": 2,
        "_links": { "self": { "href": "/products/123" } }
      }
    ]
  }
}
```

This embedded approach reduces the need for multiple requests while still maintaining proper hypermedia controls for further navigation.

Dynamic pathways: conditional actions and availability

In real APIs, not all actions are available to every user or in every situation. Your hypermedia API needs to conditionally present actions based on resource state, user permissions, and business rules.

To make actions contextual, the simplest approach is to include or exclude links based on conditions:

```
{
  "name": "Healing Potion",
  "inStock": false,
  "_links": {
```

```
      "self": { "href": "/products/123" },
      "notify": {
        "href": "/notifications/product-123",
        "method": "POST"
      }
      // No "add-to-cart" link when out of stock
    }
  }
```

This response omits the add-to-cart link entirely when the product is unavailable, guiding clients toward notification options instead.

Sometimes, though, it's better to include all possible actions but mark their availability:

```
{
  "id": "order-456",
  "_links": {
    "cancel": {
      "href": "/orders/456/cancel",
      "method": "POST",
      "available": false,
      "reason": "Order already shipped"
    }
  }
}
```

This pattern explicitly shows that cancellation exists but isn't currently available, with a reason that clients can display to users, such as a grayed-out button with hover text explaining why.

Reusability

Remember that building an API means that you want to expose your data to multiple different client types, such as web, mobile app, desktop app, and so on. The contextual actions you provide should be relevant to all of them and express the capabilities of your application in the current state, rather than the current client. Otherwise, you risk creating a point-to-point integration rather than a reusable interface to your application.

By carefully managing which actions you present and when, you create an API that gracefully guides clients through complex business processes without requiring them to understand every rule and condition. Clients simply follow the available paths presented to them, creating a more intuitive and less error-prone experience.

Choosing the right hypermedia format

Selecting the right hypermedia format for your Magic Items store API is like choosing the right packaging for your products. This decision affects how clients interact with your API, how easily they can discover capabilities, and how well your API evolves over time.

Why your format choice matters

The hypermedia format you choose directly impacts several critical aspects of your API ecosystem. Different formats provide varying levels of guidance for navigating your API, significantly affecting client experience as users interact with your resources. Developer adoption is also influenced by your format choice, as some formats are inherently easier to understand and implement than others, potentially accelerating or hindering integration efforts. When considering long-term maintenance, certain formats make it easier to add new capabilities without breaking existing clients, facilitating smoother API evolution over time. Additionally, the performance characteristics of your API are affected by format verbosity, which directly influences payload size and parsing complexity, potentially impacting response times and resource utilization.

> **Common Hypermedia formats**
>
> When choosing a standardized hypermedia format, you have a plethora of options. We are not going to dive into each one of them, but if you are interested in the topic, these are some of those with the highest adoption: HAL (`https://datatracker.ietf.org/doc/html/draft-kelly-json-hal-11`), JSON-LD (`https://json-ld.org/`), Siren (`https://github.com/kevinswiber/siren`), and JSON:API (`https://jsonapi.org/`). For error handling, there is currently an internet standard worth following, called problem+json (`https://www.rfc-editor.org/rfc/rfc9457`).

Choosing your format: strategic considerations

Different hypermedia formats represent different philosophies about how to implement HATEOAS principles. Rather than selecting based on technical sophistication alone, consider practical factors such as client ecosystem support, team familiarity, and performance requirements.

Whichever format you choose, consistent implementation is key to creating a truly navigable API. This decision fundamentally shapes how clients will interact with your API, directly influencing the next critical aspect of your design: the impact on your overall API architecture and implementation.

Overcoming implementation challenges

We've established our hypermedia strategy and selected an appropriate format. Now let's address the implementation challenges that inevitably arise during development. We've found that selecting the right libraries for your chosen format can significantly streamline development, while thoughtful performance optimization prevents response bloat as link collections grow. Additionally, we'll examine testing approaches we've developed to verify those critical state transitions and navigational paths. In this section, we'll work through these practical challenges with solutions we've successfully applied in production environments. Let's transform our carefully crafted designs into maintainable, efficient code that delivers on hypermedia's promises. These implementation challenges become particularly evident when addressing client-side consumption patterns.

Client library considerations

When implementing hypermedia in production APIs, client-side consumption presents unique challenges. Most standard HTTP client libraries were designed for hardcoded endpoints, not for discovering and following dynamic hypermedia controls. This creates a fundamental mismatch that you'll need to address through strategic decisions.

Think about the range of client library options available to you. You can choose between generic hypermedia clients, such as HAL browsers or Siren parsers, for specific hypermedia formats that you are using. While generic clients provide immediate hypermedia support, they may not handle your domain-specific needs efficiently. To address this issue, you should consider building client libraries that can assist developers in handling hypermedia links and navigating the API. It is really important to design your client's libraries to work even when hypermedia controls are absent or limited. This allows for graceful degradation during API evolution or partial updates, much like how retail websites still function when certain navigation elements are unavailable.

Incremental adoption strategies and handling backward compatibility

Transforming your API from a conventional endpoint-based design to a fully hypermedia-driven system is not a one-step challenge. For successful adoption, you should follow an evolutionary path that considers existing client integrations while gradually introducing more hypermedia controls. This incremental approach allows both your team and your API consumers to adapt at a manageable pace.

A good first step is expanding your existing response formats rather than replacing them entirely. Add a simple `_links` object to your current JSON responses, introducing basic navigation controls without disrupting the familiar data structure. This "hypermedia-lite" approach lets clients that ignore these controls continue functioning while allowing newer clients to discover and leverage the navigation capabilities.

```
{
    "name": "Healing Potion",
    "price": 29.99,
    "_links": {
      "self": { "href": "/products/potion-123" }
    }
}
```

The preceding example shows adding the first hypermedia controls to your API response.

As your application evolves, gradually expand these controls to include more sophisticated state transitions and related resources. When introducing new features, implement them first through hypermedia controls rather than new endpoints, allowing clients to discover functionality organically rather than through documentation alone.

Backward compatibility becomes particularly crucial when introducing hypermedia to established APIs. Remember that "the externally observable behavior of an API cannot be changed once published." Unlike internal software, where you control all components, API consumers may be organizations or individuals you've never met, running applications you cannot update. Breaking these integrations can be very costly to your consumers and ultimately to you. When adding hypermedia controls, ensure your API still responds to existing request patterns. To retain general backwards compatibility, do not delete anything and do not change processing rules. Instead, focus on adding hypermedia properties and metadata and consider leveraging content negotiation to serve different representations based on client capabilities. This approach offers enriched hypermedia responses to newer clients while maintaining simpler formats for legacy systems.

```
Accept: application/vnd.magicitems.v1+json
Accept: application/vnd.magicitems.hypermedia+json
```

These two examples of content negotiation headers show a possible approach to content negotiation using the vendor-specific (vnd) media format with and without hypermedia enabled.

While versioning plays an important role in this evolution (a topic we'll explore deeply in *Chapter 13*), the ideal approach minimizes the need for explicit versioning by designing for backward compatibility from the start.

Testing becomes especially critical during this transition. Implement comprehensive test suites that verify both new hypermedia functionality and continued support for legacy request patterns. By taking a thoughtful, incremental approach to hypermedia adoption, your API can evolve gracefully without forcing consumers into disruptive upgrades. This balance of innovation and stability creates a foundation of trust with your developer community while still enabling your API to embrace the full power of hypermedia controls.

In this section, we explored the practical aspects of bringing hypermedia to life in your API. We examined essential design patterns for collection navigation, state transitions, and resource discovery that create intuitive pathways through your data. We have talked about how to select the right foundation for your specific needs by choosing a fitting standard. We have also addressed real-world implementation challenges, showing what to consider while choosing client libraries and how to adopt hypermedia incrementally without disrupting existing clients, ensuring backward compatibility through thoughtful evolution. With these foundational implementation patterns established, we now turn to an emerging frontier: designing hypermedia APIs specifically for AI consumption. As AI increasingly becomes an API consumer alongside human developers, special considerations arise for making your hypermedia controls interpretable and navigable by machine learning systems.

Designing hypermedia APIs for AI consumption

As AI systems increasingly become key consumers of APIs, they bring unique requirements that differ from those of human developers. AI agents rely entirely on structured, predictable patterns to navigate and utilize APIs autonomously, making hypermedia's self-describing nature an ideal fit. This section explores how to design APIs that are optimized for both human and AI consumers, unlocking new possibilities for intelligent automation and integration.

Understanding AI API consumption patterns

Unlike human developers who rely on intuition and documentation, AI systems depend on semantic clarity, consistent link relations, and machine-readable affordances to interpret and navigate APIs effectively. We will dive deeper into the unique ways AI interacts with hypermedia controls, providing insights into how you can design APIs that support autonomous decision-making and seamless navigation for intelligent systems.

How AI systems interpret and navigate API structures

AI systems interact with APIs differently from humans. While humans can understand many things from the context and documentation, AI depends on machine-readable structures. Hypermedia APIs are ideal for AI as they embed navigational controls in responses, allowing autonomous resource discovery. For example, an AI in a Magic Items store API could start at the root (/) and follow links such as `related_items` to explore the catalogue without hardcoded URLs.

Semantic clarity is critical for AI systems to interpret API structures effectively. Specific formats, which use standardized vocabularies, provide explicit meaning for properties such as `price` or `category`. This allows AI agents to understand the domain context of resources, enabling more intelligent decision-making. For instance, an AI agent could identify items labelled as "on sale" and prioritize them when recommending products to users.

Key differences between human and AI consumption

In the case of hypermedia, the main difference between humans and machines is how each uses hypermedia controls. Humans use implicit context and documentation, while AI needs consistent link relations and machine-readable affordances in responses. For example, a human understands a cancel link, but an AI needs explicit metadata such as HTTP methods or a description.

AI systems also process state transitions differently. While humans can guess workflows from the context or business logic, AI agents depend on hypermedia controls to guide them through valid transitions. For example, if an order is in the `processing` state, the API should explicitly include links for allowable actions such as `cancel` or `track shipment`. Without these controls, the AI cannot determine what actions are possible. Even providing API descriptions in machine-readable files, such as OpenAPI Specification may not be enough for machines to infer all the required information to understand workflows or more contextual processes.

Another key distinction is scalability. Humans typically interact with APIs at a slower pace and in smaller volumes, while AI systems can process large datasets rapidly and execute complex workflows autonomously. This makes performance optimization, such as sparse field sets or caching, especially important for APIs consumed by AI.

By designing APIs with semantic clarity, consistent link relations, and actionable state transitions, you ensure that both human developers and AI systems can navigate your API effectively. This dual optimization unlocks new possibilities for automation, intelligent integration, and seamless interaction across diverse use cases.

AI capabilities: pattern recognition, context understanding, and reasoning

AI systems are really good at identifying patterns, understanding context, and reasoning through complex scenarios. Pattern recognition allows AI to detect relationships within data, such as identifying recurring trends or anomalies. For instance, in our Magic Items store API, an AI could analyze customer purchase histories to recognize patterns such as frequent purchases of healing potions during winter months or spikes in demand for rare artifacts before major events. This ability is foundational for tasks such as recommendation systems, fraud detection, and inventory optimization.

Context understanding is what enables AI to interpret data in relation to its environment. In contrast to simple pattern recognition, context-aware AI considers factors such as user preferences, historical interactions, and external conditions. For example, an AI-powered assistant might recommend items not only based on prior purchases but also by factoring in seasonal trends or current promotions. In **natural language processing (NLP)**, contextual understanding allows AI to grasp the meaning of words based on their usage. For instance, distinguishing whether "staff" refers to employees or a magical item, depending on the conversation.

Reasoning takes these capabilities further by enabling AI to synthesize information and draw meaningful conclusions. For example, if an AI notices that a customer has added multiple ingredients to their cart but no brewing equipment, it might infer that they need a cauldron and suggest it as an additional purchase. Reasoning also helps AI adapt dynamically. It could revise recommendations when new data becomes available or adjust workflows based on changing customer behaviors.

By combining pattern recognition, context understanding, and reasoning, AI systems can navigate APIs autonomously and intelligently, offering personalized experiences and unlocking new possibilities for automation and decision-making. These capabilities make hypermedia APIs particularly powerful for AI consumption, as their self-describing nature provides the structured pathways needed for effective exploration and interaction.

Current limitations and expected evolution in AI API interactions

Today's AI systems face significant challenges when interacting with APIs, particularly those lacking good hypermedia controls. While capable of impressive language processing, modern AI struggles with several fundamental limitations that impact effective API navigation and utilization.

Contextual understanding barriers

AI systems often struggle to maintain context across complex API workflows. Unlike humans, who intuitively understand that adding an item to a cart naturally precedes checkout, AI may fail to recognize these implicit relationships without explicit guidance. For example, when interacting with our Magic Items store API, an AI agent might successfully retrieve product details but struggle to understand that the add-to-cart link represents the next logical step in a purchasing workflow rather than just another resource to explore. Without semantic context, AI systems may treat all links as equally relevant rather than understanding their roles in business processes.

API discovery and navigation challenges

Current AI systems lack efficient mechanisms for exploring unfamiliar APIs. They often resort to trial-and-error approaches or require extensive training on API descriptions, such as an OpenAPI document. When API structures change or new capabilities are added, AI systems may continue using outdated patterns, missing new, more efficient pathways. This limitation becomes particularly evident when dealing with complex state transitions that require understanding which actions are available at each state.

Future integration patterns

The combination of hypermedia-driven APIs with semantic payloads is emerging as the foundation for truly autonomous AI interactions. By embedding machine-readable contexts through standardized formats designed for this purpose and implementing consistent hypermedia patterns, APIs are becoming self-describing environments that AI can navigate with minimal human intervention.

As these technologies mature, we can expect a new generation of agentic AI systems capable of performing complex tasks through APIs without human oversight: from orchestrating entire procurement workflows to managing sophisticated customer interactions, all by following and interpreting the hypermedia controls that guide them through your digital ecosystem.

AI-navigable APIs: designing for machine consumption

When designing APIs for AI consumption, creating clear pathways for discovery and navigation becomes as important as the functionality itself. Your API's entry point serves as the front door to your digital storefront. As we have already mentioned before, AI systems need programmatically discoverable capabilities.

To start off, implement a well-structured root endpoint that provides navigational links to key resources and capabilities.

```
GET /
{
  "name": "Magic Items Store API",
  "_links": {
    "products": { "href": "/products" },
    "orders": { "href": "/orders" },
    "schema": { "href": "/schema" }
  }
}
```

This approach enables AI consumers to discover your API's capabilities programmatically rather than requiring hardcoded knowledge. Including a dedicated introspection endpoint (/schema) further enhances discoverability by providing detailed metadata about available resources and operations.

It is also important not to overwhelm AI systems with all possible operations at once. Reveal capabilities contextually based on the current state and relevance. When an AI requests product information, include links to related operations such as add-to-cart or check-availability directly in the response:

```
GET
/products/healing-potion
{
  "id": "healing-potion",
  "name": "Healing Potion",
  "_links": {
    "add-to-cart": {
      "href": "/cart/items",
      "method": "POST"
    },
    "similar-products": { "href": "/products/healing-potion/similar" }
  }
}
```

This pattern reveals capabilities progressively as the AI navigates through resources. This is somewhat similar to how, in real life, physical stores might present related items near a product (e.g., sponges next to dish detergent). This way, AI systems can discover additional functionality contextually without being overwhelmed by all possible operations at once.

Consistency

Consistency in navigation patterns is particularly crucial for AI consumption. When AI systems encounter predictable patterns, they can more effectively learn and navigate your API. Apply uniform linking structures, consistent relation naming, and standardized operation patterns across your entire API. For example, ensure collection resources always include the same pagination controls, as we explained earlier in this chapter:

```
GET /products?page=2
{
  "items": [
    { "id": "invisibility-potion", "name": "Invisibility Potion" }
  ],
  "_links": {
    "self": { "href": "/products?page=2" },
    "first": { "href": "/products?page=1" },
    "prev": { "href": "/products?page=1" },
    "next": { "href": "/products?page=3" }
  },
  "page": {
    "size": 10,
    "totalElements": 128,
    "totalPages": 13,
    "number": 2
  }
}
```

This consistency ensures AI systems can develop reliable expectations about how to navigate collections, regardless of the specific resource type.

AI using OpenAPI documents

OpenAPI documentation provides the blueprint that helps AI systems understand your API structure, but standard specifications often lack the semantic richness needed for optimal AI interpretation. Enhance your OpenAPI documentation with detailed descriptions, examples, and annotations:

```
paths:
  /products/{productId}:
    get:
      summary: Retrieve a specific product
      description: >
        Returns detailed information about a magical item in the
inventory…
      parameters:
        - name: productId
          in: path
          required: true
          description: The unique id of the magical item
          schema:
            type: string
            example: healing-potion
      responses:
        200:
          description: Successfully retrieved product details
          content:
            application/json:
              schema:
                $ref: '#/components/schemas/Product'
              example:
                id: healing-potion
                name: Healing Potion
                description: Restores 50 hp instantly
                price: 29.99
                category: potions
```

With these detailed descriptions, examples, and semantically rich field names, AI systems can better understand not just the structure of your API but the meaning and purpose of its resources and operations.

By optimizing entry points, implementing progressive disclosure, maintaining consistent navigation patterns, and enhancing OpenAPI documentation, you create an API that's not only functional for human developers but navigable for AI systems. This dual-purpose design future-proofs your API for the emerging landscape of AI-driven integration while maintaining a clear, intuitive experience for traditional consumption.

State machines and decision trees in API design

When designing APIs for complex workflows, traditional stateless approaches often fall short, leaving clients to manage intricate process flows independently. Modern API design recognizes that resources move through well-defined lifecycle states, with each state offering unique capabilities and transition paths. By modelling these workflows explicitly, we create more intuitive interfaces for both human developers and AI agents.

Modelling complex workflows as state machines

State machines provide a structured way to model complex workflows by representing each step as a distinct state and defining transitions between them. In an API, this approach ensures that workflows are not hardcoded on the client side but instead dynamically guided by server-provided links. For example, in an order fulfilment process, states could include *order placed*, *payment processed*, *item shipped*, and *order completed*. Each state would expose specific actions – such as cancelling or tracking – based on its current status, ensuring clients (human or AI) only perform valid operations.

Explicit state transitions with hypermedia

Explicit state transitions in hypermedia APIs make workflows transparent by embedding actionable links directly into responses. This eliminates ambiguity and allows clients to navigate workflows without prior knowledge of the API's logic. For instance, when an order is in the *processing* state, the response might include links for *cancel* or *track shipment*, clearly indicating available actions. This explicit approach ensures that AI systems can autonomously follow valid transitions while human developers gain clarity about workflow rules.

Context preservation in multi-step processes

Preserving context across multi-step workflows is critical for maintaining continuity. This involves passing relevant data between states to avoid redundant queries or loss of information. For example, in a checkout process, the API might carry forward details like selected items, payment method, and shipping address between states such as *cart review* and *payment confirmation*. Context preservation can be achieved through session tokens or embedding contextual metadata within responses. This ensures that both human users and AI systems can seamlessly progress through workflows without requiring repeated data inputs.

Guiding AI through decision trees

AI systems often rely on decision trees to navigate complex workflows by evaluating conditions at each step and choosing appropriate paths. APIs can facilitate this by providing structured decision points with clear criteria for branching. For example, an AI agent managing inventory might query an API to determine whether to reorder stock based on thresholds. This structured approach allows AI agents to evaluate conditions programmatically and take appropriate actions without manual intervention.

By combining state machines, explicit transitions, context preservation, and decision tree guidance, APIs can model workflows that are intuitive for human developers while enabling autonomous navigation for AI systems. These design patterns ensure seamless interaction across complex processes while maintaining flexibility for future enhancements.

Modelling API workflows in OpenAPI

The Arazzo Specification defines an OpenAPI-based approach for documenting API workflows. While Arazzo helps articulate functional use cases with deterministic semantics beneficial for both human developers and AI agents, it fundamentally differs from hypermedia-driven approaches by requiring predefined workflow definitions separate from the API responses themselves. Unlike contextual hypermedia systems, where navigation options are dynamically embedded within responses, allowing clients to discover possibilities at runtime, Arazzo's static documentation approach sacrifices true runtime adaptability and self-discovery for predictability. This makes Arazzo less resilient to API evolution and more dependent on out-of-band knowledge, reinforcing the client-server coupling that hypermedia principles were specifically designed to eliminate. It is still a great way to document API workflows for developers. You can learn more about the Arazzo Specification here: https://www.openapis.org/arazzo.

Practical examples and futureproofing

Designing APIs optimized for AI consumption requires forward-thinking patterns that not only address current needs but also adapt to evolving AI capabilities. By focusing on structured content discovery, intelligent manipulation, and robust search and filtering mechanisms, you can ensure your API remains relevant and effective as AI systems become more autonomous and sophisticated.

API patterns optimized for AI

AI systems thrive on predictability and structure. Implementing consistent patterns across your API makes it easier for AI agents to understand and interact with resources. For example, providing a unified schema for resource representation ensures that AI systems can parse responses uniformly across different endpoints. Take a look at a product catalogue using a standardized structure for all items:

```json
{
  "id": "potion-123",
  "type": "product",
  "attributes": {
    "name": "Healing Potion",
    "price": 29.99,
    "category": "potions",
    "tags": ["health", "restoration"]
  },
  "_links": {
    "self": { "href": "/products/potion-123" },
    "related": { "href": "/products/potion-123/related" }
}}
```

This pattern ensures that AI systems can rely on consistent attribute names (e.g., name, price, tags) and link relations (self, related) across all resources, reducing the need for custom parsing logic. However, this approach also has its drawbacks. Strict adherence to a standardized structure might limit the API's ability to represent complex or unique resource types that don't fit neatly into the predefined schema. Moreover, applying a comprehensive structure to all resources might introduce unnecessary complexity for simpler endpoints that don't require all the standardized fields. Remember, it's always important to balance these standardized patterns with the specific needs of your API and its users.

Content discovery and manipulation

AI systems often need to discover content dynamically and manipulate it based on contextual goals. APIs can facilitate this by embedding metadata that describes the relationships between resources and their manipulable attributes. For example, a search endpoint might include filters for narrowing results:

```
{
  "_links": {
    "search": {
      "href": "/search{?q,category}",
      "templated": true }
  },
  "_templates": {
    "fields": [
      { "name": "q", "type": "string", "description": "Search query" },
      { "name": "category", "type": "string", "description": "Product
category" }
    ]}}
```

This structure enables AI systems to dynamically modify queries based on user preferences or external conditions, such as filtering products within a specific price range. When choosing a templating system, try following some established formats, such as HAL-FORMS or JSON Schema, to avoid potential integration challenges.

Search and filtering patterns for AI consumption

Search and filtering are critical for enabling AI systems to find relevant data efficiently. APIs should provide robust query mechanisms with clear documentation of supported filters, sorting options, and pagination controls. Here's an example:

```
GET /products?category=potions& page=2
{
  "_links": {
    "self": {"href": /products?category=potions& page=2"},
    "next": {"href": "/products?category=potions& page=3"},
    "prev": {"href": "/products?category=potions& page=1"}
  },
  "_embedded": {
    "items": [
```

```
{
  "id": "potion-456",
  "name": "Mana Potion",
  "price": 25.99
}]}}
```

This design allows AI systems to programmatically navigate search results while maintaining context about the current query parameters.

Adapting to evolving AI capabilities

As AI systems grow more capable, APIs must evolve to support advanced reasoning and decision-making processes. This includes providing richer semantic annotations, dynamic workflows, and real-time updates. For example, an inventory management API might offer decision-making guidance based on stock levels:

```
{
  "_actions": [
    {
      "name": "reorder-stock",
      "method": "POST",
      "href": "/inventory/reorder",
      "fields": [
        { "name": "productId", "value": "item-789" },
        { "name": "quantity", "value": 50 }
      ]}]}
```

This response provides an AI-friendly decision tree structure. When a condition is met (stock is low), it suggests an action to reorder stock. The _actions array specifies the API endpoint, HTTP method, and required fields for the reorder operation, enabling AI systems to autonomously execute inventory management tasks based on predefined conditions.

Summary

In this chapter, we've explored how hypermedia APIs bridge the gap between human developers and AI systems. Starting with true RESTful design principles, we tackled the practical side of implementing hypermedia patterns in your APIs. From pagination and filtering to collection management, we covered concrete solutions to common challenges.

We dove into how AI navigates API structures, highlighting the importance of semantic clarity and consistent patterns. We showed how to create an AI-friendly API interface. By modeling workflows as state machines, we demonstrated how to guide AI through complex decision processes.

In the next chapter, we'll dive into API change management and explore strategies for versioning and evolution. You'll learn why change management is essential, discover the key building blocks for success, and see how to implement a practical change process using the Magic Items Store as an example. This chapter will give you the tools to manage change with confidence while keeping your APIs resilient and adaptable.

Get This Book's PDF Version and Exclusive Extras

UNLOCK NOW

Scan the QR code (or go to `packtpub.com/unlock`). Search for this book by name, confirm the edition, and then follow the steps on the page.

Note: Keep your invoice handy. Purchases made directly from Packt don't require an invoice.

13

API Change Management: Strategies for Versioning and Evolution

APIs are living, breathing systems that must evolve to meet the changing demands of technology, business goals, and user expectations. Managing these changes is both an art and a science. Effective API change management ensures that new features and updates enhance the experience without breaking existing integrations. This chapter delves into strategies for API change management, focusing on versioning and evolution while balancing stability and innovation. It emphasizes the critical importance of preserving backward compatibility and maintaining a seamless experience for existing consumers.

We will cover the following main topics in this chapter:

- The *why* of API change management
- API change management building blocks
- Implementing an API change process for Magic Items Store

By following this chapter, you will gain a deep understanding of how to manage API changes without disrupting users. You will learn how to differentiate between versioning and evolution strategies, assess when changes require a version bump, and develop a structured process for implementing these strategies. You'll be able to navigate the complexities of versioning approaches, the principles of API evolution, and practical steps to apply them in a real-world scenario. Additionally, you will explore how companies such as Stripes and Adidas adopt API evolution as a strategy for managing their API changes.

With these skills, you will be well prepared to update your API for new requirements without breaking existing implementations.

The why of API change management

Change is an inevitable part of API development. APIs evolve for several reasons, including the need to modernize legacy systems, introduce new capabilities, and enhance security measures. Modernization helps reduce technical debt, improve scalability, and adopt new architectural patterns that boost performance and developer experience. At the same time, adding new features allows APIs to meet evolving user demands, stay competitive, and unlock new business opportunities. Ensuring security is equally crucial, as it protects sensitive data, mitigates vulnerabilities, and ensures compliance with industry standards. Balancing these needs requires careful planning, effective communication, and a well-defined strategy to manage the impact on API consumers.

Let's dive into the first reason why API change is inevitable: modernization.

API modernization

Modernization efforts play a crucial role in managing technical debt and ensuring APIs remain relevant and scalable in today's fast-paced digital landscape. Over time, legacy code and outdated technologies can become a significant burden, limiting scalability, slowing development cycles, and increasing maintenance costs. Analyst reports, including those from Gartner and Deloitte, have long highlighted that legacy systems can account for a significant portion of enterprise technology, with maintenance costs absorbing 60–80% of IT budgets. This restricts innovation and drains resources that could be better used to build new features or improve user experience.

Refactoring or re-architecting APIs isn't just a technical exercise—it's a strategic move to improve reliability, reduce risk, and modernize practices.

Transitioning from monolithic systems to modular RESTful or GraphQL APIs, for example, not only boosts performance but also increases flexibility and service compatibility. Smaller, well-defined APIs are easier for teams and third parties to integrate with, reducing coupling and speeding up development. In large-scale migrations I've worked on, this flexibility consistently lowered integration overhead and future-proofed systems against changing requirements.

Modernizing APIs also opens the door to cloud-native architectures. Lightweight, stateless APIs can scale horizontally, handle large data volumes, and support real-time workloads with minimal rework. It's not just about handling today's load—it's about building systems that stay resilient and adaptable as demands grow.

Of course, modular APIs introduce their own challenges—schema management, error handling, and client versioning among them. But the long-term gains in scalability, reliability, and integration speed often outweigh the complexity.

Modernized APIs are designed with **future-proofing** in mind, allowing organizations to meet evolving security standards, such as adopting stronger authentication protocols and token-based security measures. Additionally, they facilitate **better system interoperability**, making it easier for various systems and applications to connect and share data seamlessly. This integration improves overall performance, reduces latency, and creates a more intuitive user experience.

A successful API modernization strategy isn't just about replacing old technology—it's about transforming APIs into scalable, secure, and high-performing solutions that drive business innovation. With the right approach, organizations can reduce technical debt, improve developer productivity, and adapt more quickly to changing user demands and market conditions.

> Best practice
>
> A key best practice in API modernization is to conduct a comprehensive API assessment and adopt an iterative modernization approach. The assessment helps identify pain points such as performance bottlenecks, security vulnerabilities, and outdated components, providing a clear roadmap for modernization. Rather than overhauling everything at once, an iterative approach focuses on incremental improvements, starting with high-impact areas. This reduces risks, minimizes service disruption, and allows for continuous delivery of value while aligning modernization efforts with business priorities.

Now, let's explore the second reason for API change: introducing new capabilities.

New API capabilities

To stay competitive in today's fast-paced market, businesses must continuously introduce **new API capabilities** that align with evolving user needs and industry demands. New features not only enhance the value of APIs but also enable businesses to expand their service offerings, improve integrations with third-party platforms, and unlock new revenue streams. For example, Stripe continuously evolves its API to introduce new payment methods and fraud detection capabilities, while Slack's API regularly adds features such as message threading and workflow automation, expanding its integration possibilities for developers.

However, balancing innovation with stability is critical to avoid disruptions. Poorly managed API changes can lead to broken client integrations, increased support costs, and a loss of trust from developers and partners. A notable example is Facebook's API changes, which caused significant disruption when it restricted access to user data after the Cambridge Analytica scandal. While the change was necessary for privacy protection, it was implemented with minimal warning and inadequate alternatives for developers, causing frustration and leading many to abandon their integrations.

Another case is X/Twitter's sudden deprecation of free API access, which caught many developers off guard and forced them to rapidly adjust or shut down their applications. These incidents highlight the importance of API change management strategies, backward compatibility, and proactive communication to maintain user trust during API evolution.

A well-structured API change management process ensures that businesses can introduce new capabilities confidently while preserving a strong relationship with their developer community. Clear documentation, adequate lead time for changes, and transparent communication can help smooth transitions and foster long-term trust.

Now, let's dive into the third reason for API change: security updates.

Security updates

Security updates are essential to ensure that APIs remain resilient against emerging threats and comply with evolving security standards. These updates safeguard sensitive data, protect systems from exploitation, and maintain user trust in the API ecosystem.

A great example is Stripe's transition from API v1 to API v2, which introduced stronger authentication models and improved request validation. By implementing more secure access methods and improving idempotency handling, Stripe reduced the risk of unauthorized access and ensured more reliable request processing. These changes reflect Stripe's commitment to staying ahead of evolving security risks while maintaining a seamless developer experience.

Similarly, Twilio's approach to securing webhooks and media files demonstrates how security updates can protect sensitive data in real-time communication services. Twilio recommends using **HTTPS** and **TLS encryption** to secure communications and prevent man-in-the-middle attacks. For media files, such as call recordings or images sent via messaging services, Twilio supports **HTTP basic authentication**, ensuring that only authorized users can access this content. Twilio also provides **request validation using HMAC-SHA1 signatures**, enabling developers to verify that incoming requests are genuinely from Twilio and not malicious actors.

These examples highlight the importance of proactive security updates in protecting APIs from potential vulnerabilities. Regular audits, adopting modern security protocols such as **OAuth 2.0**, and validating requests help organizations maintain a secure API environment. Combining these practices with clear documentation and developer tools ensures a smooth implementation of security updates without disrupting user integrations.

Now that you understand *why* API change management is important, let's delve into its core building blocks—the essential components that help ensure API evolution is smooth, well communicated, and aligned with business goals.

API change management building blocks

API change management is a strategic process that balances the need for innovation with the importance of stability and reliability. Evolving an API is not merely a technical necessity; it requires careful planning, communication, and a well-defined change strategy that aligns with business goals and user expectations. Each change—whether introducing new features, improving performance, or addressing security—must be evaluated for its potential impact on consumers to ensure a smooth transition.

Successful API change management consists of several key building blocks. Let's dive into the first one: **strategic prioritization and planning**.

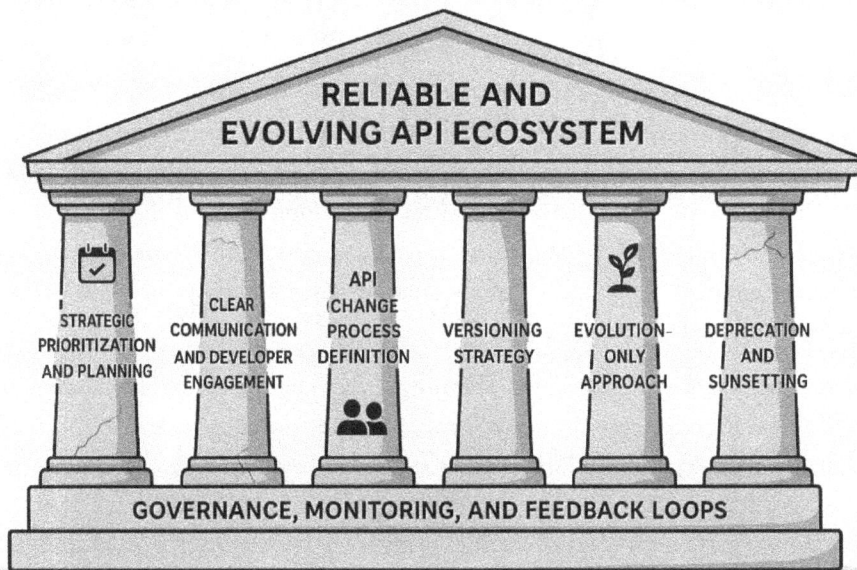

Figure 13.1 – API change management building blocks

🔍**Quick tip**: Need to see a high-resolution version of this image? Open this book in the next-gen Packt Reader or view it in the PDF/ePub copy.

📖**The next-gen Packt Reader** is included for free with the purchase of this book. Scan the QR code OR go to `https://packtpub.com/unlock`, then use the search bar to find this book by name. Double-check the edition shown to make sure you get the right one.

Strategic prioritization and planning

API change management begins with a clear strategy and well-defined priorities. Not all API changes are created equal—some are urgent security fixes, others are performance optimizations, and some are business-driven feature enhancements. Strategic planning ensures that changes are aligned with both **technical feasibility** and **business objectives**, avoiding unnecessary disruptions while delivering maximum value. Successful planning involves collaboration across multiple teams, including product, engineering, security, and developer relations.

One critical aspect of planning is identifying the *why* behind each change. Changes driven by business goals might focus on expanding the API's capabilities to unlock new markets or meet evolving customer demands. For example, a payment API might need to support additional currencies or alternative payment methods to enter new regions. On the other hand, technical improvements might aim to reduce latency, improve scalability, or modernize a legacy component to reduce maintenance costs. These reasons must be weighed and prioritized in the context of available resources and technical debt.

Risk assessment plays a crucial role in planning. Every change introduces some level of risk—whether it's breaking existing integrations, impacting performance, or increasing infrastructure costs. By assessing the potential impact of each change, teams can decide which ones to tackle first and what mitigation strategies to put in place. For instance, deploying a new version of an API might require extra performance testing to ensure it can handle expected traffic.

A **roadmap** is an essential tool for strategic planning. It provides a timeline for upcoming changes, offering both internal teams and external developers visibility into what's coming next. This roadmap should balance short-term needs with long-term goals, ensuring the API remains stable while evolving over time. It also helps manage dependencies between teams, aligning release schedules and reducing the chances of conflicts or delays.

Now that you have grasped the importance of strategic prioritization and planning for API change management, let's dive into the second building block: **clear communication and developer engagement**.

Clear communication and developer engagement

Effective communication is the cornerstone of successful API change management. Even the most well-planned change can backfire if developers are caught off guard. Communication should be timely, transparent, and multi-channel to reach all affected stakeholders. It's not just about announcing changes—it's about explaining their rationale, providing guidance, and engaging with developers throughout the process.

One key component of communication is **proactive notification**. API providers should notify developers well in advance of any significant change, especially for breaking changes. Notifications can take several forms, including **changelogs**, **email updates**, **blog posts**, and **developer portal announcements**. For instance, when GitHub introduced new rate limits for its API, it communicated the change months in advance through multiple channels, ensuring developers had ample time to adapt.

Documentation plays a crucial role in communication. Each API update should come with detailed release notes, migration guides, and updated reference documentation. These resources help developers understand how to adjust their integrations and minimize the risk of downtime. Comprehensive documentation is especially critical for complex changes, such as those involving authentication or new request formats.

Another aspect of developer engagement is **community support**. Providing a **sandbox environment** or **early access program** allows developers to test changes before they go live. Offering direct support through forums, Slack channels, or dedicated developer relations teams can also make a big difference in building trust and ensuring smooth transitions.

In addition to effective communication with your API users, you need to define your API change process.

API change process

An effective **API change process** begins with a strategic decision: should your API changes be managed through versioning, continuous evolution, or a hybrid approach? Each strategy has its unique advantages, depending on the API's target audience, complexity, and how frequently it evolves. Selecting the right approach helps reduce friction and ensures a smooth experience for developers while balancing innovation and stability.

The API change process is inherently characterized by trade-offs. For instance, when versioning an API, two essential factors to consider are API cost and API quality:

- **API cost**: Maintaining multiple versions imposes costs on both API providers and users. Upgrading between versions may require significant changes, and some users may struggle to keep pace. Providers face the dilemma of either retiring old versions—which can upset users—or maintaining them indefinitely, which increases operational overhead.

- **API quality**: A robust versioning strategy facilitates continuous improvement. New versions often bring enhanced functionality, security updates, and performance optimizations. Users who delay upgrading might miss out on these benefits, effectively paying a hidden cost for remaining on an older version.

This balancing act paves the way for identifying the API change process that best aligns with your requirements.

Versioning strategy

Versioning is a fundamental strategy in API change management, providing a structured framework for introducing changes—especially breaking ones—without disrupting existing consumers. It allows API providers to evolve their offerings while preserving a stable and predictable experience for developers. When done correctly, versioning ensures that new features and improvements can be introduced with minimal friction, even as older versions continue to serve long-term integrations.

There are different approaches to versioning, and selecting the right one is essential for long-term API success. Some providers adopt global versioning, where the entire API is versioned uniformly, often through URI-based or header-based methods. This approach offers clarity and a consistent upgrade path for consumers, but can increase operational complexity when managing multiple active versions. On the other hand, resource-based versioning allows individual resources to evolve independently, offering more flexibility but at the cost of added complexity in implementation and governance.

Global API versioning

Global API versioning assigns a single version identifier to the entire API, signaling which major set of functionalities is being delivered. This approach is ideal when introducing significant, breaking changes that require a clear demarcation between versions. However, it comes with notable trade-offs:

- **URI versioning**:

    - *Example*: `https://api.example.com/v1/products`

    - While explicit and clear, embedding v1 in the URL forces consumers to hardcode a specific version. This design makes gradual upgrades challenging because the URL itself is tied to a particular version.

- **Query parameter versioning**:

    - *Example*: `https://api.example.com/products?version=1`

    - Decoupling versioning from the URL structure offers more flexibility. However, it can complicate caching mechanisms and may require additional server-side parsing.

- **Header-based versioning**:

    - *Example*: `Accept-Version: 1.0`

    - Using custom headers keeps the URLs clean and consistent across endpoints. The trade-off is that both API providers and consumers must implement custom header handling, and the versioning information may be less discoverable for new users.

> Best practice
>
> Global versioning is effective for managing breaking changes, but can be operationally expensive as the API evolves. Providers must balance the need to support legacy versions against the benefits of pushing new updates.

A critical best practice is avoiding the inclusion of v1 in your URLs. When you do not hardcode the version into the base URL, the default endpoint always represents the latest stable release. This approach encourages a design where consumers interact with the most current, secure, and optimized version, reduces technical debt by minimizing fragmentation in the API structure, and simplifies the upgrade path since consumers do not need to change their base URL with every version update.

While global versioning provides a straightforward method for managing large-scale changes, its one-size-fits-all approach might not be optimal for every scenario. For APIs that require more granular control, resource-based versioning offers an alternative. Let's now transition to exploring how individual resources can be versioned independently.

Resource-based versioning

Resource-based versioning allows individual endpoints or resources to evolve independently rather than enforcing a uniform version across the entire API. This granular approach provides flexibility for incremental updates:

- **URI-based versioning at the resource level:**

    - *Example*: `https://api.example.com/products/v2`

    - In this model, only the specific resource (i.e., `products`) is versioned. Other resources continue to operate at their current version until an update is warranted.

- **Content negotiation (media type versioning):**

    - *Example using custom media types*: `Accept: application/vnd.example.products.v2+json`

    - This method leverages HTTP's content negotiation capabilities. It keeps the URL structure uniform while allowing the server to determine the appropriate resource version based on the `Accept` header.

The following are the advantages:

- **Incremental adoption**: Consumers can upgrade individual resources as needed, rather than switching the entire API

- **Targeted updates**: Changes to one resource do not require modifications to others, reducing the risk of widespread disruption

These are the challenges:

- **Complexity**: Managing different versioning strategies across various resources can lead to inconsistency if not tightly coordinated

- **Documentation overhead**: Detailed, resource-specific documentation is essential so that API consumers clearly understand which version of each resource they are interacting with

Versioning is not always the answer to every API change. Many changes—such as performance improvements or adding optional fields—can be introduced without versioning if they maintain backward compatibility. However, breaking changes such as altering response formats, modifying authentication mechanisms, or removing fields typically require a new version. The key challenge for API providers is to distinguish between these change types and apply versioning judiciously to avoid unnecessary fragmentation.

> **Best practice**
>
> A robust versioning strategy must be complemented by clear communication and governance. Developers need to know when a new version is available, how it differs from the current one, and how to migrate seamlessly. This involves proactive announcements, comprehensive documentation, and well-structured deprecation policies. Without these elements, even the most carefully planned versioning strategy can lead to confusion and frustration among consumers.

Versioning provides a structured solution for managing API changes, but it can introduce long-term maintenance overhead and operational complexity. Providers must carefully plan the life cycle of each version, including defining support timelines and deprecation strategies. For those concerned about reducing maintenance costs while optimizing developer experience, an evolution-based approach may offer a more practical and seamless alternative.

Evolution-only approach

The **evolution-only** approach to API change management prioritizes continuous improvement while maintaining backward compatibility. In this strategy, APIs evolve without introducing new versions, allowing providers to roll out enhancements incrementally. By carefully managing non-breaking changes, such as adding optional fields or improving response formats, the evolution-only approach ensures that existing integrations remain intact and unaffected. This approach is particularly effective when stability and seamless upgrades are critical for maintaining user trust.

One of the main advantages of the evolution-only model is its ability to avoid fragmentation. All consumers remain on the same version of the API, simplifying support and maintenance while reducing the need for complex versioning infrastructure. Since no new versions are created, providers can focus on enhancing the current API without managing multiple active versions. However, this simplicity comes with the added responsibility of rigorously preventing accidental breaking changes, which can have significant consequences for API consumers.

For evolution-only APIs to succeed, a set of strict extension rules must be followed to maintain compatibility. These rules include ensuring that no fields or functionality are removed, no processing rules are altered, and any new features introduced are optional. This discipline minimizes the risk of breaking existing clients and keeps the API surface manageable over time. It also demands that clients adopt a flexible and forgiving implementation, ignoring unknown fields and gracefully handling unexpected data—often referred to as Postel's law.

Note

Postel's law, also known as the robustness principle, is a design guideline for computer systems, particularly in networking protocols. It advises that software should be conservative in what it sends (output should strictly adhere to the relevant standards and specifications) and liberal in what it accepts (input can be more flexible, allowing systems to process data even if it deviates slightly from the strict standard).

Originally articulated by Jon Postel, this principle has been fundamental in the development of the internet, helping ensure interoperability among diverse systems while maintaining robust communication.

When a breaking change is unavoidable, the evolution-only strategy requires creating a new resource variant rather than altering the existing one. This preserves backward compatibility while offering new functionality. For example, if an optional query parameter needs to become mandatory, the new resource might have a different URI (/new-resource) while the old resource remains available. This ensures that existing clients can continue using the original resource without disruption while new clients adopt the updated variant.

In the evolution-only model, deprecation and sunsetting are critical components for managing resource variants over time. Deprecated variants should be marked clearly in documentation and at runtime, with sufficient notice and guidance provided for consumers to migrate. Regular monitoring of deprecated resources ensures a smooth transition before they are eventually removed. This process, combined with continuous monitoring and communication, helps maintain a healthy API ecosystem without the need for explicit versioning.

While the evolution-only approach focuses on maintaining backward compatibility without introducing new versions, some situations require a more flexible strategy to balance continuous improvements with breaking changes. This is where the hybrid model comes into play, offering a structured yet adaptable framework for managing change. Let's explore how combining evolution with versioning can help API providers achieve both stability and rapid iteration.

Hybrid model (combining versioning and evolution)

The **hybrid model** is one of the most flexible strategies in API change management. It combines continuous evolution for non-breaking changes with versioning for breaking changes, offering the best of both worlds. This approach enables APIs to evolve at a rapid pace while maintaining a structured process for handling significant updates that may disrupt existing integrations.

In a hybrid model, **non-breaking changes**—such as adding optional fields, expanding response payloads, or improving performance—are introduced within the existing version to ensure backward compatibility. These incremental improvements allow developers to adopt changes without requiring immediate action or risking service disruptions. Continuous evolution keeps the API fresh and adaptable, meeting user demands without the overhead of managing multiple versions.

However, when a **breaking change** becomes necessary—such as removing fields, modifying authentication mechanisms, or altering response formats—a new version is introduced. This gives developers a clear migration path and ample time to adjust their integrations. By providing transparent communication and detailed migration guides, API providers can minimize friction and maintain developer trust during these transitions.

An essential component of the hybrid model is the **deprecation and sunsetting strategy**. When a new version is released, the older version must be carefully phased out. Clear deprecation policies ensure developers know how long the old version will be supported and provide them with the tools and time needed to migrate. Regular monitoring of deprecated versions helps determine when it's safe to sunset them, ensuring a seamless transition for all stakeholders.

The hybrid model offers the perfect balance between stability and innovation, allowing API providers to meet the evolving needs of their consumers while maintaining reliable and predictable services. In upcoming sections, we'll delve further into the details of how to implement a hybrid model effectively, including best practices for versioning, deprecation planning, and maintaining a consistent developer experience.

After exploring the flexibility and adaptability of the hybrid model, it's valuable to see how this approach is successfully implemented in real-world scenarios. One notable example is Stripe's API change management process, which combines predictable versioning with continuous evolution. Let's take a closer look at how Stripe has mastered the balance between stability and innovation while maintaining an exceptional developer experience.

Use case: Stripe API change management process

Stripe's API release process is a benchmark for effective planning and strategic change management. Over the years, Stripe has continuously improved its API to meet evolving global payment standards while maintaining backward compatibility and minimizing disruption for its vast developer ecosystem. The recent introduction of a predictable release cadence and versioning system further demonstrates Stripe's thoughtful approach to API evolution.

Under the new model, Stripe combines semi-annual major releases with monthly feature updates, striking a balance between stability and innovation. Each major release includes breaking changes and is thoughtfully named after a plant, reflecting the idea that APIs are growing systems that need to be carefully nurtured and maintained. Monthly releases, in contrast, are backward-compatible and allow for safe adoption of new features without requiring developers to overhaul their integrations.

The **Acacia release**, the first API version under this new process, exemplifies Stripe's focus on predictability. Developers can now plan their engineering cycles more effectively, knowing when to expect breaking changes and how long they have to implement them. The release process is tightly integrated with Stripe's SDKs for each supported language, ensuring that SDK versions remain directly associated with API versions. This eliminates confusion and simplifies dependency management for development teams.

Another pillar of Stripe's success in API change management is its redesigned developer changelog. Unlike traditional changelogs that list every update, Stripe's new changelog helps developers understand which changes apply to their specific API version. It offers step-by-step upgrade guidance, detailed summaries of platform updates, and filtering options to focus on relevant changes. This level of clarity allows developers to adopt changes faster and with more confidence, ultimately leading to a more efficient development experience.

By adopting this structured and transparent release process, Stripe empowers its developer community to innovate while reducing the risks associated with API changes. Predictable updates, comprehensive documentation, and real-time communication ensure that API consumers can stay in sync with Stripe's evolution without sacrificing stability. Stripe's model serves as a best practice for companies seeking to modernize their API strategies while maintaining a seamless user experience.

The following timeline visually illustrates Stripe's regular API release cadence, highlighting planned updates and moments where breaking changes are introduced:

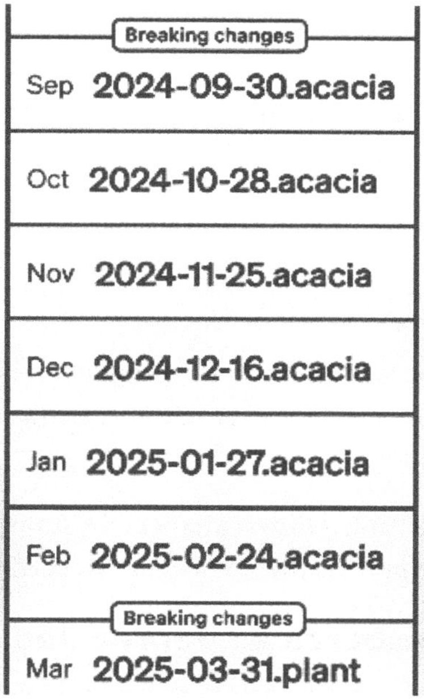

Breaking changes

Sep **2024-09-30.acacia**

Oct **2024-10-28.acacia**

Nov **2024-11-25.acacia**

Dec **2024-12-16.acacia**

Jan **2025-01-27.acacia**

Feb **2025-02-24.acacia**

Breaking changes

Mar **2025-03-31.plant**

Figure 13.2 – Stripe API release process

As we've seen with Stripe's API change management process, **structured planning** and **transparent communication** are critical for seamless API evolution. However, introducing breaking changes requires even more careful handling to avoid disruptions. This is where a well-defined deprecation and sunsetting strategy becomes indispensable. Let's explore how deprecation can be managed effectively to ensure smooth transitions and maintain developer trust.

Deprecation and sunsetting

Deprecation and sunsetting are indispensable phases of the API lifecycle, ensuring that APIs evolve sustainably without sacrificing user trust or system stability. While change is inevitable, forcing abrupt transitions risks alienating developers and disrupting business operations. A well-orchestrated deprecation and sunsetting strategy balances the need for progress with the duty of care owed to existing consumers.

At a high level, deprecation signals that an API feature or version is entering its end-of-life phase, giving developers ample time and guidance to migrate. Sunsetting marks the irreversible removal of the deprecated functionality. Both require careful design—not just technical adjustments, but thoughtful communication, monitoring, and migration support.

Without a deliberate deprecation policy, APIs either calcify (paralyzed by fear of breaking changes) or decay (fragmented with half-supported legacy versions). Properly managed deprecation and sunsetting enable continuous evolution while preserving developer confidence, controlling technical debt, and ensuring a sustainable platform trajectory.

In real-world implementations—such as Stripe's phased version releases or Adidas's structured deprecation protocols—deprecation is treated not as an afterthought but as a core responsibility of API stewardship.

From experience leading multiple large-scale API programs, the APIs that succeed long-term aren't just the ones that ship features fast; they're the ones that help developers *survive change* without feeling abandoned.

Effective deprecation and sunsetting follow a predictable, transparent life cycle. The following subsections show a field-tested process that organizations such as Adidas and Stripe employ.

Mark the feature or resource as deprecated

The first critical move in the deprecation and sunsetting process is to formally announce the beginning of the end-of-life journey for a resource, feature, or version. At this stage, deprecation is no longer an internal technical decision—it becomes a public, contractual signal to your developers and ecosystem.

Done well, this step sets the tone for the entire deprecation life cycle. It tells developers, both human and programmatic, that change is coming, provides them with the necessary context, and empowers them to plan migrations proactively.

Clear, visible deprecation signaling is not a luxury; it is an essential responsibility.

Without it, developers may unknowingly build new integrations on deprecated surfaces, stakeholders may be caught off guard, and trust in the platform can erode rapidly. In contrast, early and explicit deprecation helps do the following:

- Reduce migration friction
- Minimize surprises in production environments
- Preserve the platform's reputation for reliability and developer empathy

A guiding principle

If a client can still discover or integrate with a deprecated feature without a clear warning, the deprecation process has failed.

To avoid this, deprecation signaling must happen on two essential surfaces:

- At runtime, for automated detection by systems, tooling, and monitoring infrastructure
- In documentation, for human developers seeking understanding, guidance, and next steps

Both are equally critical. Many operational failures happen when only one surface is addressed and the other is neglected.

Let's break down each surface in more detail.

Marking at runtime

At the protocol level, APIs must embed machine-readable signals indicating that a resource or feature is deprecated and scheduled for removal.

Key techniques include the following:

- **Sunset HTTP header**: Add a `Sunset` header to all responses from the deprecated resource. This header specifies the intended shutdown date, giving clients a concrete, predictable deadline to act upon: `Sunset: Wed, 30 Sep 2025 23:59:59 GMT`.

  Clients monitoring API responses can surface these headers in their observability tools or CI pipelines, triggering proactive migration efforts. To learn more about this header, refer to the official RFC 8594 documentation at `https://datatracker.ietf.org/doc/html/rfc8594`.

- **Deprecation HTTP header (optional but valuable)**: In addition to specifying a sunset date, consider including a `Deprecation` header simply marked as `true`. This immediately flags the resource as deprecated, even if the removal timeline is not finalized: `Deprecation: true`.

- **Link header to migration guidance**: Use a `Link` header with a `rel="deprecation-guide"` relationship type, pointing to migration documentation or upgrade instructions. Here is an example: `Link: <https://developer.example.com/migrate-api-v2>; rel="migration-guide"`.

This allows both humans and machines to discover next steps without manually hunting through release notes.

> Best practice
>
> Use all three headers in combination—`Sunset`, `Deprecation`, and `Link`—for maximum clarity and machine accessibility, and treat runtime deprecation headers as part of your API contract during the migration period.

Marking in documentation

While runtime signals target automated detection, human developers need clear, unmissable guidance when they interact with your API documentation, SDKs, and developer portals.

Key practices include the following:

- **Clear deprecation labels**: Every deprecated resource, method, field, or operation should be prominently labeled as Deprecated with visual indicators such as badges, colored warnings, or banners.
- **Detailed deprecation notes**: Next to the deprecation label, provide the following:
  - A brief explanation for the deprecation (e.g., replaced by a newer, more secure model)
  - A direct link to the recommended alternative or migration guide
  - Expected sunset date, if available
- **SDK and client library annotations**: If you provide SDKs (auto-generated or manually written), mark deprecated methods or classes with standard language-specific annotations (e.g., @deprecated tags in Java, Python, or TypeScript).

  This ensures IDEs and linters can warn developers during local development—not just when running integration tests.
- **Release notes and changelogs**: Every deprecation must also be recorded in your changelog or release notes, including the following:
  - Deprecation announcement date
  - Migration path and recommended alternative
  - Timeline for sunset (or tentative horizon if undecided)

Best practice

Documentation should not merely mention deprecation—it should guide action. Every deprecated feature should answer three questions for developers: What is happening? Why is it happening? What should I do instead?

The importance of dual-channel signaling

Why invest effort in both runtime and documentation visibility? Because developers discover and interact with APIs through multiple channels:

- Some discover deprecated endpoints while browsing the portal
- Others detect deprecation only through observability alerts or monitoring dashboards
- Some rely exclusively on SDKs, where runtime signaling inside the client code is critical

Failing to cover both surfaces increases the risk that deprecation warnings will go unnoticed by significant parts of your user base, leading to last-minute crises during sunset.

Dual-channel visibility transforms deprecation from an event into a partnership. You are helping developers succeed—not punishing them for depending on you.

Deprecate the narrowest viable unit

A critical discipline in deprecation is scoping deprecations as tightly as possible:

- If only a specific field in a payload is being removed or replaced, mark only that field as deprecated, not the entire resource
- If only a particular query parameter or operation is obsolete, deprecate only that specific part

Over-broad deprecations (e.g., marking an entire resource as deprecated because of a minor field change) cause unnecessary migrations, inflate developer workloads, and create skepticism about future deprecation notices.

Conversely, precise, minimal deprecations do the following:

- Reduce migration effort
- Increase developer confidence that future deprecations will be manageable
- Strengthen the API provider's reputation for thoughtful change management

For example, suppose a `discountPercentage` field in the `/products` response is outdated. You should do the following:

- Annotate only `discountPercentage` as deprecated
- Recommend using a new `discountAmount` field instead
- Leave the `/products` resource itself fully operational and unmarked

This surgical approach minimizes churn and respects the investment developers have made in their integrations.

Marking a feature or resource as deprecated is the first public step in the end-of-life process—and arguably the most important. It establishes the tone for whether developers will experience the deprecation as a predictable, manageable migration or as an unexpected breaking change.

Key principles to remember are as follows:

- Announce deprecation both at runtime and in documentation
- Provide actionable, not just descriptive, deprecation notices
- Scope deprecations narrowly to minimize disruption
- Treat deprecation visibility as part of your long-term API contract

When deprecation is handled thoughtfully at this step, every subsequent phase—informing users, monitoring usage, and final sunset—becomes dramatically smoother.

Once a resource or feature is formally marked as deprecated, the next vital step is to proactively communicate the change to the developers who rely on it. Signaling alone is insufficient if developers are not made aware—or worse, if they are left guessing about what the deprecation means for their integrations.

Inform and educate consumers

Effective communication during deprecation must be multi-channel, empathetic, and action-oriented. This phase is about more than making announcements; it's about helping developers succeed through the transition.

Too often, API teams underestimate the need for active outreach, assuming that developers will regularly check changelogs or documentation updates. In reality, most integrations are "out of sight, out of mind"—developers integrate once and rarely revisit unless prompted. Without proactive communication, deprecations risk becoming hidden landmines, detonating only when least convenient.

At a minimum, deprecation communications should achieve four outcomes:

- Developers are aware of the change
- Developers understand the reasons and implications
- Developers know the migration path
- Developers feel supported through the transition

Let's explore how to achieve each of these outcomes thoughtfully.

Proactive notification across multiple channels

Relying on a single channel—such as a changelog post—is not enough. Developers engage with your platform through diverse touchpoints, and you must reach them where they are, not where you hope they'll be.

Proactive notification strategies should include the following:

- Email communications to registered developers and API key owners
- Developer portal announcements, prominently displayed near API documentation and dashboards
- In-product notifications if your API is consumed via a SaaS platform or admin console
- SDK or CLI warnings, such as console messages or compile-time alerts, if official client libraries are in use
- Community engagement, posting in relevant forums, Slack communities, Discord servers, or partner channels
- Release notes and changelogs, clearly listing deprecated elements and linking to migration guides

> Best practice
>
> Use layered redundancy—send multiple notices across multiple channels over time. One email or one portal banner is rarely enough. Developers are busy, and migration work competes with other priorities. Timely, repeated nudges make all the difference.

Actionable migration guidance

Awareness alone does not solve the problem. Developers must be provided with concrete steps for what to do next.

Every deprecation communication should include the following:

- **The migration path**: What is the alternative resource, field, or method?
- **Behavioral differences**: How does the new functionality differ from the deprecated one, if at all?
- **Code examples**: Before/after comparisons in popular client languages.
- **Gotchas and edge cases**: Anything that might break assumptions during migration.

Migration guides should aim to be **turnkey**—giving developers enough context and examples that they can migrate without needing to open a support ticket.

> Best practice
>
> Write migration guides from the perspective of a tired developer at 5 P.M. on a Friday, trying to finish the task quickly. Clarity, brevity, and examples matter more than formal completeness.

Personalization for high-impact consumers

For business-critical APIs, not all consumers are equal. Key partners, major enterprise clients, and heavy-volume users deserve personalized deprecation outreach.

Depending on the size of your ecosystem, do the following:

- Identify top consumers through API analytics
- Assign account managers or developer advocates to reach out directly
- Offer migration planning support calls or individualized timelines if justified

This is especially important when contractual obligations are involved. Breaking an integration with a major customer can have business and reputational consequences far beyond a simple technical change.

> Best practice
>
> For strategic clients, treat major deprecations almost like mini-change management projects: involve customer success, technical account managers, and engineering teams early.

Support channels and safety nets

Even the best documentation and migration guides will not prevent every problem. Developers encountering difficulties during migration need to know where to turn for help.

You should offer the following:

- **Dedicated support channels** (e.g., a special Slack migration room, or ticketing priority queues)
- **Office hours** with your engineering team for hands-on troubleshooting
- **Fallback timelines** or escalation paths for customers genuinely unable to meet deadlines

> Best practice
>
> Position support as empowering developers—not merely fixing errors. Framing support positively (*"We're here to make your migration easier"*) encourages engagement and reduces frustration.

The tone of deprecation communications

Perhaps most importantly, the tone of all communications around deprecation should be empathetic, clear, and supportive—not adversarial or defensive. Good deprecation messaging is not *"You must migrate or else."* It is *"We are evolving the platform to serve you better. Here's how we'll help you succeed."*

Practical example: SDK and API migration at Apideck

One recent real-world example of thoughtful deprecation communication comes from Apideck's revamp of their Unified API SDKs in 2025. This was not a small change: Apideck transitioned from auto-generated OpenAPI SDKs to a new generation powered by Speakeasy, fundamentally improving method design, error handling, pagination, and developer ergonomics across all supported languages.

Recognizing the significant impact on existing integrations, Apideck approached the migration communication with intentionality and precision across multiple dimensions:

1. **Framing the change through value**: Rather than starting with a dry deprecation notice, Apideck led with a blog post (`https://www.apideck.com/blog/redefining-our-sdks-developer-experience`) that framed the migration as a developer experience upgrade. The announcement highlighted tangible improvements—such as better method naming, streamlined pagination, improved debugging, and stronger type safety—so that customers could immediately understand the *benefits* of moving, not just the *costs*.

2. **Providing detailed migration paths**: For each supported language (Node.js, Python, PHP, and .NET), Apideck published clear, structured migration guides (`https://developers.apideck.com/guides/sdk-migration`) detailing the following:

   a. Changes to method signatures

   b. Expected migration efforts

   c. Specific examples of old vs new SDK usage

   d. Differences in error handling and pagination

3. **Visible warnings inside the product**: Inside customer dashboards, clear banners and in-app notifications informed users that the old SDKs were deprecated and linked them directly to migration guides and resources.

4. **Deprecation messaging inside existing SDKs**: Rather than silently letting older SDKs go stale, Apideck embedded runtime deprecation warnings directly into the SDKs themselves. These warnings nudged developers in active environments, redirecting them toward the new SDKs at the moment of highest relevance.

5. **Multi-channel communication and reminders**: Deprecation announcements were sent not just once but reinforced over time through the following:

   a. Targeted email communications

   b. Slack community posts

   c. Direct customer success outreach for strategic partners

   d. Reminders in release notes and monthly updates

6. **Monitoring migration progress actively**: Behind the scenes, Apideck tracked SDK usage analytics to monitor migration adoption over time. This allowed them to do the following:

   a. Identify lagging customers early

   b. Prioritize support outreach where needed

   c. Validate readiness before formally sunsetting the old SDKs

This is an example of a Slack reminder sent to all Apideck customers still using old SDKs:

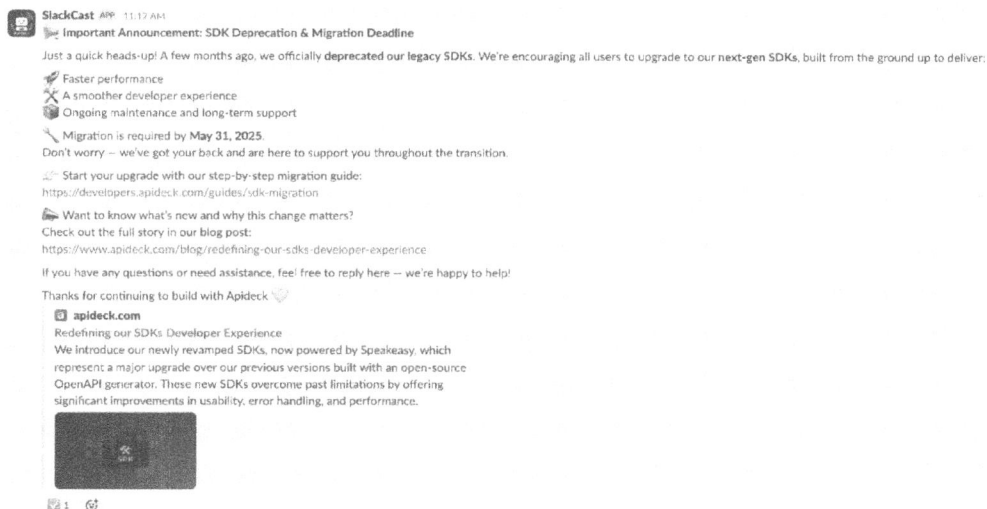

SlackCast APP 11:17 AM
📣 **Important Announcement: SDK Deprecation & Migration Deadline**

Just a quick heads-up! A few months ago, we officially **deprecated our legacy SDKs**. We're encouraging all users to upgrade to our **next-gen SDKs**, built from the ground up to deliver:

⚡ Faster performance
✖ A smoother developer experience
🛠 Ongoing maintenance and long-term support

🔧 Migration is required by **May 31, 2025**.
Don't worry — we've got your back and are here to support you throughout the transition.

📖 Start your upgrade with our step-by-step migration guide:
https://developers.apideck.com/guides/sdk-migration

📰 Want to know what's new and why this change matters?
Check out the full story in our blog post:
https://www.apideck.com/blog/redefining-our-sdks-developer-experience

If you have any questions or need assistance, feel free to reply here — we're happy to help!

Thanks for continuing to build with Apideck 💙

🔗 **apideck.com**
Redefining our SDKs Developer Experience
We introduce our newly revamped SDKs, now powered by Speakeasy, which
represent a major upgrade over our previous versions built with an open-source
OpenAPI generator. These new SDKs overcome past limitations by offering
significant improvements in usability, error handling, and performance.

Figure 13.3 – Apideck API/SDK deprecation communication

By making migration a measured process rather than a deadline-driven scramble, Apideck helped users transition smoothly while building long-term trust in their platform evolution.

This migration demonstrates how proactive communication, empathetic framing, layered support, and continuous monitoring can transform a high-risk change into a high-trust opportunity. It shows that when handled well, even major breaking changes can become proof points that strengthen developer confidence rather than eroding it.

Informing and educating consumers during deprecation is about much more than sending a notice. It is about building a trust bridge through a transition that could otherwise feel risky, frustrating, or costly.

The most successful deprecations share common traits:

- Proactive, multi-channel notification
- Actionable migration guidance with examples
- Personalization for critical customers
- Responsive support channels
- Empathetic and clear communication tone

By investing in thoughtful communication early, you dramatically reduce the chances of migration chaos and instead create an environment where developers view your platform as a reliable, trusted partner, even when change is unavoidable.

API change management is a multifaceted process that requires a combination of strategic thinking, disciplined execution, and continuous communication. Each of the building blocks—strategic prioritization and planning, evolution-only approaches, hybrid models, and deprecation and sunsetting—provides a structured way to manage change while preserving a reliable and predictable experience for API consumers. These elements work together to ensure that your API can evolve to meet changing business and user demands without compromising stability.

At its core, effective API change management is about balancing innovation with reliability. It empowers API providers to introduce new capabilities, modernize legacy systems, and secure their APIs, all while maintaining the trust and satisfaction of developers. A successful change management strategy requires clear communication, realistic timelines, and thoughtful migration paths to minimize disruption and foster continuous growth.

By integrating these building blocks into your API lifecycle, you create a framework that adapts to both technical and business needs. Whether you're iterating rapidly in a start-up environment or managing a high-stakes enterprise API, this structured approach will help you manage change with confidence and ensure long-term success.

Now that we've covered essential API change management building blocks, let's deep dive into how we apply what we learned in Magic Items Store APIs.

Implementing an API change process for Magic Items Store

To ground the principles we've discussed in a real-world context, let's walk through a practical example of how an API change process was implemented at Magic Items Store.

In this section, we'll follow the full life cycle of how Magic Items Store identified technical debt, introduced a structured change process, managed deprecation, and laid the foundation for sustainable future evolution.

Each phase of this transformation will demonstrate how proactive planning, clear communication, and disciplined governance can turn even a legacy API into a developer-friendly platform.

Background: addressing early API design issues

Magic Item Store's first-generation API was developed under tight deadlines, with a strong focus on launching quickly rather than establishing consistent design patterns. As the business scaled, several shortcomings emerged:

- **Inconsistent resource naming**: The `/catalog` endpoint was used to retrieve products, which became confusing as the API expanded to support additional catalog-related elements such as banners and promotions
- **Unstructured data models**: Different endpoints followed varying response formats (e.g., a mix between camelCase and snake_case), making integration difficult for developers
- **Lack of a formal versioning or change management strategy**: Changes were made ad hoc, sometimes leading to unexpected breaking changes

To address these challenges, Magic Items Store introduced a structured API change management process to ensure stability, scalability, and a smooth transition for API consumers.

Phase 1: Establishing an API change process

The first phase of Magic Item Store's evolution focused on putting foundational change management principles in place—creating clear policies that would govern future API improvements without sacrificing backward compatibility or developer trust.

Step 1: Defining the change policy

To ensure API stability while allowing for continuous improvements, Magic Items Store adopted a clear API change policy based on three principles:

- **Backward compatibility first**: Any change that would break existing consumers must be handled through a new resource variant, never by modifying existing resources
- **Consistent extension rules**: Adding new functionality should always be non-breaking, ensuring that existing clients can continue working without modification
- **Transparent deprecation process**: When retiring outdated resources, developers must be given sufficient notice and clear migration guidance

This structured approach ensured that Magic Items Store could evolve its API safely while maintaining trust with developers.

Step 2: Creating a new resource variant for products

One of the most significant pain points in Magic Item Store's API was the use of /catalog to retrieve products. Initially, this seemed like a logical decision, as the catalog contained all items listed in the store. However, as the business evolved, this design choice led to confusion:

- The /catalog endpoint returned more than just products, including promotions, banners, and discontinued items
- API consumers expected only purchasable products, but instead had to filter out irrelevant data manually
- Expanding the catalog model further risked making the problem worse

To resolve this, Magic Items Store introduced a new, dedicated /products resource while keeping /catalog for broader catalog-related elements:

- /products now exclusively returns purchasable items
- /catalog remains available for legacy clients, but is marked as deprecated
- Filtering inconsistencies were fixed, aligning with a standard query structure

Example API call before and after

To illustrate the change, consider the following example. This shows retrieving products from the legacy /catalog endpoint (now deprecated):

```
GET /catalog?filter=active
 {
  "items": [
    {
      "id": "123",
      "title": "Running Shoes",
      "status": "active",
      "category": "footwear"
    },
    {
      "id": "124",
      "title": "Promotional Banner",
      "status": "marketing",
      "category": "misc"
    }
  ]
}
```

Here are the issues:

- Response included marketing banners, requiring additional filtering
- The term `catalog` was too broad and ambiguous

Now, let's see how the same product data is retrieved using the newly introduced /products endpoint, which provides a cleaner and more focused interface:

```
GET /products
  {
    "products": [
      {
        "id": "123",
        "name": "Running Shoes",
        "category": "footwear"
      }
    ]
  }
```

Let's look at the improvements:

- /products now returns only relevant, active products
- Naming aligns with RESTful best practices
- API consumers can now query without extra filtering logic

Phase 2: Managing the deprecation of /catalog

With a cleaner design now available, the next focus was on managing the transition without disrupting existing clients. Phase 2 involved carefully orchestrating deprecation communications, providing migration guidance, and introducing sunset mechanisms over time.

Before diving into the steps, it's important to understand that deprecation is not a single announcement—it's an ongoing process of helping developers adapt comfortably at their own pace.

Step 1: Announcing deprecation with clear communication

Magic Items Store rolled out a structured deprecation campaign using multiple communication channels:

- The API documentation was updated to clearly mark /catalog as deprecated
- A changelog entry described the upcoming changes, linked to migration guides, and detailed the timeline for removal

- Developer dashboards displayed a visible warning banner about the pending deprecation
- Targeted email notifications were sent to API key holders actively using /catalog, ensuring that no active consumer missed the news

Additionally, Magic Items Store published comprehensive migration guides, offering side-by-side examples of how to move from /catalog to /products.

These guides outlined what developers needed to update in their integrations and helped teams estimate the migration effort required.

Step 2: Implementing a sunset strategy for /catalog

To provide developers with ample time to transition, Magic Items Store followed a structured deprecation process:

Sub-step 1: Deprecation notice in API responses

Requests to /catalog included a Sunset HTTP header, warning developers of its eventual removal:

```
Sunset: Wed, 30 Sep 2025 23:59:59 GMT
Deprecation: true
Link: <https://developer.magicstore.com/migrate-products>;
rel="deprecation-guide"
```

This ensured developers had clear guidance on when the endpoint would be removed and how to migrate.

Sub-step 2: Grace period for developers to transition

Magic Items Store provided a six-month transition window, during which the following took place:

- /catalog continued functioning normally
- API usage analytics monitored migration progress
- Developer support was available to help with integration changes

Sub-step 3: Final sunset and removal of /catalog

Once the migration period ended, /catalog was officially sunset. Any requests to it returned a 410 Gone response with migration guidance:

```
HTTP/1.1 410 Gone
Content-Type: application/json
 {
```

```
    "error": "The `/catalog` endpoint has been removed. Please use `/
products`."
}
```

Phase 3: Future-proofing API strategy

With the success of the /catalog migration, Magic Items Store established long-term API governance practices:

- API changes must follow a structured governance process to avoid future inconsistencies
- All breaking changes require a new resource variant, ensuring backward compatibility
- A hybrid API evolution approach was adopted, allowing non-breaking changes within existing endpoints while introducing new versions only when necessary
- Strict deprecation and sunsetting guidelines were put in place to maintain a seamless developer experience

By implementing a structured API change management process, Magic Items Store successfully transitioned from a disorganized, inconsistent API to a stable, scalable, and developer-friendly ecosystem.

Here are the key takeaways from Magic Item Store's API transformation:

- Legacy endpoints were gracefully deprecated with minimal disruption
- Backward-compatible changes were managed effectively through clear extension rules
- API evolution became predictable, balancing stability with continuous improvements
- Developer communication improved, ensuring that changes were well documented and announced proactively

Summary

In this chapter, we explored how to manage API changes effectively—balancing the need for innovation with the responsibility to preserve stability and developer trust. API change management is not just a technical exercise; it's a strategic discipline that ensures your platform evolves without disrupting existing users.

We began by understanding why change is inevitable, whether due to modernization, introducing new capabilities, or reinforcing security. Each driver demands careful planning to avoid broken integrations and to maintain a competitive advantage.

We introduced the building blocks of API change management and discussed versioning strategies—global, resource-based, and evolution-only models—and when to apply each. We highlighted how companies such as Stripe successfully balance rapid innovation with predictability by combining continuous evolution with structured versioning cycles.

A key theme was the importance of deprecation and sunsetting. Properly signaling deprecated resources through runtime headers, documentation, and proactive outreach ensures developers have time and support to migrate confidently, minimizing friction.

The Magic Items Store case study showed these principles in action, demonstrating how a once inconsistent API evolved into a structured, scalable platform through disciplined change management, clear migration paths, and transparent communication.

By mastering these strategies, you can lead your API through continuous evolution, turning inevitable change into a catalyst for growth and stronger developer relationships.

Get This Book's PDF Version and Exclusive Extras

UNLOCK NOW

Scan the QR code (or go to packtpub.com/unlock). Search for this book by name, confirm the edition, and then follow the steps on the page.

Note: Keep your invoice handy. Purchases made directly from Packt don't require an invoice.

14

Unlock Your Book's Exclusive Benefits

Your copy of this book comes with the following exclusive benefits:

- ☁ Next-gen Packt Reader
- ✦ AI assistant (beta)
- 📖 DRM-free PDF/ePub downloads

Use the following guide to unlock them if you haven't already. The process takes just a few minutes and needs to be done only once.

How to unlock these benefits in three easy steps

Step 1

Have your purchase invoice for this book ready, as you'll need it in *Step 3*. If you received a physical invoice, scan it on your phone and have it ready as either a PDF, JPG, or PNG.

For more help on finding your invoice, visit `https://www.packtpub.com/unlock-benefits/help`.

> **Note**: Did you buy this book directly from Packt? You don't need an invoice. After completing Step 2, you can jump straight to your exclusive content.

Step 2

Scan this QR code or go to `https://packtpub.com/unlock`.

On the page that opens (which will look similar to *Figure 14.1* if you're on desktop), search for this book by name. Make sure you select the correct edition.

<packt>   Q Search...   Subscription 🛒 👤

Explore Products   Best Sellers   New Releases   Books   Videos   Audiobooks   Learning Hub   Newsletter Hub   Free Learning

Discover and unlock your book's exclusive benefits

Bought a Packt book? Your purchase may come with free bonus benefits designed to maximise your learning. Discover and unlock them here

Discover Benefits   Sign Up/In   Upload Invoice

Need Help?

1. Discover your book's exclusive benefits   ∧

Q   Search by title or ISBN

CONTINUE TO STEP 2

2. Login or sign up for free   ∨

3. Upload your invoice and unlock   ∨

Figure 14.1: Packt unlock landing page on desktop

Step 3

Once you've selected your book, sign in to your Packt account or create a new one for free. Once you're logged in, upload your invoice. It can be in PDF, PNG, or JPG format and must be no larger than 10 MB. Follow the rest of the instructions on the screen to complete the process.

Need help?

If you get stuck and need help, visit `https://www.packtpub.com/unlock-benefits/help` for a detailed FAQ on how to find your invoices and more. The following QR code will take you to the help page directly:

Note: If you are still facing issues, reach out to `customercare@packt.com`.

‹packt›

packtpub.com

Subscribe to our online digital library for full access to over 7,000 books and videos, as well as industry leading tools to help you plan your personal development and advance your career. For more information, please visit our website.

Why subscribe?

- Spend less time learning and more time coding with practical eBooks and Videos from over 4,000 industry professionals
- Improve your learning with Skill Plans built especially for you
- Get a free eBook or video every month
- Fully searchable for easy access to vital information
- Copy and paste, print, and bookmark content

At www.packtpub.com, you can also read a collection of free technical articles, sign up for a range of free newsletters, and receive exclusive discounts and offers on Packt books and eBooks.

Other Books You May Enjoy

If you enjoyed this book, you may be interested in these other books by Packt:

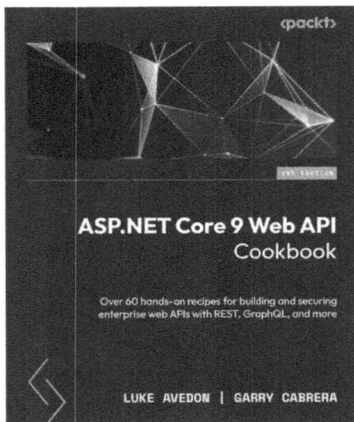

ASP.NET Core 9 Web API Cookbook

Luke Avedon, Garry Cabrera

ISBN: 978-1-83588-034-0

- Implement HybridCache with stampede protection to replace distributed and in-memory caches
- Perform unit, integration, and contract testing to ensure robustness and reliability
- Optimize API performance using output and response caching with tag-based invalidation
- Design custom middleware for rate limiting, centralized exception handling, health checks, and more
- Streamline API troubleshooting using Serilog's structured logging and Seq's powerful log visualization for quick insights
- Secure your APIs with authentication, authorization, and HTTPS enforcement

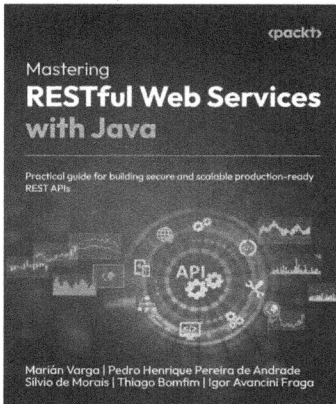

Mastering RESTful Web Services with Java

Marián Varga, Pedro Henrique Pereira de Andrade, Silvio de Morais, Thiago Bomfim, Igor Avancini Fraga

ISBN: 978-1-83546-610-0

- Design clean, modular REST APIs that support real-world business workflows
- Implement secure authentication and authorization flows using modern identity standards
- Deploy your application to the cloud with strategies that ensure reliability, elasticity, and cost-efficiency
- Use the OpenAPI specification to define precise contracts and promote consumer-driven API development
- Leverage Java records and virtual threads to write concise, scalable, and concurrent service logic
- Apply structured testing techniques to validate behavior, resilience, and security across your API layers

Packt is searching for authors like you

If you're interested in becoming an author for Packt, please visit authors.packtpub.com and apply today. We have worked with thousands of developers and tech professionals, just like you, to help them share their insight with the global tech community. You can make a general application, apply for a specific hot topic that we are recruiting an author for, or submit your own idea.

Share your thoughts

Now you've finished *RESTful API Design Patterns and Best Practices*, we'd love to hear your thoughts! Scan the QR code below to go straight to the Amazon review page for this book and share your feedback or leave a review on the site that you purchased it from.

https://packt.link/r/1835885292

Your review is important to us and the tech community and will help us make sure we're delivering excellent quality content.

Index

U

ubiquitous language 65
  business terminology 66
  characteristics 65
  usage 66, 67
  used, for aligning APIs 74
Uniform Resource Identifiers (URIs) 88

V

value objects 67
versioning 332
  evolution-only approach 335, 336
  Global API versioning 333, 334
  hybrid model 337
  resource-based versioning 334, 335

W

Web API Design Maturity Model (WADM) 125
  affordance-centric 129
  database-centric 126, 127
  object-centric 127, 128
  resource-centric 128, 129
Webhooks 91
WebSockets 91

Y

YAGNI principle 52
  reference link 52

www.ingramcontent.com/pod-product-compliance
Lightning Source LLC
Chambersburg PA
CBHW081041220326
41598CB00038B/6950

* 9 7 8 1 8 3 5 8 8 5 2 8 4 *